THE W

Kirsty,
with love,
Shona x

THE WEST HIGHLANDS

Roger Higham

ERIC DOBBY PUBLISHING

First published in Great Britain 1994 by
Eric Dobby Publishing Ltd.,
12 Warnford Road,
Orpington, Kent BR6 6LW

Copyright © Roger Higham 1994

ISBN 1-85882-023-5

Designed by Vera Brice
Maps by Vera Brice and Leslie Robinson
Line drawings by the author

Set in Ehrhardt by Poole Typesetting (Wessex) Ltd, Bournemouth
Printed and bound in Spain

Front cover:
Glencoe, Scotland.
Photo: J. Hinde Ltd (PSI).
Reproduced by kind
permission of the Telegraph
Colour Library.

Back cover:
Loch Eil, Western Highlands,
Scotland. Photo: R. Matassa
(PSI). Reproduced by kind
permission of the Telegraph
Colour Library.

CONTENTS

MAPS

KEY

∴ Ancient monuments

† Churches, cathedrals or monastic sites

▉ Castles

BLACK AND WHITE PLATES
(by the author)

COLOUR PLATES

ACKNOWLEDGEMENTS

The author and publishers would like to thank the following for allowing them to reproduce copyright material in this book:

The Bodley Head: extract from Rosemary Sutcliff's *The Hound of Ulster*.

Methuen (Octapus): extracts from H. V. Morton's books.

William Collins: extract from W. H. Murray's *The West Highlands of Scotland*.

1

Cowal

One of the most attractive features of the West Highlands of Scotland is the superabundance of water in its scenery. Most of it, admittedly, comes straight down from the sky, but sufficient quantities as an adjunct to the mountains produce that degree of the spectacular that delights the senses. Water therefore is seldom out of the picture during the course of this book, which attempts to describe the area to the north and west of Clydeside, running up the mountainous and deeply indented coastline of Scotland as far as Cape Wrath. Attention will also be given to some of the off-shore Inner Hebrides. The mainland coastline is only 225 miles in length as the crow flies (a hooded crow, of course, a specifically Highland species), but allowing for all the convolutions of the peninsulas and sea-lochs, there are over 2,000 miles of sea-shore.

It is impossible to describe in detail every glen, mountain, village and loch in this area, it would take a book three times the length of this and a lifetime of personal acquaintance. W. H. Murray, in his celebrated *West Highlands of Scotland*, asserts that 'No man can hope to see and know the entire west coast on one summer's journey. He must know in advance which district he prefers to see first, go there, and truly come to feel that he knows it, before moving on to another.' If anyone, after reading

Loch Gilp

Loch Ridden

this book, becomes inspired to visit one of these areas, get out of his car, put his boots on and walk for miles, thoroughly to let its magic seep into his soul, then it will have served its purpose.

The Firth of Clyde separates the Highlands from Ayrshire and the environs of Glasgow. You can cross it in several ways; there is, to start with, a tunnel from Govan to Partick; there is the more exciting ferry crossing from Gourock to Dunoon, and there is the Erskine Bridge between the two. The latter is by far the most convenient way of entering the West Highlands, because it leads without undue stress to Loch Lomond, long considered not only one of the most beautiful of fresh-water lochs, and certainly the longest, but also a first-rate introduction. 'We emerged through a pass in the hills,' writes Sir Walter Scott in the words of his hero, Francis Osbaldistone in *Rob Roy*, 'and Loch Lomond opened before us. I will spare you the attempt to describe what you would hardly comprehend without going to see it. But certainly this noble lake, boasting innumerable beautiful islands, of every varying form and outline which fancy can frame, its northern extremity narrowing until it is lost among dusky and retreating mountains, while, gradually widening as it extends to the southward, it spreads its base around the indentures and promontories of a fair and fertile land, affords one of the most surprising, beautiful, and sublime spectacles in nature.'

It is much easier to drive along the A82 by Loch Lomondside now than it used to be, because it has been widened and is faster. You may find that the majority of the population of Glasgow, if it happens to be a public holiday or any weekend, shares Sir Walter's opinion. The first sight of the loch from the road is of the Duck Bay Marina, accompanied by a spacious car-park and picnic site. The blue waters of the loch support an astonishing number of sailing craft, motor-boats, sail-boards, water-skiers and every other mode of aquatic travel. Some of the mariners being less skilled than others, a rescue-boat is maintained in the lochside village of Luss; a Sunday paper article of

June, 1989 illustrates its importance. Loch Lomond, it claims, could become a death-trap if funds are not found to keep the rescue-boat in the water. Funded originally by the Royal Society for the Prevention of Accidents, for fourteen years the same boat, a twin-engined Avon inflatable, crewed by volunteers, has been saving weekend windjammers from total immersion at least thirty times every summer. Let us hope that the aforesaid involuntary submariners show their gratitude with their cheque-books in sufficient quantities to keep the rescue work afloat.

Glasgow Fair fortnight brings the heaviest influx of visitors. It occurs in early July each year, and its effects can be encountered all over the south-west Highlands and islands. Another Sunday paper, in July, 1989, pointed out that not all the visitors have innocent enjoyment in mind, as professional thieves have moved in and are doing brisk business, frisking the visitors. Two Australian girls left their minibus for a few minutes to take photographs of the magnificent scenery. When they returned, it had been cleaned out: travellers' cheques, jewellery, passports and money were gone. At the Duke Bay Marina an unattended boat was sailed to the far side of the loch, heaved out of the water on to a trailer and driven away. Policemen say that the more tourists there are, the better, 'because it cuts down the seclusion'. I cannot recall that factor worrying Fagin and the Artful Dodger unduly.

Loch Lomond, 24 miles long, covers an area of 27½ square miles. Its foot, at Balloch, is only four miles from the Clyde, where the Leven river performs its function as outflow. It may well once have been a sea-loch: 12,000 years ago its basin was occupied by a massive glacier, whose ice scoured out the rock. The loch's surface is now about 20 feet above sea-level. The northern reaches, narrow and comparatively unfrequented, reach a depth of 653 feet at one point. There are over thirty islands in the southern stretch and many of them are nature reserves for the multitudinous varieties of wildfowl which winter there: species of duck, geese, divers (even the Great Northern, familiar to Arthur Ransome fans), Whooper swans, grebes, and hawks.

There are few villages on the west bank, and virtually none on the east, whose only minor road terminates at the Youth Hostel under Ben Lomond, Rowardennan Lodge. At 3,192 feet, Ben Lomond is the most southerly Munro. This term, bandied about in mountaineers' jargon, is frequently heard in the Highlands; a Munro is a name given to 276 separate mountains, each of 3,000 feet or more, and is so called because they were first listed by one Sir Hugh Munro. Ben Lomond means Beacon Hill. Before the thirteenth century the loch went by the same name as the river, Loch Leven, but as clan warfare intensified, the beacon no doubt gained in significance.

The Celtic Gaels, originating from Ireland, began to enter western Scotland in the third century AD, and after much division eventually merged with the Picts, who were probably also Celtic. Their society was tribal, like most primitive societies, their lives revolving around the tribe, or clan. *Clann* in the Gaelic means children, and they felt themselves all to be the children of a common ancestor within their tribe. The Gaelic Celts of Northern Scotland constituted the last tribal society of Europe until the British government deliberately destroyed it in the second half of the eighteenth century. The clan was a close-knit family unit, sometimes small but often very diverse, with dozens of branches; the chief of each clan commanded total loyalty and obedience from all clansmen, in return for which he could exert total jurisdiction: the law began and ended with the Chief. As land became insufficient to feed the multiplying mouths of the clans, so raiding and reiving developed into a way of life, and, lacking any overall authority, clan warfare became both commonplace and brutally violent.

The three clans occupying Loch Lomondside were the MacGregors, MacFarlanes and Colquhouns. The Colquhouns (pronounced Cohoon) inhabited the west bank and the glens Luss and Fruin, and their Chief's headquarters was in Luss.

The MacFarlanes lived on the north-western sides, from Glen Douglas up to Inverarnan, and Clan Gregor's land was around the upper east side, from Inverarnan to Ben Lomond. The two latter clans, living in more mountainous and less fertile regions, became addicted to cattle-rustling, principally at night (the moon around Loch Lomondside was known as MacFarlane's Lantern). The most celebrated affair occurred in 1603, when the Colquhouns raided the MacGregors, and the MacGregors retaliated by making deep inroads into Glen Fruin, fighting a bloody battle in which nearly 300 Colquhouns perished, helping themselves to everything they could carry away from the neighbourhood of Luss, and burning what they could not. The consequence was that Colquhoun of Luss, the Chief, took 220 Colquhoun widows laden with the gory apparel of their late husbands, to see King James VI at Stirling. This worthy, soon to be James I of England, is well known to have had a horror of violence, so he outlawed the whole of Clan Gregor, proscribed their name, and forfeited all their land for ever.

Clan Gregor remained outside the law, but obstinately refused to go away. The famous Rob Roy, about whom Scott could have written a much more exciting novel had he chosen to do so, was well acquainted with this area. There is a Rob Roy's Cave a short walk north of the Inversnaid Hotel to the north of Ben Lomond, and there is a Rob Roy's House deep in Glen Shira, west of Loch Fyne. The Government built a fort at Inversnaid in 1713 to keep the MacGregors in check: Rob Roy and his band attacked and sacked it.

The MacFarlanes dwindled. Neil Munro in his novel *Doom Castle* portrays them as a poor, shiftless, thieving bunch, not more than thirty or forty strong, an occasional nuisance to the mighty Campbells of Inveraray. They did have a castle on an island in Loch Lomond, at Inveruglas opposite Rob Roy's Cave, and they held it until the mid-seventeenth century when Oliver Cromwell's men destroyed it. The MacFarlane battle-cry was 'Loch Sloy!' Loch Sloy was a narrow fresh-water loch in their

7

heartland, between Ben Ime and Ben Vorlich. Now it is a catchment reservoir for the North of Scotland Hydro-Electric Board, draining water from 32 square miles of mountain, and has been dammed to make it bigger. Neil Munro also wrote about a much later MacFarlane, the puffer skipper known as Para Handy. He was just as proud of his ancestors: 'I'm a MacFarlane, and a MacFarlane never was bate yet, never in this world!'

The Colquhouns remained. One of them, Sir James, planned and built Helensburgh, named after his wife, on Gare Lochside in the eighteenth century. Another rebuilt Luss in 1850: its stone cottages today are the prettiest on the lochside, roses climbing about them all summer, and brilliant with rhododendrons in the spring. Another branch inhabits Rossdhu House with its park and gardens.

The only other village of any size on Loch Lomondside is Tarbet. Its name, *Tairbeart* in the Gaelic, means isthmus, so there are quite a number of similarly named places in northern Scotland. Some of them are narrow enough to have carried the reputation of being places where ships could be dragged from water to water; here, Loch Long is only a mile and a half to the west, and during King Haakon's expedition to Scotland in 1263 to try to maintain his hold over large parts of the West Highlands and islands, he sent his son-in-law Magnus, with 40 ships, into Loch Long up to Arrochar. Magnus and his men dragged some of the ships to Tarbet, whence they ravaged and burnt Luss and some of the islands.

At the head of Loch Long, Arrochar can be reached by an alternative route, if you have plenty of time. Now that the A82 is so much improved, the contrast is greater: the road by Loch Long is narrow and takes time, but it is quieter and scenically just as attractive.

In Dumbarton there is a roundabout of crucial importance: coming from the direction of the Erskine Bridge, if you stick to the A82 and go straight on, you come to Loch Lomond. Turn left through Dumbarton town, you are on A814 and Clydeside; through Cardross, accompanying the railway, and you come to Helensburgh. This Colquhoun-inspired town has a naval tradition, but nowadays it is as much a holiday centre as Duck Bay Marina. It too has a yacht marina, there is a golf course, an information centre, and plenty of hotels and boarding-houses. In Upper Colquhoun Street there is also Hill House, owned by the National Trust for Scotland. The remarkable Scottish architect Charles Rennie Mackintosh built it in 1904, for Walter Blackie, the Glasgow publisher; although he used the framework of traditional Scottish design, his own adaptations created something quite exceptional in modern domestic architecture. It is open all year round, every day from 1 pm to 5 pm.

The long naval connection of the Gare Loch is maintained still. I remember seeing in 1962 the dismal sight of great grey rusting aircraft-carriers waiting to be broken up, some in the process of dismemberment, like horses in a knackers' yard. Now there is the submarine base at Faslane; you might see one of the dark grey serpentine monsters lying at anchor in the loch. You will certainly see the high wire fences topped with rolls of barbed wire that surround the base with impenetrable security.

At Garelochhead the road leaves the lochside, goes over and then under the railway, and finally drops steeply to Loch Long, another sea-loch indenting from Clydeside. There are fine views across its narrow waters, first the opening to Loch Goil, and then the succession of craggy heights running northward on its far shore, *Clach Bheinn*, the Saddle, and *Cnoc Coinnich*. The road still calls itself A814 but is narrow, not single-track, but oncoming vehicles pass each other with nervous apprehension, it leaps from side to side and up and down and is clearly eager to throw all unwary travellers into the loch. Locals take it at nonchalant speed. It is nonetheless a pretty road, through shady woodland, the bright loch-water shining beneath the rods of local fishermen. There is another naval base along it, where you might see a supply ship moored. Ten miles of this road separate

Garelochhead from Arrochar, and it does take time.

Arrochar is full of hotels and excellent holiday facilities, such as camping and caravan sites, all down by the head of Loch Long, because it is situated below a range of mountains known as the Arrochar Alps. The nearest of these, across the loch-head westward, is officially called Ben Arthur, but at least since 1799 it has been called *An Greasaiche Crom*, the Crooked Shoemaker, and it is usually known as the Cobbler. The tallest of its jagged peaks looks from some angles like a shoemaker bending over his last. There is also the great Ben Ime, 3,318 feet, and several other imposing heights within the vicinity, and Arrochar is therefore a popular rock-climbing centre.

The road, now called A83 having joined that from Tarbet, rounds the loch-head and starts to climb away from Loch Long. At Ardgartan it swings round into Glen Croe, where the foaming white water of the Croe tumbles past a log-cabin Youth Hostel and there is plenty of excellent walking and climbing. The road climbs up through pine-woods the long way up Glen Croe, to the saddle between Ben Ime and its neighbour *Beinn an Lochain*, known as Rest-and-Be-Thankful, at 860 feet. Its importance as a hill-pass has long been recognized, not only by the Highlanders, but by the Government too after the traumatic events of the Jacobite rising of 1745–46. One General Caulfield was sent, with soldiers as his labourers, to reconstruct the old pony-track and make it a real road. Its remains can still be seen below the modern road, down in the glen. The pass received its apposite name from the inscription on a now-vanished stone seat. It is the gateway to Argyll, but first we shall turn to Cowal.

Two roads lead off to the west of the Rest-and-be-Thankful; one is General Caulfield's, which of course takes you back into Glen Croe. The other, a single-track road with passing-places (a familiar Highland phenomenon), wriggles through a lonely, high glen between *Beinn an Lochain* and Ben Donich, joins the road B839 that runs from Loch Fyne and is called Hell's Glen, and dips to Lochgoilhead.

This is the country of Cowal, a 32-miles-long peninsula projecting south-westward from the mainland, between the Firth of Clyde and Loch Fyne. It is variously spelt with one or two ls, apparently according to taste, and derives its name from one Comgall (or Comgal), grandson of King Fergus of Dalriada, whose land it was. These were the early Scots of the third century, who came from Ireland and made their homes in *Earra-ghaidheal*, the Coast of the Gael — Argyll. Cowal is a rather peculiar place, because, from its proximity to the populous areas of Glasgow and Ayrshire, it would appear to be overrun by retired business-men and day-trippers, not to mention fishermen, sailors and golfers. Yet one has only to leave the coast roads and principal thoroughfares to find as much solitude as anywhere else in northern Scotland.

Lochgoilhead, formerly and properly called Kinlochgoil, has no long history, since it owes its existence to the Industrial Revolution. None of its houses dates from earlier than the nineteenth century, and only its church bears traces of an older habitation. It is first heard of in 1442, called the 'Church of the Three Holy Brethren of Kinlochgyll', although who the three brethren were is uncertain. We shall encounter a good many of the associates and followers of the great St Columba around the West Highlands, so they may well have been of their company. The church, whatever its origins, became a burial place for the family of Campbell of Ardkinglas from the early fifteenth century.

The settlement lies on three sides of the head of Loch Goil (*Gobhal*, meaning fork, perhaps because the loch forks off from Loch Long). Perched on its farthest hillside is a large square keep-like structure in Scottish baronial style, called Drimsynie, which in addition to being an hotel boasts a swimming-pool and a curling-rink, and is set about on the lower hill-slopes with wooden summer chalets and caravans, which in summer share the loch-side beauties with clouds of local midges. The older hotel, round the curve of the bay, is the Lochgoilhead Hotel; it offers excellent and inexpensive accommodation and commands a splendid view down the loch, of the high hills opposite, and the gulls crying and wheeling over bobbing boats anchored in the sparkling water. The loch is deep, 240 feet or thereabouts, and the enclosing hills can give a claustrophobic feeling, especially in winter when the mists hang down over them and the world closes in. The hills are called Argyll's Bowling Green, a phonetic transliteration of the Gaelic *Buaile na Greine*, the sunny cattle-fold. The Campbells would drive their — and the Duke of Argyll's — cattle from Loch Fyneside south to the Clyde by way of Hell's Glen to Lochgoilhead, and across the Árdgoil hills to Loch Long, whence they would be ferried to market.

A narrow road beneath the chalets and caravans runs along the western lochside through beautiful woods of oak and birch. They were acquired by the Forestry Commission in 1966 and have not yet all been replanted with conifers. The road passes a huge boatyard and what is called a Boat Centre, with lines of yachts and motor-cruisers at anchor for hire. Five miles of this road, not too strenuous a walk, bring you to Carrick Castle, a solitary watch-tower which stands guard at the water's edge over a few houses, shop and hotel, some ducks and geese on the lochside green and a couple of children playing with bicycles. Carrick (from *carraig*, rock) stands on a small rocky peninsula projecting into the loch, an island when the castle was built. It consists of a rectangular tower-house, ingeniously built so that it is quite difficult to find a way in, and once inside even harder to find a way up or down between floors. It dates from the late fifteenth century (although there is evidence of reconstruction from an earlier building), and was possibly built as a hunting seat from which King James IV of Scotland could pursue the unfortunate wild boar, the last of which was hunted down and killed in about 1690. In 1651 Carrick was reinforced and garrisoned by Archibald Campbell, 8th Earl and 1st Marquis of Argyll, against Cromwell's men. Argyll had opposed Montrose, Charles I's supporter in the Highlands (and suffered for it) but was so shocked by the King's execution that he joined in the proclamation of Charles II. His men were among those routed by Cromwell at Worcester. His support of Charles II did him no good: he was executed soon after the Restoration for having conspired with Cromwell against Charles I.

Carrick was ruined in 1685 when the 9th Earl of Argyll also involved himself in politics, thereby also forfeiting his head. He supported Monmouth's bid for the throne against the Catholic James II (VII of Scotland), was easily crushed, and provided, with the downfall of the second Campbell chief within 25 years, the clan's numerous enemies with their chance of revenge. John Murray, Marquis of Atholl, brought his clansmen to exact the price of so much past Campbell cruelty.

Carrick is ruined, and dangerous, and is therefore fenced off. Work on its restoration is under way, but will take years. Close by is a little jetty where fishermen cast their lines into the loch: in 1965 they had a fisherman's tale to beat all, because a large white whale swam into the loch. It is not far from the entrance from Loch Long, and the little single-track road stops here.

Hell's Glen is the fearsome name of the wild and deep valley where another single-track road winds down from Loch Fyne-side. There is a scattering of croft-houses but plenty of sheep and wildlife. The old cattle-droving days gave the glen its name, when the felonious MacFarlanes and MacGregors would use the steep wooded slopes for ambushing the Campbells on their way to Loch Long and relieving them of the burden of taking their animals any farther. The little road joins an excellent wide highway, A815, on the eastern shore of Loch Fyne, not far from Ardkinglas and the head of the loch. Turning left, you come soon to the hamlet of St Catherine's, from which until 1964 a ferry used to transport passengers across to Inveraray, whose white Georgian buildings can be clearly seen, and on a still sunny day shine like snow and reflect perfectly in the lambent loch-waters.

At Strachur the road departs from the lochside to Dunoon.

The village is the largest on east Loch Fyneside and is glorified by the Creggans Hotel, made famous by the late Sir Fitzroy MacLean and Lady MacLean. Otherwise it is a rather straggling collection of houses strung out along the lochside and up the valley of the river Cur, which gives the village, Strath Cur, its name. The nucleus is around the church, off the road to the left in the Dunoon direction. The church was built only in 1787, but built into its walls are some old carved grave-slabs, showing warriors and their broadswords, which were found in a ruined chapel near the saw-mill at Ballemeanoch on the Cur, not far away. The churchyard is circular, which means that it may be the site of an ancient Celtic village.

The village of Strachur is not in Strathcur at all: you climb quite steeply from the lochside and then descend into the strath, and the Cur springs from the hills to the east (those on the western side of Loch Goil, in fact). In the valley you enter deeply wooded country anciently called Glenbranter Forest, but now titled Argyll Forest Park, where there are hill and forest walks. Coloured maps showing the routes, the kind of country they cover, and the time it takes to walk them can be obtained from the Information Centre in Dunoon or the Forestry Commission's offices nearby.

Down the glen, shortly before the waters of Loch Eck come into view, there is on the left of the road a cairn memorial. For six years the now-demolished Glenbranter House nearby was the home of the celebrated comedian and singer, Sir Harry Lauder. His name may well mean nothing to today's generation, to whom the Beatles are history and Bing Crosby pre-history, but one or two of them may have heard the song, 'Keep right on to the end of the road': its sentiments are still valid, and always will be. Lauder had the monument erected in memory of his son John, killed in the war of 1914–1918.

Loch Eck is long and narrow, with high and steep wooded hills on both sides. It is six miles long, around 400 yards wide, and the hills rise sharply to 2,000 feet and more. The hillside woods are mainly Forestry Commission spruce and pine, but by the waterside there are descendants still of the indigenous rowan, birch, oak, and sycamore. Along the shores there are occasional caravan sites and clusters of self-catering chalets, for the loch is famous for its fishing. In its depths is reputed to live a rare fish called a powan, a fresh-water herring which is found otherwise only in Loch Lomond. Judging by the number of anglers dangling their lines in both lochs, the poor old powan is likely to become rarer still. Since it is so sheltered, Loch Eck is normally placid, its still shining waters reflecting the luxuriantly green hillsides and the craggy cliffs; but I have seen it whipped up so furiously by a raging gale that clouds of water went flying twenty or thirty feet above the surface.

Beyond the head of the loch, to the right of the road, are the Younger Botanic Gardens. They are worth visiting, especially for their trees, the tallest of which were planted by James Duncan between 1870–1880. The gardens were later bought by the Younger brewing family, who gave them to the nation in 1928. Like many of the great West Highland gardens, they are at their best in springtime, when the rhododendrons and azaleas are in bloom.

A road departs from the head of the loch to Strone Point, around which the villages of Kilmun, Strone, and Blairmore form a more or less continuous line of summer houses, villas or cottages, mostly built by Glaswegian industrialists in the nineteenth century. This is the eastern shore of Holy Loch. Kilmun Church is near the original cell of St Mun, an early missionary, who gave the loch its name. The church is the burial-ground of the Earls and Dukes of Argyll, Chiefs of Clan Campbell. It is a long way from either Loch Awe or Inveraray, but there is a story. Celestin, son of Sir Duncan Campbell, the Black Knight of Lochawe, had gone to the Lowlands to be educated but had died there instead. He was fetched back over the Clyde, but at Kilmun a howling snowstorm prevented any further progress. At that time the whole of Cowal belonged to the Lamonts, so

Campbell asked the Lamont Chief if his son might remain and be buried at Kilmun. 'I, Great Lamont of all Cowal,' he replied, 'do grant unto thee, Black Knight of Lochow [former spelling of Lochawe], a grave of flags, wherein to bury thy son in thy distress.' The grateful Campbell did so, endowed the church, and in 1442 founded a college there. It will soon become clear how long Campbell gratitude to the Lamonts lasted.

Holy Loch may well have got its name from the missionary activities of St Mun and St Fintan, but for years the principal activity carried out there was anything but holy, because it used to be the base of U.S. nuclear submarines. There were usually some to be seen there, and always the depot and supply ships were at anchor or moored to a jetty. It was the main ballistic missile base for American submarines outside the U.S.A. About 1600 Poseidon warheads armed them, and together with the Royal Naval 10th Submarine Squadron at Faslane, the strike capacity harboured in this corner of Scotland was formidable. The U.S. base is now closed, and only the submarines from Faslane may be seen in the Clyde. Controversy surrounds them still, from the C.N.D. protesters encamped near the Faslane gates to the destruction of a Carradale fishing boat and its crew when its tackle got entangled with one of the submarines. The latter incident caused immense resentment against the dark, sinister-looking ships, but even now their visible presence cannot be underestimated.

On the western lochside at Sandbank there are large sheds where the (unsuccessful) America's Cup challengers *Sceptre* and *Sovereign* were built. Yachting is important on Clydeside, and any day dozens of white and multicoloured sails may be seen on Holy Loch, where once the great steamships were paramount. The road skirts the lochside and comes to Hunter's Quay, where Western Ferries run a half-hourly service of car-ferries to Gourock across the Clyde. Hunter's Quay is named after a former landowner, Robert Hunter, who built the first

Cowal

pier there and encouraged the development of yachting as a potentially lucrative activity. Behind the adjacent village of Kirn is the 18-hole Cowal Golf Course, a phenomenon in the West Highlands where nine holes are usual.

Dunoon, the capital of Cowal, is built around a double East and West Bay, divided by Castle Hill. It has been made a prosperous seaside town by the multitudinous Glaswegians who fill it to over-flowing at all holiday times. Caledonian Mac-Brayne Ltd run another ferry service from its pier, again to Gourock, so there is good access. The pier was originally built by the father and uncle of Robert Louis Stevenson, and, as will appear, they were also responsible for a number of West Highland lighthouses.

What is left of the ruined Dunoon Castle stands on top of a prominent hill which has been the site of some kind of fortification since the days of early Dalriada, and probably before that too. The English forces of Edward III captured it in 1334, but eventually they were ousted by King Robert Bruce's grandson, Robert the Steward, assisted by Dougal Campbell of Lochawe. When the steward became King Robert II and founded the royal family of Stewart, in 1371, he appointed the Campbells as hereditary keepers of Dunoon, a right confirmed thereafter by successive Scottish kings. Cowal, however, was Lamont country, and despite the incident of the interment of the unfortunate Celestin Campbell, strife between the two clans was probably inevitable. The gruesome horror of the final conflict in 1646 at Toward Castle, the Lamont stronghold, is typical of Highland feuding fury.

At the foot of Castle Hill is a red sandstone pedestal bearing a statue of 'Highland Mary'. This is Mary Campbell, born at Auchamore Farm near Dunoon, with whom Robert Burns had one of his more serious affairs. She died of a fever at Greenock, and Burns wrote:

Oh pale, pale now, those rosy lips,

17

I aft hae kissed sae fondly!
And closed for aye the sparkling glance,
That dwelt on me sae kindly!
And mould'ring now in silent dust,
That heart that lo'ed me dearly!
But still within my bosom's core
Shall live my Highland Mary.

Burns might have married her, and had he done so, she could have exerted a more benign influence over his life than did Jean Armour. But the fever took Mary, and Burns eventually married Jean instead. Several times, however, he subsequently wrote of Mary, in tones like those above, of heart-felt regret. The statue was erected in 1896.

Behind the crumbled remains of the mediaeval castle stands a nineteenth-century mansion called Castle House, built by Lord Provost James Ewing of Glasgow in 1822. It is now Dunoon's public library.

The A815 road runs along the sea-shore to Innellan, which is a string of stately villas and modern houses, some of which are hotels; there is also Knockamillie Castle, even more ruinous than Dunoon, two pony-trekking centres, a nine-hole golf course, and the White Heather Farm, which grows exactly what its name implies. Farther on beyond the lighthouse at Toward Point and around the tip of this peninsula, there appear behind a screen of trees the jagged ruins of Toward Castle (Toward is pronounced like Howard).

The story of the sack of Toward Castle in 1646, as mentioned above, is a sad, sick one. Sir James Lamont from his hereditary fortress proclaimed his support for King Charles I, and was besieged by Archibald Campbell, 8th Earl and 1st Marquis of Argyll. The siege failed, and Argyll proposed a truce: the Lamonts accepted and accordingly lowered their defences. The Campbells at once pounced upon them, took and sacked the castle, plundered the land, and brought some 200 bound prisoners to Dunoon. On one tree in the castle grounds they hanged 36 Lamonts, and the rest were slaughtered. In 1906 the Clan Lamont Society erected a Celtic cross on the spot as a memorial. Toward Castle, now in Argyll hands, was burnt like Carrick in 1685 by the Marquis of Atholl, and it was never restored.

Another story is told about Toward Castle by Seton Gordon in his *Highways and Byways in the West Highlands*; it illustrates the sanctity of Highland hospitality and is much more warming. It seems that a young Lamont and the son of MacGregor of Glen Strae were out hunting near Glen Coe. They quarrelled, and Lamont knifed and killed MacGregor with his *sgian dubh* (the black knife worn by Highlanders in their hose). From a short distance away MacGregor's attendants gave chase, and Lamont, greatly ashamed of what he had done in a fit of sudden anger, managed successfully to elude them. At nightfall he arrived at the MacGregor home at Stronmilchan (near the head of Loch Awe, which means that Lamont had accomplished at least 25 miles of very hard going). He was ignorant of the fact that the father of the man he had just murdered lived there, so he knocked and asked for hospitality and shelter against his hunters. The request was granted. When the MacGregor attendants turned up, told the bitter tale, and discovered that the murderer was actually in the house, they clamoured for his blood. MacGregor of Glen Strae refused to give Lamont up, pointing out the duties of a host to his guest whatever the circumstances. Instead, he escorted him to Loch Fyne and saw him safely into a boat on his way to Cowal.

Years later, the MacGregors made their murderous intrusion into Glen Fruin, the Colquhouns petitioned the King, and Clan Gregor was ruined. MacGregor of Glen Strae made his way to Toward Castle, where he was welcomed by Lamont, and permitted to stay for his remaining years.

The only trouble with this edifying story is that the last part of it at least is pure fiction. Alexander MacGregor of Glen Strae, following the proscription of 1603, was eventually arrested by the authorities, taken to Edinburgh, and executed in 1604. Alas for the milk of human kindness: in Highland history it is strictly rationed.

Near Toward Castle's ivy-shrouded ruins stands a great house called Castle Toward, built in 1832 for another Lord Provost of Glasgow. The road after this is single-track, and on the eastern shore of Loch Striven it passes Inverchaolain Church, whose graveyard is full of Lamonts. A few miles farther on the road terminates, and the only way forward for a motorist is backward, back to Toward Point, Innellen and Dunoon: this is the West Highlands, and mountains seldom admit convenient short cuts.

A reminder of this truism occurs when you have trailed back through Sandbank on A815 and turned left on the B836, a minor road that ventures into the wild and treeless Glen Lean. On the barest, highest stretch at the top, at 350 feet, Loch Tarsan has been created for hydro-electric power. Its water drops from this height to sea-level at Loch Striven in less than a mile through a tunnel in the hillside, and is converted into electricity at the power station at the loch-head. Water can do it, even if a motorist cannot. Loch Tarsan is well stocked with trout, if not electric eels, so is frequented by fishermen, but they must be hardy, as this is a bleak and savage tract with very few inhabitants. The road descends less precipitously than the water to the power station.

Loch Striven is largely untroubled by the works of man, since apart from the B836 skirting its head, and the little track from Toward along part of its eastern shore, there is no access to it. *Cruach nan Capull*, 2,005 feet, on its eastern flank, flaunts heather on its hillsides in August rivalled by nowhere else in Cowal. Stop by the wayside, just before the road leaves the lochside to climb over the hills, and enjoy the view.

Your road cuts across another of Cowal's peninsulas, that between Lochs Striven and Riddon, and drops down to

Auchenbreck. There are two ways of proceeding from here. You can take the right fork where A886 runs off to Glendaruel, or you can go left, on A8003 along the west side of Loch Riddon to Tighnabruaich. Either way you will in due course return to Strachur.

Glendaruel is fertile, a land of corn, hay, and root-crops, among the wooded hillsides. It therefore supports several clachans, or villages; one is called Clachan of Glendaruel, whose church is called Kilmodan. The church is early seventeenth century, but is named after St Modan, a follower of St Columba, who established a cell in the vicinity. A well, also bearing his name, still exists up on the hillside.

Around a bridge over the river there was once a battle fought, between the Scots and an army of Norwegians under one Mechan, son of Magnus Barefoot, in 1110. The Norwegians had the worst of it, and the Scots began to heave their corpses into the river. The river had been called *Ruadh-thuil*, red water, because of its peaty colour: by a subtle Gaelic pun it was renamed *Ruadh-fhuil*, bloody water. The Anglicized version, Ruel, of course loses this.

If you go along the Loch Riddonside road, A8003, stop at one of the laybys, high above the water, at the engagingly-named Buttock Point. Here is a splendid view of the lower loch, of the island of Bute, and the passages on both flanks of the island known as the Kyles of Bute. Bute has only low hills in its northern end, and does not seem to be part of the Highlands, whereas Arran, which has heights of over 2,000 feet, does. Like Dunoon, Bute is a playground for Glasgow, but it is for the former reason that it is omitted from this work.

Facing Bute on the Cowal shore is Tighnabruaich, a plea-santly irregular hillside village which has prospered now as a holiday centre. It has a school for sailing, a Youth Hostel, reputedly good fishing, and is the base of the cruiser *Beagle*, formerly a seine-net trawler, which takes its passengers on wildlife exploration cruises. At Kames, where there is a nine-hole golf course, you turn sharp right by the hotel and go as far as Millhouse, where you turn sharp right again, from which you will gather that you are now heading north again. The road is the usual Highland variety, single-track with passing places, and goes eventually to Kilfinan. The country is pleasantly mild and green, with sheep pastures and arable crops. From some of the high points you can see across Loch Fyne to the Knapdale hills. Kilfinan is small, but has a good-looking hotel. Seton Gordon, writing in 1934, says: 'At Kilfinan I conversed with an old man who told me that when he was a boy 100 pupils attended the local school, and all of them were able to converse both in Gaelic and in English. Now, he said, there were no more than seven pupils at the school, and none of them was able to speak Gaelic.' The clearance of the Highlands of its native Gaelic-speakers and their partial replacement by English-speakers is still continuing.

The little road, dignified by the title B8000, reaches Loch Fyneside at Otter Ferry, which has nothing to do with otters but is named from the long sandy spit or *oitir*, projecting into Loch Fyne. No otters, and no ferry either, currently. The narrow road runs by the green pastures of the foreshore, which contrast with the darker trees hanging on the high hills and the sparkling loch water. From Lephinmore you can see Minard Castle across the loch, a grey waterfront shape set among trees; it is a fairly recent construction, but soon on the Cowal side you come to a little bay and the ivy-hung tower of Lachlan Castle on its far side, and this is far from recent. It is not open to the public, which is a pity, for it is said to contain something unique in castle-building: in the courtyard there are two residential blocks facing each other. At first floor level a timber gallery used to run across above the entrance, with a door to the hall at one end and the north-east spiral stairway at the other. A similar gallery at second-floor level ran from the stairway along the inner face of the eastern block, giving access to the two rooms in it. Galleries like this were often constructed in town-houses, and sometimes were built on the outside walls of castles for defence of the wall below, but incorporation into the domestic arrangements inside is very rare.

The castle still belongs to the Chief of Clan Lachlan (*Mac Lochlainn* means Son of the Norseman) and has been held by successive Chiefs for 700 years. The fifteenth Chief brought 250 fighting men to Prince Charles in the 1745 Jacobite rising; after the disaster of Culloden, in 1746, the castle was ordered to be destroyed, but it was not seriously damaged. Neither, however, was it reoccupied: the family built another house nearby.

Running inland to avoid the bluff on which the castle stands, the road passes Strathlachlan Church, a little white chapel built in 1792 with a belfry which is said to date from pre-Reformation days, a little square stone bell-hanging frame.

Soon the road from Glendaruel joins the A8000 and follows the lochside to Strachur to complete the circuit of Cowal.

2

Arran

There are two ways of going to Arran: one is to take the ferry from Ardrossan, on the Ayrshire coast, which takes about 55 minutes. The other is to go down to Claonaig where a much smaller boat takes half an hour to reach Lochranza, but does so only during the summer months. Both are car ferries, and both are run by Caledonian MacBrayne. Timetables can be obtained by writing to their head office at this address:

Caledonian MacBrayne Ltd.,
Registered Office,
The Ferry Terminal,
Gourock PA19 1QP, Scotland.

Their telephone number for reservations is 0475 34531.

Arran is mountainous, and can be seen standing out against the western horizon from anywhere along the Ayrshire coast. It is screened from the Atlantic by the long peninsula of Kintyre on its western flank; its northern coast faces the mouth of Loch Fyne, its southern, the open sea. It is elliptical in shape, about 165 square miles in area, and its coastline is 60 miles long. The island is roughly divided into two sections, the mountainous and rugged north, where several peaks, with Goatfell the highest, exceed 2,000 feet, and south of a lateral road known as 'the

24

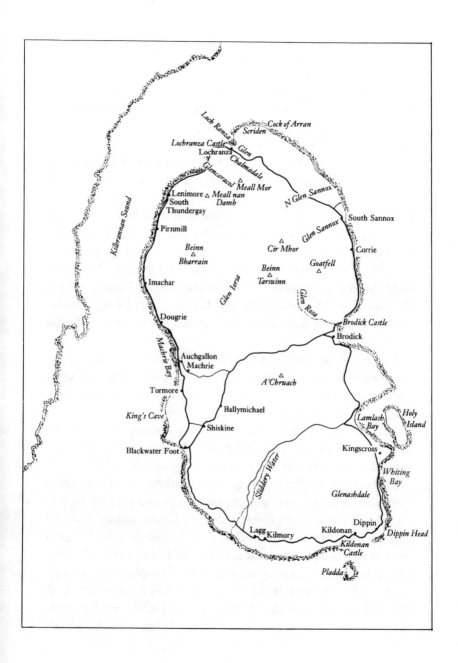

String', a much lower lying, yet still hilly area which is more fertile and enjoys a mild climate, which permits the growth of exotic plants like palm trees. North or south, it rains a good deal.

If it is not raining, and the entire island is not obscured by dark and misty clouds, it is clearly visible from the moment the steamer leaves Ardrossan. To your right are the low islands of Great and Little Cumbrae, and Bute; to your left, out in the sea beyond the Firth of Clyde, the curious hump of Ailsa Craig rides the horizon like some apocalyptic monster lurching up from the primeval depths. Sea-birds of many kinds repay attention with binoculars and bird-book; perhaps the dark, mysterious and sinister shape of one of the nuclear submarines will appear and head swiftly towards Ailsa and the sea. As the ferry draws nearer, the high rocky outline of Holy Island stands out, like some stalwart sentinel guarding Lamlash Bay, to its right the high green promontory between it and Brodick; behind Brodick stand the giants with their heads in the clouds, the dim, formidable, hazy mountains, their peaks communing with the heavens.

Brodick is scarcely a sprawling metropolis, but most of its houses appear to be hotels, guest-houses or boarding-houses. It has certainly expanded mightily since 1932: a photograph of this date in H.V. Morton's *In Scotland Again* shows a little two-funnel paddle-steamer at the pier with a group of somewhat basic buildings on the foreshore, the bay-side road, and precious little else but a few cottages. Nowadays, in addition to the generous facilities for accommodation, it boasts tennis courts, a bowling green and putting green, and an 18-hole golf course. There is more: there is Brodick Castle and its beautiful gardens, and a group of white-washed former farm buildings at the northern end of the village, called the Isle of Arran Heritage Museum, open from May to September. It depicts life in Arran as it used to be and, by all accounts, it was a bit primitive. A Glasgow merchant went to Arran in 1783 and found that 'its situation for trade is excellent, but the laziness of the people obligeth them to overlook that advantage, and were it not necessity they would not even plant their few potatoes, sow their oats, or venture a mile from their shore in search of their fish.' This experience is quoted by R. Angus Downie in his *All About Arran*, and he adds that even in 1874, in *A Fortnight in Arran*, W. Mitchell writes of the cottages, that 'in many there is only a but and ben, where the one is the house and the other the byre.'

Downie also quotes one Landsborough who says in an unfashionably grandiose manner in his *Arran*, 'In few places on this fair earth is there beheld so delightful a mingling of beauty and grandeur as in the near view of Brodick. Grandeur you certainly expect; for these magnificent mountains are seen from afar, and form the greatest ornament of our western coast. But you are not prepared for the remarkable beauty and sweetness given by the rich clothing of wood on the mountains skirts, down to water's edge; nor for the fine effect produced by Brodick Castle, rising in ducal grandeur amidst the embowering foliage of many venerable trees; nor for the solemnising of the deep-retiring glen, winding along the Rosa, till it seems lost in the embrace of the approximating mountains.'

Downie himself says that the main part of Brodick lies about half a mile round the bay from the pier. So it does, but it is connected by a continuous line of hotels with the pier and the hillroad to Lamlash.

Brodick Castle stands on a lower slope of Goatfell, but high above the bay and to the north of the village. It is in the care of the National Trust for Scotland, who will charge for entrance to both castle and gardens (except for members). The castle is mostly nineteenth century, but if you look closely at parts of the eastern end you will see older masonry. The site itself was used by the Vikings, who gave Brodick its name (Broad bay), but there are walls left from the late thirteenth or early fourteenth century, parts of a late sixteenth-century tower-house doubled in size to house Cromwellian troops in the mid-seventeenth century (when a battery was built at the extreme eastern end), and the rest was added in 1844 when the 10th Duke of Hamilton wanted to make his castle presentable as a home for his heir.

Arran belonged to the Norwegian kings, at least in theory, until 1263 when King Haakon tried to confirm his jurisdiction over large parts of the West Highlands and islands, and failed. Eventually his heir sold Arran back to the Scots. Not long after this came the failure of the male line to the Scottish throne, a prolonged dispute, the intervention of King Edward I of England, and the wars of independence. Robert Bruce, grandson of one of the claimants in 1290 to the vacant throne, made an attempt to seize the throne and got himself crowned in 1305, but could not maintain himself. In the winter of 1306–1307 he was taking refuge in the island of Rathlin, off the Antrim coast; in the spring of 1307 his lieutenant, James Douglas, suggested action in the form of a raid on English-held Arran. Douglas himself and a small band sailed over to Kintyre, thence to Arran, where they landed on the west coast. By night they crossed the island and lay hidden in the woods by Brodick Castle, which was held for the English by Sir John de Hastings, another claimant to the crown. In the morning Douglas's little band ambushed and killed a party bringing provisions to the castle, and retreated to the depths of Glen Cloy (where the 'String' road runs down to Brodick). Ten days later Bruce arrived with 300 men in a fleet of galleys and joined Douglas. There is, it seems, little evidence that Bruce and his men captured the castle, and the table they will show you where he sat, and the room in which he slept, might or might not be genuine. They sent a man called Cuthbert to the mainland to discover the political situation, and arranged a signal in the form of a beacon fire if things looked promising. When the guards subsequently reported a fire on Turnberry Point, Bruce and his unimpressive invasion force made for Ayrshire.

But though the beams of light decay,

'Twas bustle all in Brodick-bay.
The Bruce's followers crowd the shore,
And boats and barges some unmoor,
Some raise the sail, some seize the oar;
Their eyes oft turn'd where glimmer'd far
What might have seem'd an early star
On heaven's blue arch, save that its light
Was all too flickering, fierce, and bright.

So Sir Walter Scott wrote, in *The Lord of the Isles*; Cuthbert met them on the shore, in great distress. He had not lit the fire since he had heard only discouraging reports. Bruce dithered, not knowing whether to go forward or back, but his brother Edward flatly refused to go to sea again. Bruce carried on, and after many vicissitudes (and some appalling acts of terrorism by Douglas) succeeded. Yet it was only the death of the stern and efficient Edward I that enabled him to exert eventual control.

There have been Earls of Arran. The first was Sir Thomas Boyd, who married a sister of King James III and was granted land in Arran and the earldom, but lost both after two years, in 1469. The next was James Hamilton; he was involved in a murderous power-struggle with Archibald Douglas, Earl of Angus, who had married the widowed Queen Margaret (Henry VIII's sister). The climax came in April, 1520, when supporters of Hamilton and Douglas fought each other in the streets of Edinburgh, which squalid affair the worthy citizens called 'Cleanse-the-Causeway'. Arran lost and fled to France, and Angus was later divorced by the queen. Twenty years later, with James V dead and the infant Mary on the throne, Arran rose to power again as Governor of Scotland. But when he arranged a treaty with Henry VIII of England that Mary and Edward, Prince of Wales, should be married, opposition to him strengthened, rumours whispered that Arran had sold queen and kingdom to the English, and lacking the will to resist he caved in. The treaty was annulled, the French alliance was renewed, and Henry VIII had missed a chance of a lifetime.

The Hamiltons continued to rule Brodick Castle and Arran for centuries, becoming Dukes of Hamilton under Charles I. The castle was frequently attacked: in 1558 the Earl of Sussex burnt all Kintyre and Arran during the religious disorders of the age; in 1646 the Campbells raided Arran and burnt Brodick, because Hamilton tied himself up with Montrose, and in 1652 came the Cromwellian soldiers under Major-General Deane to hold the castle. They were not popular: a foraging party was attacked and wiped out somewhere between Corrie and South Sannox, on the east coast.

The 12th Duke had no male heirs. When he died in 1895 Brodick went to his only daughter, later Duchess of Montrose. When she died in 1957 she bequeathed the castle and its gardens to the National Trust for Scotland. Her daughter, Lady Jean Fforde, augmented the gift with a vast area of mountainside including Goatfell.

The gardens are beautifully landscaped, and grow a wide variety of indigenous and exotic plants, shrubs and trees. They are laid out on the slopes between the castle and the sea, and while you are strolling up and down and around the paths and steps, look out for two items of further interest: one is the Bavarian Summer-House, a little polygonal wooden hut on a prominent point overlooking the bay, with diamond-pane windows, deep eaves, and inside on the split-log walls and on the ceiling, decorated with beautiful designs fashioned entirely out of hundreds of different kinds of fir-cones. The other attraction is an Ice-house, a deep subterranean cavern con- structed in the days before freezers, for storing ice and perishable foods; a fair way from the castle kitchens, but probably a better bet than resorting to curry powder when the meat went off.

The mountain area of Brodick's bequest is administered by the Countryside Rangers of Scotland, who have a headquarters in a row of cottages near the castle. In one of them they have set up a small exhibition showing, in a light-hearted manner, what to wear and what not to do when climbing, the geological formation of Arran, its wild residents and visitors, and of what the National Trust estate at Brodick consists. The Rangers were established by the Countryside (Scotland) Act of 1967; their task is to provide information, help and advice to visitors and show them how to enjoy the countryside without making a nuisance of themselves to its inhabitants, human and animal; to encourage good behaviour in the course of savouring the splendours of nature, to provide assistance in emergencies (such as rescuing people who have got themselves into trouble on the mountain), and to help to supervise conservation work. At Brodick they oversee gangs of volunteers to keep tracks in good repair and to try to keep under control the ubiquitous rhododendrons, which grow like weeds and are treated as such. They teach newcomers the basics of natural history and woodcraft, and they keep a watch on the wildlife of the district, making habitats secure against possible depredation, either by man or beast. There are several recommended trails around the Brodick estate, lasting from half an hour to two hours. If you want to climb Goatfell, and are inexperienced, a Ranger will accompany you and keep you from falling off it. One of them, a tough, capable, keen-eyed character, was in residence in the little office attached to the exhibition.

Goatfell is a high, pointed mountain of 2,866 feet; it stands aloof from Brodick in chill, awesome majesty. Tree-clad up to about 1,000 feet, the rest is bare rock and the last time we saw it, in mid-April, snow-clad. The first recorded ascent of it was in 1628 by Lugless Willie Lithgow, who told the Marquis of Hamilton (later Duke) that the view from the summit was 'A larger prospect no Mountaine in the world can show, pointing out three Kingdomes at one sight: Neither any like Ile or braver Gentry, for good Archers, and hill-hovering Hunters.'

This opinion was corroborated some 300 years later when H.V. Morton climbed it, arriving at the summit 'more exhausted

Goatfell, Arran

than when I climbed the higher Ben Nevis.' He had to be quick, because he had spotted a storm coming in from the Atlantic. 'But what a view! I consider the view from Goatfell on a clear day finer than that from Ben Nevis. From the Ben you look over miles of mountain-tops; from Goatfell you see land and water.

'I looked to the south-west and, far off on the very edge of the sea, I saw Ireland. It looked like a dark blue ridge on the horizon. At my feet was the Firth of Clyde, blue on this glorious day as the Bay of Naples, and, across fifteen miles of sunlit water, was the mainland of Scotland. I could see Ardrossan dead opposite. I could even see the tiny cranes on the dockside.

'Ayr lay in a fume of grey smoke, then the coast rose to the uplands of Galloway, remote and faintly blue, where the Merrick lifts himself above his wild neighbours.

'But to the north and north-east, incredibly lovely, lay the fretted coast-line of the Firth and of Argyll, a country so indented that its coast measures over 2,000 miles, a greater distance than from Ireland to Newfoundland. I looked away to the great mountains, far off over the blue sea: Ben Cruachan to the north; the Paps of Jura to the north-west; Ben Lomond to the north-east.

'I have never seen a more perfect blend of sea, mountain and coast scenery. It would be worth waiting a whole year for a day like this and the view from Goatfell.'

You have to be lucky, of course. Most people (including Morton) do not have the time to wait for the right day, and can visit Arran a dozen times, still waiting.

Goatfell is the highest: there are nine others in northern Arran, all over 2,000 feet. They are *Cir Mor, Beinn Nuis, Beinn Tarsuinn, Caisteal Abhail, Beinn Bharrain, Cioch na h-Oighe, Am Binnein, Beinn Chliabhain,* and *Beinn Bhreac,* and all are climbable, if you follow the carefully mapped out trails and guides provided by the Rangers.

On Goatfell's western side, the Rosa water has carved out the deep and beautiful Glen Rosa on its way to Brodick Bay. There is no road, only tracks, normally entailing the employment of Shanks's pony, but ponies of the usual description can be hired at the Glenrosa Farm Stables from Mr and Mrs Davidson. The coast road, after Brodick Castle, creeps along a narrow fringe of land permitted on the edge of the sea by the massive flanks of Goatfell. It rounds Merkland Point to Corrie, crossing on the way the Corrie Burn which is also known as the White Water because most of it is spray, so tumultuous is its descent from the dark mountain. On either side of it lie huge boulders of granite, the more northerly of the two estimated at over 2,000 tons. The other is a mere pebble, only 15 feet high and weighing just the 620 tons. The White Water carves a deep glen between Goatfell and its neighbour *Am Binnein,* 2,172 feet, a bare granite mountain of little charm.

Because of the shortage of land between mountain and sea, Corrie's pretty one-storey cottages, characteristic of many Highland sea-front villages, are built in ribbon-like rows. There is an hotel, and one or two craft shops, which have multiplied and proliferated throughout the Highlands. They sell an assortment of knitted and woven woollen goods, pottery, brooches, necklaces and bracelets of polished local stone, metal articles, and an array of carved horn implements. The quality is usually high, and so are the prices.

At one time limestone was quarried from an adjacent hillside and exported from Corrie's quay; there was increased demand for it in 1801 when the Crinan Canal was being constructed to connect Loch Fyne with the Sound of Jura and obviate the long trip round the Mull of Kintyre.

Further large lumps of granite litter the wayside between Corrie and Sannox, and from the latter a track leads up the famous Glen Sannox to the mountain *Cir Mhor*, from which spring not only the Sannox water but also that of Glen Rosa. Morton calls Glen Sannox 'one of the chief glories of the island'. Its three miles constitute, he says, the wildest Highland scenery that can be imagined. 'The hills rise up on each side of the glen, bare, steep, and terrible. At first you compare this glen with Glen Coe, but your second thought will be more accurate: Glen Sligachan in Skye. It has the same desolate grandeur, the same eerie quality, the same air of the world's end.'

Here too, if you do not fancy putting one foot before the other and venturing into Morton's world's end as a pedestrian, you can hire a pony from Mr J. McKinnon, of the Sannox Pony Trekking Centre. Sannox also has a nine-hole golf course, if you can possibly tire of wild Highland scenery.

The road now leaves the coast and ventures inland, following North Glen Sannox, until away in the hills to the left the river can be seen hurtling down a series of falls. The glen is greener and more wooded than most others in the north of the island, which perhaps accounts for the fact that it once supported the largest village in Arran; that is, until the notorious Clearances in the early 19th Century, when the whole lot, some 500 people altogether, were transported to New Brunswick and the Duke of

Hamilton raised sheep there instead. Perhaps the village was over-populated: Landsborough says that in North Sannox were 'some of the poorest cottages I had ever seen inhabited by human beings.'

Beyond the hills on the glen's east side, down on the coast, are masses of Old Red Sandstone piled up to 500–600 feet, the result of a landslide in times past. They are known, reasonably enough, as the Fallen Rocks.

The road climbs out of North Glen Sannox to a pass at 654 feet, then winds its way down Glen Chalmadale, which is deeper and steeper, with hills of over 1,000 feet on either side. At its end is Loch Ranza and the village on its shores of the same name. An attractive village, with rows of white cottages on the foreshore, Lochranza has a Youth Hostel, the landing-pier for the Claonaig ferry, a nine-hole golf course, a putting green, tennis courts, and Lochranza Castle.

The Claonaig ferry is of the type used extensively in the Highlands and islands for short trips needing to carry cars. Descended directly from the old wartime landing-craft, they have engine, wheelhouse and cabin in the stern, and a ramp instead of a bow, which is raised during the voyage and lowered when the vessel reaches the concrete slipway at its destination. They are fun to travel in, giving a sense of adventure and communion with the waves that splash over them. However, since cars drive into them, it follows that they have to reverse off, and as the angle between ramp and slipway is not always widely obtuse, danger to projecting exhaust pipes can be acute.

Lochranza Castle is tall, grey and romantic-looking, and stands on an offshore island. It has a basis of a late thirteenth-century (or early fourteenth) hall-house, but was extensively altered in the sixteenth-century. It was acquired by Robert the Steward, later Robert II, in 1360, and used by him and later monarchs as a hunting-seat. It was held by the Montgomerie family from 1452 to 1705, but by 1772 it was already ruined and roofless, and it still is. It can be visited, however, and there is a notice near the road telling whom to contact for the key – and a boat, presumably.

A few miles to the north-east of Lochranza and inaccessible by road, is the Cock of Arran on the northernmost point of the island. It is a large lump of sandstone on the beach which looks something like a cock with its wings spread, at least so sailors say who use it as a landmark. A mile farther on is the Scriden, the result of another landslide of Red Sandstone, like the Fallen Rocks, but these fell only a couple of hundred years ago, with such a crash that it was heard in Bute and various places on the Argyll coast.

West of Lochranza the mountain cliffs drop almost sheer into the water, and the road has to snake precariously along their base. At Catacol Bay, Glen Catacol emerges from a deep cleft between *Meall Mor* and *Meall nan Damh*; there is a small group of houses and an hotel called, collectively, Catacol. This is one of only a few scattered hamlets encountered by the traveller along this road, which skirts the mountains and narrowly avoids plunging into the Kilbrannan Sound. Between Lenimore (also called North Thundergay) and South Thundergay, a burn issues from the high sides of *Meall nan Damh* and flows into the sea. Its source is a loch, 1,000 feet above the sea, called *Coirein Lochain*. Downie quotes from an early writer on Arran, one Ramsay, who describes the loch in *Geology of the Island of Arran* 'The place is perfectly lonely — not a tree is near; and except the brown heath on its margin, and a few stunted rushes by the brook, the surrounding hills are almost bare of vegetation. The water is dark and deep, and the stormy blasts of the mountain never reach its still and unruffled surface.' Morton would no doubt have made another world's end out of it, had he been there.

Thundergay is an Anglicized form of its proper Gaelic name, *Ton-ri-gaoith*. Pirnmill is bigger, with a row of cottages on the shore; from here, or Imachar, or from any of these villages on the west Arran coast, there are splendid views across the

Kilbrannan Sound to the rugged Kintyre coast. On a fine day, when the white cottages dapple the green shoreline, the great hills rising behind them sheer and stark, the blue sea sparkles with a few white sails speckling its placid surface and the high hills of Kintyre beyond; when your narrow road twists, turns, rises and falls, following the contour of the hills like a Corniche, you could imagine yourself in Italy. On a normal day, when the rain sheets down like stair-rods, and you can see nothing at all, you might as well be in Brixton.

At Dougrie (*Dubhgharadh*) the Iorsa water comes dashing down from Glen Iorsa, past a fine stone house, a shooting-lodge built by a past Duke of Hamilton and decorated with antlers. Where the Machrie Water joins the sea at Machrie Bay there is a wide plain on which stand some ancient stone circles and burial mounds: eight stone circles all told. The best is at Auchgallon, consisting of fifteen stone blocks with a 47-foot diameter. There are also chambered cairns, at Tormore on the bay, and they were all built by inhabitants of Arran in the Bronze Age. The nine-hole golf course and tennis courts near Auchgallon were not. The plain is flat and fertile, which may account for the evidence of ancient habitation, but between the two river-mouths of Machrie and Blackwaterfoot there are the high cliffs of Drumadoon. A large twelve-acre Iron Age fort occupies their summit, and at their foot, a mile along the beach from Tormore, is the King's Cave.

The cave is scoured out of the cliff's white and red sandstone, 100 feet long by 44 feet wide at one point, and nearly 50 feet high. Its floor was partly excavated in 1909, and they found a rather unexciting collection of boar tusks, deer antlers, bones, a bit of a bronze ornament, and rubbish. On the walls are the remains of engraved figures of horses, deer, circles, a sword, a man, some serpents, and a wealth of fascinating modern graffiti which have nearly obliterated the former, more artistic, efforts. Its name derives from the legend of Robert Bruce and his arachnid mentor, but if this story has any truth in it, the more probable venue for it is Rathlin Island, since, when Bruce came to Arran he was accompanied by 300 men and landed on the east coast. During the eighteenth century the cave was used for meetings of the Kirk Session, and in the 19th century it was the parish school. There is no record of the scholars studying spiders.

This cave may also have been used for smuggling, for Arran was notorious for it at one time. It was also distinguished for illicit distilling. 'I have been told,' writes Downie in 1932, 'that till quite recently the curious visitor who swore secrecy could purchase in Blackwaterfoot and elsewhere liquor upon which excise had not been paid. It was also said that those who did so were actuated rather by inquisitiveness or the desire to support local industry than by the love of the stuff, for it had a crude, vile taste.'

Blackwaterfoot in Drumadoon Bay is a village clustering around the mouth of the Blackwater. There is much evidence of the tourist industry: several hotels, many houses in building, probably for holiday letting, a twelve-hole golf course, a bowling green, tennis courts, two more riding stables (one at Shiskine, a mile away on the 'String' road), and a new shop, where you cannot support local industry by buying illicit whisky. Much additional industry is supplied by flocks of small boys rivalling those of the multitudinous gulls, energetically throwing stones into the water.

Blackwaterfoot is an excellent base for exploring the paths which lead up into the hills of this southern, milder, greener, gentler part of Arran, and if it refrains from raining for half an hour you will find time to visit all the chambered cairns, standing stones, circles and signs, and all the inland scenic beauties too. Or you can go fishing.

The 'String' goes from Blackwaterfoot into the broad plain, through Shiskine and Ballymichael, then follows the Machrie water into the hills. The valley bottoms are green, fertile and wooded, but the hills are bare. The road climbs steeply between

An Tunna and *A'Chruach*, both over 1,000 feet to a pass, then descends into a lush valley, with wonderful views of the whole of Brodick Bay and the Firth of Clyde.

To see the rest of the southern part of the island it is probably best to start from Brodick and go the other way, up the hill by the ferry terminal to Lamlash. It rises to a height of 375 feet, and from this eminence, looking back, the great northern hills stand out clearly: Goatfell, *Beinn Nuis*, and *Beinn Chliabhain*. Turn the other way facing south, and before you is Holy Island, in Lamlash Bay. It is steep and high, and *Mullach Mor*, its summit, is a stiff climb to 1,030 feet from sea level. It has two lighthouses, one on the seaward, one on the landward side. It also has some important caves.

Holy Island and Lamlash acquired their names from the cell established in one of the caves by St Molaise, a contemporary of St Columba, in the Sixth Century. St Molaise, like St Columba, is believed to have been of royal extraction in Ireland, and also like him sailed to these remote islands to live, meditate, and preach the Gospel. His cave is on the western, sheltered coast of Holy Island, a low, simple cave compared with the King's Cave at Drumadoon. The island became known as Eilean Molaise, and Professor W. J. Watson, who contributes a Gaelic glossary to Seton Gordon's *Highways and Byways in the West Highlands*, says that Lamlash is for *'lean-m'Laise*, the first syllable of *eilean* having been elided in unstressed position, and that the name was primarily that of the island now called Holy Island.' The town Lamlash, to corroborate this judgment, is pronounced with the stress on the second syllable, as La M'lash.

The walls of St Molaise's cave have been carved with runic inscriptions by Norsemen, some of which may have been cut when King Haakon's fleet sheltered in Lamlash Bay in 1263: or maybe not, for some have been identified as much older than that. Modern tourists have added, as usual, their own unlovely embellishments. Below the cave is a sandstone block, seven feet high and 31 feet in circumference, known as the Judgement

Stone. Four seats have been cut out of the stone near the top, at its four corners, but their function is unknown. Guesswork might supply the answer that St Molaise and his successors, as Holy Men, would command respect and be asked to adjudicate in delicate cases brought before them. Guesswork, however, is frequently wrong. Nearby is St Molaise's Well, a spring of water which could cure all ills.

The island can be reached by boat from Lamlash, which faces it across the sheltered bay. It clusters in a heap down the steep hill-slope, provides Johnston's Marine Stores for all known nautical requirements, two self-drive cruiser-hire companies, an 18-hole golf course, the obligatory putting green, bowling green, and tennis courts, and a large brick Church of Scotland. Lamlash used once to be a naval base, one of many in the grim days of 1914–1918 on the west coast of Scotland. Instead of the fine yachts and motor-cruisers riding at anchor in the quiet bay, one can imagine the lean grey shapes of the warships, taking rare refuge from their apparently interminable task of watching for the deadly submarines and battling with the savage northern gales.

From Lamlash goes the only other cross-island road than the 'String'. It is smaller and narrower, and follows the Sliddery Water down to the coast road, which it joins near Lagg.

The main road rises from Lamlash Bay and climbs to Kingscross, which has another probably mythical connection with Bruce, because it was said to be from this point that he embarked with his ships when he saw what he thought was Cuthbert's beacon blazing at Turnberry. Quite why he should have chosen this departure point when the fleet was at Brodick, seems beyond comprehension: perhaps the story was used to explain the name, rather than the other way round.

Down at Whiting Bay is another large but rather scattered township, more exposed than Lamlash because it lacks a protecting island; however, its houses are stylish, with some of Arran's palm trees in their gardens, it offers most of the mandatory facilities such as a golf course, putting green, bowling green, hotels and guest-houses, and also has a Youth Hostel. There is a school, too: not, as is usual in the islands, a primary school, but a secondary school. Arran is therefore unique in not having to send its children away to the mainland once they have passed the primary age.

At the southern end of Whiting Bay paths lead up Glenash-dale, through which the Ashdale burn splashes on its way to the bay. A mile and a half or so up the glen, you can see the highest waterfall in Arran, *Eas-a-Chranaig*, where the water drops 200 feet in two great leaps. Another sharp climb brings you to Dippin, hard by Dippin Head, a row of 300-feet-high basaltic cliffs, which stand upon a ledge of basalt extending from the sea-edge to the base of the cliffs, like Staffa and the Giant's Causeway in miniature.

From the road west of Dippin can be seen the shore-village of Kildonan: the road runs along the top of the cliffs, the village lies on the narrow flat land below them. It has a fine hotel, which caters for under-water diving and boat-hiring, not to mention fishing, and it has a broken-down old watch-tower called Kildonan Castle, built at some uncertain time in the later Middle Ages. Off shore there is a small island called Pladda, which has a lighthouse. According to Downie, in the early 19th-century the excise cutter *Prince Augustus Frederick* 'ran down a salt smuggler. The smugglers and excisemen came to blows, which did not cease until one of the smugglers had been shot dead.' This incident occurred between Pladda and Kildonan. 'Again,' he writes, 'on 27th March, 1817, some whisky smugglers making for Ayrshire from these parts were inter-cepted by the revenue cutter, and turned and ran for the shore. Hastily beaching the smack they jumped ashore and, with the precious kegs on their back, tried to escape. Thus burdened, however, they were soon overtaken by the officers, who took possession of the whisky and started to carry it back to the cutter. The inhabitants of the nearby cottages, witnesses of the chase and the capture, now took a hand. The officer in charge, John Jeffrey, appealed to them to keep clear or take the consequences; but the native blood was up and a struggle ensued. Jeffrey ordered his men to fire, which they did, killing two men of the name of McKinnon, and one woman, Isabel Nicol. Jeffrey was put on trial and was found 'not guilty'.'

Another Arran man called McKirdy had the kind of nerve which unnerves authorities. While smuggling he encountered and beat the men in a revenue cutter. When a reward of £500 was offered for his capture, McKirdy turned up himself and claimed it! The authorities dithered, not knowing whether to reward him or hang him, and eventually compromised by pressing him into the Royal Navy; he rose so fast through the ranks that he was given command of a frigate, and distinguished himself in the long-lasting French wars of 1793–1815. Eventually, when his ship had captured a French warship, its crew ignited the powder-store and blew themselves, their captors, and McKirdy to kingdom come.

High above Kildonan, the road runs through green pastures for sheep and cattle; at Bennan Head the shore again becomes a series of precipitous cliffs. At Kilmory the road dips sharply to a deep glen where the Kilmory Water flashes through to the sea and the Lagg Inn stands guard over the aforesaid water, a nearby ancient cairn, and a reputation (sustained in my experience) for excellence. A short way up the steep gorge and out of it, the road that follows the Sliddery Water through Glen Scorrodale joins it and, climbs to 953 feet, down Monamore glen and to Lamlash. The main road, still keeping to the coast, rides high above the sea along the cliff-tops. Passengers in cars may enjoy the wide sea-scape and the views of Kintyre, and the Arran hills to their right: drivers may not, for the road seldom travels in one direction for a hundred yards at a time. At Blackwaterfoot you have completed the southern tour of the island.

Throughout these tours of the Highlands and some of the islands, you will wish to stay in hotels, or guest-houses, or self-catering chalets, or caravans, or go camping. A complete list of each of these types of accommodation can be obtained by writing to

The Scottish Highlands and Islands Hi-Line,
Bridgend Road,
Dingwall, Ross-shire IV15 9SL,

or by telephoning 0349 63434. All you need to do is state which part of the Highlands or islands you wish to visit, and you will be sent the appropriate brochure. Arran, for example, is listed in the brochure for Argyll and the Isles. You will find in it a map and gazeteer of the island, showing points of interest, and lists of Hotels and Guest-Houses, Bed-and-Breakfast Houses, Self-Catering, and Caravan and Camping Parks. The brochure has a picture of each place, its address and telephone number, a description, an approved or commended symbol if appropriate, the number and designation of bedrooms and bathroom facilities, its months of opening, its prices, and a row of symbols indicating other details, such as the availability of television, or a bar, whether dogs are accepted, and so on. It is the most efficient guide to planning a holiday that anyone could possibly imagine, and no matter how many of the brochures you want (we wanted, and received, no less than seven when planning a tour of the West Highlands), there is no charge: they are all free. Who said the Scots were mean?

3

Loch Fyneside Argyll

Earra-ghaidheal, Argyll, the Coastland of the Gael, drew the Gaelic Scots from Ireland from the third-century onwards because its sea-lochs gave it accessibility from the sea, and because of its great fertility. The land between Loch Fyne and Loch Awe became the very centre of Gaeldom, the heartland of their new kingdom.

It all started when the Scots under Cairbre Riada set up a kingdom in Antrim, in Northern Ireland, in the third-century, which was called Dalriada. In 258 they first arrived in mainland Scotland (then called Caledonia by the Romans) and settled in the area of the Crinan isthmus on the fringes of *Moine Mhor*, the Great Moss. The rock of Dunadd, from which they could overlook the entire area, was their stronghold and base. At this time the Caledonians, whom the Romans called Picti because they painted their faces, were at peace with the Romans, and did not trouble the newcomers, any more than the Romans did. The Antonine Wall, between the Firths of Clyde and Forth, had been abandoned in the late second-century, Hadrian's Wall had been strengthened, and the tribes to the north of it pacified.

From the year 244, when the Emperor Gordian III was murdered, until 284 when Diocletian came to power, the Roman Empire was in dire trouble; no less than fifty-five

Loch Fyneside Argyll

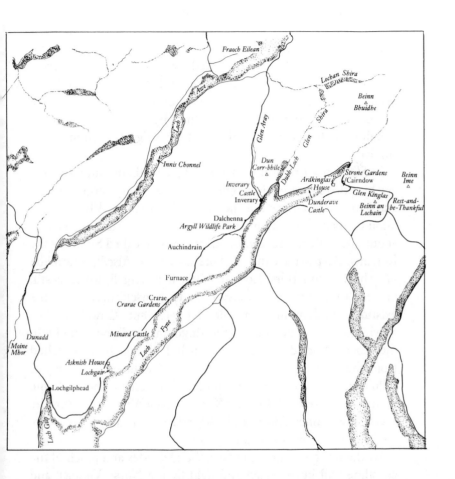

emperors were proclaimed in various parts of the empire, and most of them were murdered within a very short time (days, sometimes) of their proclamation. The defence system of Britain, reorganized by Severus in the early years of the century, held firm, and Britain remained free from the barbarian invasions, the political corruption and disruption, and the decline in prosperity suffered by the continental provinces. The Romans never tried to penetrate the Highlands, so the infant kingdom, called Dalriada like its Irish original, continued to survive.

In 500 King Erc of the Irish Dalriada died, and under Celtic law his title passed to his brother. His three sons, Fergus, Angus and Lorn left to carve out their own kingdoms in Alban, as the mountainous Scottish mainland was called. They arrived in about 503 with several thousand supporters, called Scotti by the Romans. Angus took the offshore islands of Argyll, and made Islay his headquarters. Lorn took northern Argyll, which is still named after him, and Fergus made himself master of the existing kingdom in Knapdale, Kintyre, and Cowal. Fergus survived his brothers, united the kingdoms, and penetrated into the Loch Fyneside interior. Scottish Dalriada now stretched from the Clyde to the Firth of Lorn. Centuries of struggles followed, with the ferocious raiding Norsemen and with the Pictish kings, but in 843 King Kenneth MacAlpin overthrew the Picts. The names Alban and Dalriada disappeared, and Scotland began its history as a kingdom.

By the tenth century, however, the Hebrides and much of the coastline had been seized and held by the Norse Vikings, and their tenacious grip was only broken when the Scottish hero Somerled succeeded his father as King of Argyll in 1130, beat the Vikings, and began to drive them out. His grandson Donald became King of the Isles and his successors of Clan Donald brought peace through strength to the West Highlands as Kings, then Lords of the Isles. During the struggles between Robert Bruce and King Edward I, Clan Donald and the

Campbells of Loch Awe both supported Bruce. His crushing victory over Edward II at Bannockburn confirmed MacDonald power, and initiated the rising fortunes of Clan Campbell. When in 1493, after many vicissitudes, Clan Campbell replaced Clan Donald as rulers of Argyll, they transferred their head-quarters from Loch Awe to Inveraray on Loch Fyneside.

The hills on either side of Loch Fyne are not particularly high, except at its head, where *Beinn Bhuidhe, Beinn Ime* and *Beinn an Lochain* rise to 3,000 feet or thereabouts, but the hills are grass-clad and fertile and provide, then as now, excellent grazing for cattle and sheep. In his novel *John Splendid*, Neil Munro wrote of Argyll in the seventeenth-century: 'It was a fine fat land this of ours, mile upon mile thick with herds, rolling in the grassy season like the seas, growing such lush crops as the remoter Highlands never dreamt of. Not a foot of good soil but had its ploughing, or at least gave food to some useful animal, and yet so ricky the hills and inaccessible the peaks and corries north of Ben Bhuidhe, that they were relegated to the chase. There had the stag his lodging and the huntsman a home almost perpetual. It was cosy indeed, to see at evening the peat-smoke from well-governed and comfortable hearths lingering on the quiet air, to go where you would and find bairns toddling on the braes or singing women bent to the peat-creel and the reaping-hook.'

In the chapter about Cowal, I mentioned that the Rest-and-Be-Thankful is the gateway to Argyll. The A83 road sweeps down from it, between the towering masses of *Beinn Ime* and *Beinn an Lochain*, turning sharply left at the bottom into Glen Kinglas, which it follows down to Loch Fyneside at Cairndow. To reach the village you turn off left from the main road; at the Stagecoach Inn they preserve a letter from John Keats, and his name scratched on a window. He walked to this inn at Cairndow all the thirteen miles from Arrochar, Rest-and-Be-Thankful and all, when he was touring Scotland in 1818 in company with Mr Armitage Brown, with whose cousin he was currently passionately in love. He was already ill (he died in February, 1821) so his walk was something of an achievement.

Ardkinglas House stands in its own parkland, south-west of Cairndow along the lochside. It was built in 1907, to replace an earlier house, which replaced a castle. All have belonged to a branch of Clan Campbell for 500 years. In the house that stood there in 1692 lived Sir Colin Campbell, Sheriff of Argyll. On Monday, 5th January of that year, he accepted the oath of loyalty to the crown from old MacIain, Chief of the MacDonalds of Glencoe; it should have been given before the end of the old year, but MacIain had held out to the last, out of loyalty to King James, and then had gone mistakenly to Fort William instead. In dead of winter he had taken the long, bitter road to Inveraray, been incarcerated for a whole day by a jack-in-office in Barcaldine Castle, and now Campbell of Ardkinglas told him that he was too late. 'The Proclamation,' writes John Prebble in *Glencoe*, 'had been issued five months ago, time enough for MacIain to have come before this.

'And then he stared with astonished disbelief. MacDonald of Glencoe was weeping.

'He wept without shame, tears on his leathered face and defiant moustache. His head was erect and his eyes were staring at the Sheriff, yet suddenly he was an old and broken man. Though Ardkinglas was close to the south and its colder emotions, he was as much Highland as MacIain, and he was moved by the nakedness of the MacDonald's fear. He said nothing. He waited kindly.'

Ardkinglas administered the oath to MacIain the next day, and the old man returned to Glencoe, believing himself and his clan to be free from further trouble. The terrible outcome belongs to its proper setting: Glencoe.

Adjacent also to Cairndow are Strone Gardens, where daffodils, azaleas and rhododendrons make a colourful show in springtime, and where you can see the tallest tree in Britain. It is called the 'Grand Fir' and it is 188 feet high. The gardens are open daily from April to October.

The good road A83 takes you swiftly round the lochhead, but you may be delayed for a while at a lochside establishment called the Loch Fyne Oyster Bar, which serves seafood lunches and sells local smoked salmon, trout, and kippers. When you have torn yourself away from its delights you will find the lochside road taking you through leafy woodland, and if you are concentrating on the road, as you should because it is not all that wide and it swerves with the indentations of the loch, you will miss Dunderave Castle, four miles farther on.

Dun da Ramh (Dunderave: Castle of the two oars) is a tower house, built in 1560 by the MacNaughtons of Glen Shira. This clan, whose name was formerly spelt MacNachtan, was descended from one Nectan, a character of Pictish origin. Their homeland was Tayside, in Perthshire, but they acquired land in Glen Shira and around the upper end of Loch Awe. They built a castle on *Fraoch Eilean*, an island in Loch Awe, another in the little *Dubh Loch* in the lower reaches of Glen Shira, and later on, this of Dunderave. Now accessible from the land, at the far edge of a promontory, it was once detached from it, and at high tide at least entirely surrounded by the loch-water. Neil Munro adopted it for the eponymous centre-piece of his novel *Doom Castle*. His hero, Count Victor de Montaiglon, is in Scotland bent upon revenge, and the Baron of Doom is said to be able to assist him; he has been pursued all the way round the loch-head by a gang of ferocious MacFarlanes and is trying to reach the castle as a refuge from them. Expecting the kind of castle to which he is accustomed in the fair land of France, his eye lights 'with dubiety and amazement upon a dismal tower perched upon a promontory.

'Revealed against the brown hills and the sombre woods of the farther coast, it was scarcely a wonder that his eye had failed at first to find it. Here were no pomps of lord or baron; little luxuriance could prevail behind those eyelass gables; there could be no suave pleasance about those walls hanging over the noisy and inhospitable wave. No pomp, no pleasant amenities; the place seemed to jut into the sea, defying man's oldest and most bitter enemy, its gable ends and one crenellated bastion or turret betraying its sinister relation to its age, its whole aspect arrogant and unfriendly, essential of war. Caught suddenly by the vision that swept the fretted curve of the coast, it seemed blackly to perpetuate the spirit of the land, its silence, its solitude and terrors.'

It can have been very little less dismal when the present owners, Mr and Mrs Barry Weir, went to inspect it, having seen it advertised in *Country Life*. 'You needed gumboots and an umbrella to walk around the inside,' Mr Weir is reported as saying. But it had 52 rooms, 17 acres of land and a mile of Loch Fyneside to recommend it, and the Weirs bought it for £600,000. They propose luxury flats within the castle for letting, self-catering chalets and a swimming-pool on the shore, and boats for hire on the loch. Furthermore, Mr Weir claims that his name belongs to a sept of Clan MacNaughton, so he hopes to attract American MacNaughtons to his holiday centre. In fact, the castle had already been restored in 1911 by Sir Robert Lorimer, who built Ardkinglas House, so at least Mr Weir's restoration work did not have to start from scratch.

A short way along the road from Dunderave brings you to a point of land where Loch Shira re-enters on your right, and from that point can be gained the famous first view of Inveraray, its classically styled Georgian houses shining white in the sunshine (if you are lucky), its church tower dominating behind them, the arches connecting several of the fronting buildings, the waterfront bright with boats, the still blue loch-water mirroring town, hills and all: one of the loveliest views in the Highlands. The funny thing about Inveraray, and its castle, is that neither of them existed, as such, before 1745. It is useless, for example, to say of the Court House, 'this is where MacIain gave his oath in 1692', because he didn't. All the old town buildings, and the old castle, were swept away by ducal decree, and replanted in a different place. More of that presently, however, for first the road sweeps around the head of the little indentation called Loch Shira, passing behind an elegant Georgian bridge which used to carry the road and now does not. A very minor road to the right beyond the bridge will take you into Glen Shira.

Both the bridges, old and new (the latter is far less attractive to the eye but a good deal wider), cross the Shira water as it tumbles out into the loch. The little road, although metalled, is badly pot-holed and very rough, and it divides to left and to right on either side of the *Dubh-loch*. A tiny island at its southern end is all that is left of the MacNaughton fortress guarding the entrance to their land. The right-hand road serves all the crofts in the valley. It is a beautiful, green glen, warmly wooded with great oaks and sycamores, birches and alders, and the Forestry Commission's conifer plantation higher up the eastern hillside hardly impinges. You pass by the croft-houses, and their names seem familiar . . . they would be, if you have read Neil Munro's *John Splendid*. Its hero comes from Elrigmore, the farthest croft, and he waxes lyrical about his Shira Glen, as Munro writes of it as it probably looked in the seventeenth-century.

'There, at the foot of my father's house, were the winding river, and north and south the brown hills, split asunder by God's goodness, to give a sample of His bounty. Maam, Elrigmore, and Elrigbeag, Kilblaan and Beinn Bhuidhe – their steep sides hung with cattle, and below crowded the reeking homes of tacksman and cottar; the burns poured hurriedly to the flat beneath their borders of hazel and ash; to the south, the fresh water we call Dubh Loch, flapping with ducks and fringed with shelisters or water-flags and bulrush, and farther off the Cowal hills. ...'

You pass by the farm-houses called Maam, Kilblaan, Beinn-Bhuidhe House, and Elrigbeag. It is as well to stop and leave your car just past Elrigbeag, because at Elrigmor, a much smaller house than the one Munro describes for his hero's ancestral home, there is a locked gate across the road. There is a stile, however, and the best thing in the world is to climb it and savour the rest of this delightful glen on foot.

The narrow road winds upward, high above the river which can be heard splashing along its course, between sun-dappled greenwood trees, and there appears to be no-one else in the world, even though Inveraray, a few miles away, may be enjoying one of its frequent invasions from tourists by the coach-load. At the point where the road suddenly doubles round and heads for the hills and ultimate extinction, the map (O.S. 50) shows a footpath leading across the Brannie Burn which here joins the Shira, to Rob Roy's House, but I can tell you that it does not exist. Neither does the house, which is apparently in ruins, but the famous MacGregor is said to have lived eight of his outlaw years in it. It is possible to continue, via a turning off the road which climbs the hill, farther up the glen to a dam, with a hydro-electric power station, at Lochan Shira, way up in the hills. It is a long, solitary walk.

Munro's seventeenth-century picture of Shira Glen shows it thickly populated, supported by its very fertility. It is patently still fertile, but limited in its populace to the families of the five farmhouses. The clearances have accounted for the rest. From our point of view today, its solitude makes it a veritable paradise, a blissful haven from the ugliness of crowds. In springtime it will be ablaze with colour, vibrant with birdsong; in summer, deeply tranquil, the only sounds the tumbling and splashing of the Shira water, the wind sighing in the trees, and the drowsy buzzing of innumerable insects. For me, Shira Glen is Highland landscape at its best, redolent of the subtle magic of quietness that creeps into the soul and speaks of returning there as often as possible.

The two glens, Shira and Aray, converge on a corner of Loch Fyne, separated by a ridge of hills of no great height. The ridge terminates in *Dun Corr-bhile*, 1054 feet; just to the south of it there is another, smaller peak on the very edge of the ridge overlooking the loch, and on it there are the remains of *Dun na Cuaiche*, an ancient fort, and a small stone watch-tower. Glen Aray is longer and wider than Glen Shira, and just as fertile, but what chiefly distinguishes it is that the A819 road to Loch Awe and ultimately Oban, runs through it, bearing considerable traffic.

The town of Inveraray was built around the mouth of the river. The date of its foundation is not recorded, but as it stood at the foot of the glen which leads to the heartland of Argyll, its importance was guaranteed. Until the mid-fifteenth century, the Chiefs of Clan Campbell had used the castle they built on Innis Chonnel, in Loch Awe, as their headquarters; as their lands increased they doubtless felt its inconvenience, situated too far to the south of Loch Awe and a long ride from the main routes.

Throughout the fifteenth-century the Campbells were augmenting their lands and power. Sir Duncan Campbell was created the first Lord Campbell by King James II of Scotland in 1445, and his grandson became the first Earl of Argyll in 1457. It was he who moved the family seat from Innis Chonnel to Inveraray, and built the first castle there. Town and castle clustered together about the river-mouth and the loch-side, enjoying the administrative importance of being capital of Argyll.

In 1644 the castle was taken and the town burnt by Montrose's men, led by Sir Alasdair Mac Colla Ciotach MacDonald, who was known by the Lowlanders as Colkitto: revenge was the motive for the MacDonalds' barbarity. The town rose again, on the same site. In the early eighteenth-century the castle was reckoned to be uninhabitable for a duke, and in 1744 the 3rd Duke came home to his patrimony for the first time since succeeding his brother the year before, and brought with him the English architect Roger Morris to design another castle. So he did, but in 1745 the Jacobite Rebellion broke out, the Duke was already in his sixties, and the nearest carriage-bearing road stopped at Dumbarton! No wonder that work was slow and the Duke died before it was completed.

Salvation for the enterprise came when the military road over the Rest-and-Be-Thankful was completed in 1749, and the castle was built by 1758. A four-square, symmetrical mansion, the new castle was never defensible; the plans included a spacious park to surround it, and this meant knocking down not only the old castle but the whole town too, and moving it to a new site with an entirely new range of buildings, church, court-house and all. In 1750 John Adam, brother of the more famous Robert, designed the Argyll Arms for an inn, and in 1755 the Town House, the two principal buildings along the front.

After the Duke's death in 1761 very little progress was made, because the 4th Duke was not interested, and nine years passed before anything else was done. During the 1770s and '80s work on castle and town was completed, largely under the supervision of Robert Mylne, who constructed the archways connecting the frontal buildings, and the road bridge (controlled today by a traffic light) over the Aray as it meets the loch.

In 1958 the Historic Buildings Council described Inveraray as 'an entirety designed to delight the eye from every angle of approach, both by land and water', and declared that it ought to be preserved. The spit of land projecting into the loch, on which the new town, complete with quaysides and jetty, was built, was formerly called Gallows Foreland, which calls to mind one of the judiciary duties of the dukes. Like any other magistrates, however, dukes are subject to the fluctuations of family charac-teristics, and a glance through the Campbell portrait gallery in the castle shows that some did their duties, and some did not.

The new castle is built of stone and is square, with a round tower at each corner and a high central tower. The upper storey with dormer windows, and the conical turret-roofs were added by the 8th Duke in 1877–78. The entrance to the park is in the corner of the road where, having crossed Mylne's little bridge, it swings sharp round to the left to run along the famous front; the fork towards Oban up Glenaray dives off beneath one of Mylne's arches straight ahead. You drive through the stately park, all the way round the estate, and arrive at a car park in front of the castle, facing the loch. All the rooms downstairs, and some upstairs, are made available for public inspection and there are guides who can tell you a wealth of information about the house and the family's history.

The State Dining-room, to the left of the entrance hall, and the Tapestry Drawing-room, to its right, are masterpieces of eighteenth-century taste and delicacy; the Armoury Hall in the middle uses the full height of the central tower from floor to ceiling, lit by its high windows. Its walls carry displays of arms, mainly Brown Bess muskets alternating with Lochaber axes, pikes and claymores, and in cabinets in the centre there are dirks, powder flasks, and plaid brooches. These include the belt and sporran of Rob Roy MacGregor, and a dirk handle with his name scratched on it, that was found near his house in Glen Shira. Beyond the hall there is a spacious and elegant saloon, with double glass doors opening to long, cool vistas of gardens and grounds. The walls of all these rooms are covered with family portraits of past and present Campbells and their ladies: for example the present Duchess, Iona Colquhoun of Luss; Princess Louise, a daughter of Queen Victoria, who married the 9th Duke; and one of the 'stunning, cunning Gunnings', a pair of eighteenth-century sisters who had both looks and ambition. This one, Elizabeth, married first a Duke of Hamilton, then when he died, the 5th Duke of Argyll. Upstairs there is a room full of Campbell family trees, another furnished entirely in the Victorian fashion, and one called the MacArthur room, which is haunted, and contains a 500-year-old carved oak four-poster bed said to have belonged to the MacArthurs of Loch Awe.

The bed has nothing to do with the haunting, which derives from a very peculiar story. The 8th Earl and 1st Marquis of Argyll retained a little boy who was an expert harpist, and played for the Marquis and his lady whenever so commanded. When

Colkitto's wild, half-savage marauders arrived in 1644, the Marquis decided that he ought to think first of the safety of his wife and children, and took them in a fishing boat away to Dumbarton. The castle was taken, the town burnt, and the little harpist was hanged and quartered in the brutish, feuding, Highland tradition.

Over the years since then, the legend developed that the harpist's music could occasionally be heard, but only by the Chief, be he marquis, earl or duke. The 10th Duke, Niall Diarmid, was a lifelong bachelor, and devoted his life to scholarly study. This included his family history with the guilt of the Marquis at the abandonment of his people; one morning in the 1930s his staff were astonished to find him charging along the gallery that runs around the first floor, connecting the bedrooms, shouting 'I've seen him! I've seen him!' They calmed him down, and with his unmarried sister, who also lived in the castle, elicited from him the story that he had woken to hear harp music being played. He thought it came from the MacArthur room, so he went there, and was just in time to catch sight of a little boy, who immediately disappeared. He described the boy, and his apparel.

In 1949 the Duke lay dying. Two old friends, one of them the Minister of Inveraray, sat by him. As the Duke sank from life, both men could hear the music of the harp, and the room began to darken and fill with a kind of mist, although it was a sunny summer day. The music grew louder, the room darker, then suddenly they saw the figure of the boy, outlined against the window: then the Duke died, the figure vanished, and the dark mist evaporated. Both men deposed in writing what they had seen, observing that the appearance of the boy corresponded exactly with what the Duke said he had seen fifteen years before.

Cynics may dismiss scornfully such stories, but here you are in the Highlands, where folk do not hold the supernatural in such disdain. The Campbells' family motto is 'Ne obliviscaris', which means, 'Do not forget': there is more than one way of reminding them of one ancestor's shameful neglect.

One Campbell who certainly ought to have heard the harpist was the 6th Duke, George, but by all accounts he was much too busy. He succeeded his father, the 5th Duke, in 1806. By this time, despite the massive expenditure on the rebuilding of town and castle, the Campbell fortunes were enormous, and George, who may have inherited some of his mother, Elizabeth Gunning's, less attractive features, embarked on a campaign to spend as much of it as possible. During the 29 years in which he held the ducal title he did so with such success that by the end there was not much left. He was also unfaithful to his wife, Lady Caroline Villiers, on a massive and frenetic scale. When for the first time in his life he visited Inveraray Castle in 1835, he obliged the family by doing the best possible thing for them; he dropped dead at the dinner-table. His generous bequests included debts of more than three million pounds and, despite his depravity, a number of illegitimate children that testify to an heroic fecundity. The family's fortune and power never recovered. His protrait, painted when he was still young, shows him for what he was.

The castle is open to the public from the first Saturday in April until the second Sunday in October; in April, May, June, September and October it opens from 10 am to 1 pm, and 2 pm until 6 pm, exxcept on Fridays when it is closed, and Sundays from 1 pm to 6 pm. In June the castle stays open at lunchtime, and in July and August it opens all days of the week including Fridays, from 10 am to 6 pm, and Sundays from 1 pm to 6 pm. There is a craft shop and tea-room, down in the basement, opening on to the Fosse which surrounds the castle, and in the grounds there is a museum recalling the work of the Combined Operations Training Centre at Inveraray, during the Second World War. This is open from May to September, at the same times as the castle.

The town of Inveraray is referred to by Neil Munro as Inneraora. Inner is a corruption of Inver, which means the mouth of a river, and Aora is the proper, Gaelic name for the Aray. Local people still speak of Inverara, without a hint of the final y. It is still a capital, since towns are few in the West Highlands, but its dimensions have hardly changed since it was built, save for a string of houses along the Campbeltown road, and a few more on the left of the Oban road up Glen Aray.

The first of the new town's buildings on the front is the Argyll Arms. It was less than twenty years old, a very paragon among Highland inns, when James Boswell and Dr Samuel Johnson called in, near the end of their tour of Scotland in 1773. 'We got at night to Inveraray, where we found an excellent inn' writes Boswell. 'We supped well; and after supper, Dr Johnson, whom I had not seen taste any fermented liquor during all our travels, called for a gill of whisky. "Come, (said he,) let me know what it is that makes a Scotchman happy!" He drank it all but a drop, which I begged leave to pour into my glass, that I might say we had drunk whisky together.'

Morris's inn is linked to his Town House by Mylne's arches, and beyond them the road to Campbeltown swings at right angles to advance up the main street of the town to where the parish church stands at the top. Mylne wanted it to be the central feature of the town plan, which was to be cruciform, with the church at the centre. Finished in 1792, it is in the classic Palladian style, in white harling (roughcast), granite, and free-stone. It used to have a slender steeple, but it was taken down in 1941. The interior was divided into two, one for Gaelic speakers, one for English, but there are precious few Gaelic speakers among Inveraray townsfolk today. Even in 1644, Munro has his imaginary indigenous 'Inneraora' people, Gaelic speakers to a man, complain of the Lowland shopkeepers already resident in the town.

Munro's novel *John Splendid* is about the struggles of Archibald, 8th Earl and 1st Marquis of Argyll, against the Marquis of Montrose and his rabble of Irishmen and Highlanders, and against his own conscience. Montrose had gathered reinforcements among the branches of Clan Donald, who had old scores to settle with the Campbells, and advanced rapidly through the December snows. The promise of the fat lands of Glen Aray and Glen Shira was in their minds, and the sweet thought of revenge for past crimes committed against their people. From Loch Tayside they reached Loch Awe, and began the climb and descent down Glen Aray. This is when the 1st Marquis made the fatal decision to leave his people and sail away with his wife and children, 'and the wind that carried the sound of pipes in Glen Aray,' writes John Prebble in *The Lion in the North*, 'also took him safely down Loch Fyne.' Montrose and Colkitto MacDonald's half-starved Highlanders and Irishmen fell upon Inveraray, took what they wanted and burned what they did not, killed those of the inhabitants who resisted, sacked the castle (and murdered the little harpist), and lifted from every croft and steading from Loch Fyne to Glen Orchy all the fat cattle they could find. The heather of MacDonald was raised over the myrtle of Campbell at last.

The tower visible over the northern white houses of the town belongs to All Saints Episcopal Church; built in 1886 by the Duchess of Argyll in pink granite, it contains the second heaviest ring of ten bells in the world, each bell named after a saint. The other building in the town worthy of notice can be seen on the left of the Campbeltown road as it swings left of the parish church at the top of the main street: this is the classical frontage of the Court House, with the town jail behind. As it is no longer in use for judicial proceedings, the Courtroom has been reopened and looks just as it did when the circuit court was in session. Dummy figures represent the judge, counsels, witnesses, the 15-man jury (normal in Scotland for murder trials), policemen, and the prisoner in the dock, with a tape relaying the sounds of an actual case. Visitors sit, as they should, on the public benches.

There are two prisons: the old, with eight small cells and the stink of death about them, and the new, built as a model prison in 1849, with twelve cells and facilities for the prisoners to wash and exercise. The entire display opened in May, 1989, daily from 9.30 am to 6 pm.

The Campbeltown road, still A83, first skirts the lochside, then leaves it at Dalchenna, where a 60-acre wildlife park has been established. Its creator, Malcolm Moy, wanted something distinct from the usual form of zoo, so from the minute you arrive you are surrounded by birds and animals, all willing to make personal contact with you. This last phrase does not necessarily imply that you will be eaten by lions, tigers or bears. A track takes you around the enclosures, you are encouraged to feed the creatures, and although many of the 600 different species of birds in the park are free to fly away, most of them stay put. There are Sika deer, pine-martens, badgers, goats and foxes, an albino wallaby and a white Arctic fox, whooper swans, pheasants from all parts of the world, peacocks, owls and ducks, geese, and plenty of other characters to keep you from straying away, like the birds. The Argyll Wildlife Park is open seven days a week in the summer season, from 9.30 am to 6 pm. Out of season the park closes at 3 pm.

A few miles farther on at Auchindrain, there is a museum of farming life; a *baile*, a farming township, has been set up showing eighteenth-century conditions. Weaving and other hand-crafts take place and the products are on sale at a craft shop.

About half way to Lochgilphead, and the other side of Furnace, is Crarae where there are granite quarries. Where the Crarae burn splashes down a rocky, narrow gorge on its way to Loch Fyne, Sir George Campbell of Succoth, who inherited the estate in 1920, created an extension to the existing garden, incorporating the gorge itself. It is now maintained by a charitable trust. Paths, in varying degrees of length, take visitors up and down the glen, crossing by little wooden bridges, with seats here and there for the weary. It is planted with a multitude of rare trees and shrubs, and spring and autumn are the best times to go. It is open all the year daily from 9 am to 6 pm.

A mile farther on Minard Castle stands at the lochside, a fairly modern mansion in the Scottish baronial style, converted as an hotel in 1966. Then, a glance leftward might show you Lochgair, a mile-long inlet from Loch Fyne; the eighteenth-century Asknish House stands on its shore, on the site of another Campbell castle. The road at last follows the much deeper recess of Loch Gilp, whose miles of mud-flats at low tide do not add to its beauties. At its head Lochgilphead is the market town and administrative centre for Mid-Argyll; like Inveraray it is T-shaped, a sea-front of multi-coloured stone houses, and a main street at right angles where there are shops, the Stag Hotel, and an Information Centre. There is also a nine-hole golf course nearby. Lochgilphead is on the frontier of Argyll: on its far side, beyond the roundabout, you are in Knapdale, and that is another matter.

4

Mid-Argyll

To take the road A819 from Inveraray to Loch Awe you drive
through the first of the arches attached to the Argyll Arms
Hotel. It is well graded, climbing gradually to the top of the glen
created by the Aray river. On a hilltop to your left there is a
cairn-like monument to the memory of Neil Munro the writer,
who was born in Inveraray in 1864 and died in 1930.

From the far, northern side of the pass, there is a grand view
of the great hills around Loch Awe; dead ahead looms the
massive bulk of Ben Cruachan, 3,689 feet. Study it carefully and
you will see the great dam built high up in its heart, crucial to its
mighty hydro-electric power. The road swoops down to the
lochside, by-passing Cladich to its left, swerves right, and a mile
farther on comes down to the banks of Loch Awe.

Twenty-three miles long, it is a fresh-water loch of great
beauty, surrounded by hundreds of square miles of mountain,
moorland, and wild and trackless hills. There are several stories
and explanations to account for the loch's origin: some of them,
if faintly implausible, are at least more entertaining than the real
one.

High on the slopes of Ben Cruachan there was once a magic
Well of Eternal Youth, guarded by a beautiful goddess called
Bheithir (pronounced Vair). She had to bathe each evening in

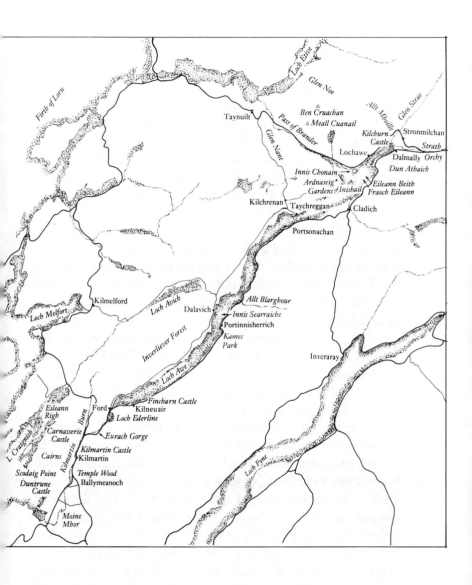

the enchanted waters to preserve her youthful loveliness. One day, however, at eventide, she fell asleep and forgot to replace the capstone on the magic spring: all night long the sacred water flowed, spilling torrents down the mountainside and flooding the great fertile strath below, creating Loch Awe. Poor Bheithir, her guardianship utterly failed, was condemned by the gods to leave their company, but she was still immortal: she had to endure the torments of mounting age. She grew wrinkled, shrivelled, hideous, and hate-filled. No longer Bheithir the Beautiful, she was called now *Cailleach Bheithir*, the Winter Hag, bringing death and darkness; her chill, shrill voice can still be heard, howling piteously and eerily around the snowy peaks and corries of great *Cruachan Beinn*.

The legends of Ossian, central to Gaelic mythology, tell another story. An old man on his deathbed called for the last survivor of his family, a daughter called Bera, and bequeathed to her the whole of the fertile strath now lying beneath Loch Awe. The only condition was that every evening at dusk she should ascend Cruachan and place a stone over the mouth of a spring there, to prevent its waters from flooding the valley. So she did, until one day when she had been hunting in Cruachan's corries she fell asleep for three days, and of course by that time the spring, gushing out in torrential volume, had flooded her heritage and Loch Awe was created.

The name Awe comes from an old Gaelic word *abh* which means water, and the loch's creation, less to a magic spring than to the action of tremendous glaciers in the unimaginable aeons before there were Gaels, or their gods, or anything else much on earth. The glaciers crawled slowly over the face of the rocks, gouging out channels, by-passing mountains and scouring out valleys, finally melting and lying in their deep beds. Loch Awe first emptied at its southern end, through the narrow Eurach gorge and out to the plain, across to Crinan and the sea; increasing glacial deposits stopped up the gap there, and instead scored the deep cleft of the Pass of Brander, pouring out the waters into Loch Etive and the Firth of Lorn.

Evidence of very early human habitation of Loch Aweside remains in numbers of cairns, standing stones, forts and duns on the hill-tops, and man-made islands called crannogs along the lochside. Much later come a few names, like St Conan, and the faint and uncertain shadows of early progenitors of Clan Campbell, Paul O'Duine and Duncan MacDuine. Loch Awe is right in the centre of Argyll's long history.

The loch lies diagonally north-east to south-west, and as A819 skirts its eastern side you can see the many islands that lie in the widest reaches, before its waters disappear through the chasmal Pass of Brander. The largest island on your left is Inishail which was a highly important burial-ground and so had a chapel, whose ruins may still be seen. Scattered about are many of the carved grave-slabs produced by the famous Loch Awe craftsmen, and an early cross. The chapel is said to have been founded in the seventh-century by St Findoca, a fact first recorded in 1257, and during the Middle Ages it was a centre for pilgrimage. Lochside folk tended to bury their dead on islands in those days, because there were wolves in the forests and they were not too choosy about whom they had for supper. The chapel was in use until 1736, when a new church, re-using some stones from the old, was built at Cladich. Inishail keeps its reputation for sanctity, for it is a place where you can sit and meditate and wonder, in peace.

To its north-east and your right is Fraoch Eilean. Clan Donald's war-cry is *Fraoch Eilean!* but this is not MacDonald country and the words have a different meaning: the MacDonald badge is heather, and the war-cry means Island of Heather. This Fraoch is the name of an Irish hero, son of King Fidhach of Connaught, who with another hero, Connal Cernach, chased some cattle-thieves across the sea to the shores of Loch Awe. He stayed around long enough to fall in love with a beauteous maiden called Gealcheann of the Golden Hair, and her mother sent him to this very island to fetch some berries from the Bush

of Eternal Youth, which grew there. She omitted to mention that
the bush was guarded by a ferocious dragon (the island is only
two acres in area: it must have been a small dragon), and she
sent him with a dog-in-the-manger purpose: she fancied Fraoch
herself, was jealous of Gealcheann, and wanted the dragon to
polish him off so that neither of them should have him. Fraoch
fought the dragon, which savaged him, and grabbed some
berries; he managed to return, but died of his injuries. The
mother ate the berries and died too, because their magic only
worked for virtuous people: they poisoned people like her.

There is a castle on Fraoch Eilean, invisible now because of a
screen of trees. It is late twelfth-century, one of the oldest stone
castles in Scotland, and its construction is attributed to Dughal,
son of Somerled. In 1267 King Alexander III granted it to the
MacNaughtons, who were related by marriage to Dughal of
Lorn, and they held it until 1308; but they joined their kinsmen
the MacDougalls of Lorn in opposition to Robert Bruce, and
lost. Bruce gave the castle to the Loch Awe Campbells, who had
supported him, and they still hold it.

The island to the right of Fraoch Eilean is Eilean Beith, and
beyond near the shore, and now accessible by a causeway, is
Innis Chonain, traditionally the burial-place of St Conan. The
Campbells of Blythswood built the nineteenth-century mansion
on the island.

Still on the eastern lochside, the A819 dives into a Forestry
Commission conifer plantation, and only emerges at the loch-
head, where you can see the impressive ruins of Kilchurn Castle
on a causewayed island, which formerly was properly isolated. It
has a splendid strategic position, as it commands the widest
section of the loch to the south-west, and to the north-east the
three glens formed by the tributary rivers, Strath Orchy, Glen
Strae, and that of *Allt Mhoille*, which leads from Glen Noe and
Loch Etive. It was first built as a tower-house by Sir Colin
Campbell of Glenorchy's wife Margaret in 1450, while he was
abroad. Successive Campbell chiefs added to it as a suitable

power-base, but as their power expanded and they acquired castles farther afield, its importance waned. In the late seventeenth century barrack blocks were built into it for a garrison, but after the 1745 rising it was evacuated, and thereafter decayed. In 1953 the Department of the Environment (then the Office of Works) took it over, patched it up and rendered it safe, and now anyone may visit it, at any time, for no charge.

Just beyond the point where Kilchurn comes into view, the road crosses over the railway and comes to a T-junction with the A85. Left is towards Oban (and a little way along, the path giving access to Kilchurn); right is to Crianlarich, Perth, and all points south. It is also the way to Glen Orchy, but before that, in Strath Orchy, is the village of Dalmally.

You can motor through Dalmally in about half a minute, but it is worth stopping for a fortnight because there is so much to be explored in the hills and glens around it. If for example you take the road to the railway station, cross the bridge over the railway and carry on into the woods and up to *Dun Athaich*, you will see the monument to the famous Gaelic poet Duncan Ban MacIntyre.

Duncan Ban (which means Duncan the Fair) was born in 1724 at a place in Glen Orchy called *Druim liaghart*, a name which now is not even on the O.S. map. His first song was composed after he had fought in the Battle of Falkirk, as a young man of twenty one. He was sent to serve on the Government side as a substitute for a local gentleman, and in the retreat from this last Jacobite victory he either lost or threw away the sword which the gentleman had lent him. Since he could not return the sword, the gentleman refused to pay him the agreed sum for the substitution. Duncan's satirical song about the situation so enraged the gentleman that he set about Duncan one day with a stick, yelling at him to 'go and make a song about that.' He did — to the Campbell Earl of Breadalbane, who made the man pay Duncan his due: the vast sum of £16.17s.6d.

Most of Duncan's life was spent in Edinburgh, but his poetry, for which his name is revered in the Highlands, is about his homeland. He composed only in Gaelic, and one hopes that eventually a better translation will be made than this of the last verse of his best-known poem, *Ben Dorain*:

> Let the wild herd seek their bed,
> Let them slumber, free of dread,
> Where yon mighty moor is spread,
> Broad and brawly;
> Where, with joy, I've often spied
> The sun colour their red hide,
> As they wandered in their pride
> O'er Ben Dorain.

In the wooded hillsides of *Dun Athaich* there are plenty of opportunities for walkers to go and visit the ruined township of Ardteatle, or the Iron Age fort of *Tom a'Chaisteal*, before reverting to what was the old military road down the lochside at Achlian. Just off this same old road not far from Dalmally station and above the village are the remains of the old MacNab township, Barachastlain. Once Duncan MacNab set up a smithy below the ridge in the early fifteenth century, and his fame was such that he was commissioned to provide all the metalwork needed in the building of Kilchurn Castle. His excellence resulted in Campbell patronage for 300 years as their hereditary armourers. They all worked at Duncan's original smithy and lived in his home, but in 1876 it was swept away to make room for the railway. The MacNabs had already deserted the township above the smithy, but its ruins are still visible.

Dalmally's church is built on a hillock on an island in the Orchy river. St Conan's presence in the neighbourhood lent distinction to the site so that Dalmally's early name was *Clachan Diseart*, Township of the Holy Retreat. St Conan's Well is not far distant, to the east of the hotel, on the north side of the main road. There was certainly a church on the same site in the fourteenth century, recorded as the burial-place of the Mac-

Gregors of Glen Strae. Many of the Loch Awe school of carved grave-slabs mark the MacGregor burials, and also those of Campbells of Glen Orchy, MacIntyres of Glen Noe, and MacNabs of Barachastlain. The present church was built in 1811 by the 4th Earl of Breadalbane; it is octagonal, with a square tower and a little spire. The colours of the west window behind the pulpit should be seen when the afternoon sun shines through, for they harmonise with the glorious tints and hues of Glen Orchy and Loch Aweside.

Of the two homes of the MacGregors of Glen Strae — either their castle, whose site was near Castles Farm, or their house *Tigh Mor* at Stronmilchan — little remains. Both were totally destroyed by the relentless Campbells in their ferocious campaign to extirpate the MacGregors. Their crowning success came in 1611: MacGregor lands had been forfeited, their castle destroyed, and even their name proscribed; the successor to the executed Alasdair as Chief fled to Stirlingshire, where he was eventually persuaded to make over the ownership of Glen Strae for ever to Black Duncan Campbell of Glen Orchy.

The sites of these two MacGregor homes lie on the old military road, which skirts the loch-head much farther back than either the present road or the railway. The A85 swings round quickly, following the lochside to Lochawe village on the northern shore. The railway made this village, bringing tourists to its large and imposing hotels near the end of the nineteenth century. In 1881 Walter Douglas Campbell of the Innis Chonain mansion house started to rebuild St Conan's Church, but it was not finished until 1930. Its style is a mixture of Gothic and Romanesque, with a dash of Byzantine; its material, granite, hewn from the side of Beinn Cruachan in great chunks and rolled down to the building-site.

Visitors to Lochawe wanted fishing, and still do: licences are obtainable. There are also fish-farms in the loch, as there are in most of the West Highlands' freshwater and sea-lochs, for they are now big business. In one of the recent great storms the Loch

Awe fish-farms broke up, and the fish escaped into the loch. Within hours the lochside was stiff with anglers, mostly up from Glasgow, helping themselves, a highly profitable exercise which went on for months. Visitors also wanted cruises on the loch, and an echo of this remains today, for the old steamer pier is back in use for a real steamer. The Dalriada Steam Packet Company have started to operate cruises in the venerable little steamboat *Lady Rowena*. Three different cruises are available, at different times on different days; a time-table is posted at the entrance to the lane down to the pier. One is called the Castle Cruise, to the mouth of the Orchy at the loch-head, with a view of Kilchurn, then to Fraoch Eilean and the Black Islands beyond Inishail; another, called the Portsonachan Lunch Cruise, goes to the old ferry inn at Portsonachan on the eastern shore, where passengers can enjoy a good lunch, and back again, an hour each way. The third goes to the Ardnaseig Gardens on the point opposite Innis Chonain, and as far as possible up the Pass of Brander.

This western arm of the loch which reaches far into the pass always appears gloomy, because of the great lowering northern hills overhanging it so precipitously. These are the heights of Beinn Cruachan, where high up in Coire Cruachan the Hydro-Electric Board built a great dam and flooded the corrie, at a height of 1,200 feet. They tunnelled into the granite mountain itself and built a power station, and an extraordinary feat of engineering it was. They built the dam, cut the tunnels into the solid rock, cut galleries and tunnels for the pipes, hollowed out a machine-hall, and opened it all in 1965 as the second biggest pumped storage station in the world (the biggest is in Luxembourg). It has four generating turbines, with a capacity of 400 megawatts, and its average annual output is 450 million units. Two steep shafts blasted into the rock enable it to drive the water back into the reservoir: the electricity is stored by using it this way, to rebuild the potential water-power. If you go to the visitor centre on the lochside you can find out all about it.

During the summer months, the Board will take visitors right into it with minibus tours; more energetic enthusiasts may feel they would like to walk the five miles of the tracks from Lochawe village, and outright mountaineers will want to do it the hard way by climbing up the west bank of the *Allt Cruachan* (by the falls) to reach the dam. From the reservoir a track shows you clearly how to reach the *Bealach an Lochain*, the pass below *Meall Cuanail*, and from there with a bit of hard going you can reach the higher of the two peaks of Beinn Cruachan. Proper equipment is essential, but it is not beyond any fit person: my wife did it, some years ago, with her father and brothers, which was very brave in this wholly Campbell country, as they are McDonalds.

Arthur Gardner did it, and describes it in his book *The Peaks, Lochs and Coasts of the Western Highlands*; he and his companions had tried one day to climb Cruachan, but the weather had broken and snow-storms forced them to abandon the attempt. 'Our next attempt', he says, 'was made under very different conditions. The morning was a perfect one, and, wishing to run no risks of a change, we made straight for the nearer summit, which we reached with little trouble, and no difficulties beyond one or two steep pitches'.

'The view from the second, or Taynuilt peak, which is only 70 or 80 feet lower than the main summit, is much the finest, as it juts out towards Loch Etive in such a way as to command that beautiful arm of the sea from end to end, while the spurs of the main peak cut off the dreary moorland which forms the middle distance in the view from the highest summit'. He could see, he says, the Isle of Rhum, 60 miles away; some of the Outer Hebrides; the Glencoe peaks, and of course 'the familiar bluff outline of Ben Nevis asserted its supremacy, while farther away still ridge beyond ridge melted away into the distance'.

The Pass of Brander is narrow, dark, and possessed of its own ghoulish reputation: its very name, *am Brannraidh* in Gaelic, means Place of Ambush, and there have been plenty of those in the gruesome history of the Highlands. The most significant was in 1308.

Robert Bruce, on returning to the mainland from Arran, was still struggling to maintain himself as undisputed King of Scotland. John MacDougall, Lord of Lorn, opposed him; the MacDougalls had already inflicted a defeat on him in the dark days of 1306 at Tyndrum, and torn from his cloak the trophy that became known as the Brooch of Lorn. The Lord of Lorn was usually an ally of the Lord of the Isles, and Angus MacDonald of the Isles had already given Bruce his backing, but John MacDougall had married the daughter of Red John Comyn of Badenoch, and Bruce had killed this rival in a desperate struggle in the church of the Greyfriars in Dumfries, in 1306. MacDougall of Lorn was bound to uphold the family honour.

Bruce advanced into the Pass of Brander, the key to Lorn, knowing that the MacDougalls would attempt an ambush. Sure enough, high up on the walls of the pass they were poised to receive him, with great boulders to roll down on his men. Bruce therefore sent his staunch lieutenant James Douglas high up into the hilltops with a strong band of archers. Bruce's men began to attack the MacDougalls uphill, dodging the boulders; Douglas's archers simultaneously peppered them with arrows from above. The MacDougalls were routed, flying down to the ford *Creag an Uillt*, near modern Bridge of Awe, where Bruce's men cut them off and continued the slaughter until the Awe flowed red. Bruce took all Lorn from the MacDougalls and gave it to Campbell of Loch Awe.

On the eastern side of the loch a minor road called B840 leaves the A819 at Cladich and follows the lochside. This side is easier of access than the western side, passes through some pleasant green-wood from the ancient forest and some interesting sites. The first is Portsonachan, the 'Blessed Port' from which a ferry crossed the loch to Taychreggan on the other side, still called North Port. The rights to run the ferry were held for

400 years by one family, the MacPhedrans; during the thirth-eenth century Sir Neil Campbell is said to have given these rights to MacPhedran, his helmsman in perpetuity, because of his doughty and skilful striving to rescue his master's galley during a more than usually stormy loch-crossing. After a fierce clan battle in 1770 the Campbells took the rights back from them, and in the nineteenth century the estate was bought by Malcolm of Poltalloch, who rebuilt the old drovers' inn as the Portsonachan Hotel. The ferry ran until about 1945. The hotel today is in good shape, providing lunches for *Lady Rowena*'s passengers, and around it is a holiday village with chalets and a caravan site.

The road runs along the very edge of the loch, which means that it goes in a straight line for no more than ten yards at a time, and it is single-track so one has to watch out for oncoming traffic; there is not much of it. Hills rise steeply up to great heights behind. At a farmhouse called Blarghour there are ruins on the hillside of a large deserted township, and on the far side of the descending stream, *Allt Blarghour*, a little track leads up to a stupendous waterfall of 90 feet, once reckoned to be one of the greatest attractions of Loch Awe. Along the lochside road you come unexpectedly to another castle on the offshore island Innis Chonnel. It seldom appears among the picture postcards of West Highland castles, but its grim grey thirteenth-century walls are impressive enough, its doleful atmosphere is just as menacing as Munro's Doom, or Dunderave, and it was the principal seat of Clan Campbell until the building of Inveraray in the mid-fifteenth century.

The name Campbell, unusually among Highland names, comes from a physical peculiarity: *Cam-beul*, the crooked mouth (another is Cameron, from *Cam-sron*, crooked nose). One Gillespic Cambell is recorded in 1266 as holding land in Menstrie and Sauchope in Clackmannanshire. His descendants claimed that Gillespic was connected by marriage, a few generations back, with Aife, daughter of Paul O'Duine, known as Paul an Sporran, the Royal Treasurer, and that he was descended from the legendary hero Diarmid. This is why the Campbells are sometimes called Clan Diarmid. In 1292 Colin Campbell, said to have been the son of Gillespic, supported the claim of Robert Bruce (the grandfather of King Robert) to the throne, following the death of Margaret, the Maid of Norway, in 1290.

This Colin Campbell was the '*Cailean Mor*' who founded the fortunes of his family: he was knighted by Alexander III in 1280, was killed in battle fighting the MacDougalls of Lorn, and was buried in Kilchrenan, up the road from Taychreggan on Loch Aweside. His son Neil Campbell, the first '*MacCailean Mor*', had been astutely married to a sister of the Robert Bruce who was later to be king. There were three Robert Bruces at this period: the old 'Competitor' who was about eighty when he claimed the throne, his son, and his grandson the future king. Neil Campbell joined Bruce in 1296, and was given Lorn after the battle in the Pass of Brander. After Bannockburn in 1314 he was given all the Earl of Atholl's land: the Campbells were on their way. Their lateral branches, such as the Campbells of Glen Orchy, became equally powerful, and bit by bit the clan annexed, swindled or fought their way to be lords of all Argyll.

The castle of Innis Chonnel continued in use by the Campbells, under hereditary captains, first MacArthurs, then MacLachlans, during the sixteenth and seventeenth centuries, and was used by them for the incarceration of their more valuable captives. One such was the infant son of Angus MacDonald of Islay, who was kept there for twenty years until rescued by MacIain of Glencoe.

Just past the little offshore island of *Innis Searraiche*, where there is a ruined chapel and a burial ground, still in use, is Kames Park, a wide green meadow with the Kames river flowing through it on its way to the loch; on either bank there are two more deserted townships. Kames, the southern one, is distinguished by a huge boulder sitting on a little hillock, known as the Devil's Rock. It seems that the Devil threw it to stop his Sunday peace being disturbed by the singing of the Kames parishioners.

The eastern shores of the loch here are more open and less wooded than the opposite side; in this southern end of the loch itself is the deepest water, reaching something like 300 feet in places. Here lurks the *Beathach Mor*, the Great Beast of Loch Awe, a frightful monster with a horse-shaped head, a scaly back and no less than twelve gigantic legs. To see it, you need to have put away a good few drams of malt whisky and, when you have seen it, plenty more to restore the nerve.

Near the southern end of the loch stands Fincharn Castle, on a rocky headland. It is of thirteenth-century origin and used to be a stronghold of the MacMartins, until its lord decided to exercise his ancient *'droit de seigneur'* on a young and lovely retainer about to be married. The bridegroom, not surprisingly, was so incensed that he managed to burn the castle down, and it has never been repaired.

At Kilneuair, 'Chapel of the Yews', is the ruined church of St Columba; it is roofless, but still has aumbries, piscina and font, and there are many carved grave-slabs in the churchyard. It was built in the fifteenth century, with stones from an older church at Killevin near Auchindrain on Loch Fyneside: they were brought across the great bleak wilderness stretching between the two lochs called Leacan Muir, along a still usable rough track, by a hand-to-hand human chain, all the twelve miles.

Nearby is the head of the loch, the road through the village of Ford, and the Eurach Gorge close by the little Loch Ederline. Ford was formerly called *Ath na Cro*, Ford of the Cattle, from a crossing-point quite near the present bridge. The village has an hotel, and used to have two, but the Crown Inn, where Keats stayed during his Highland tour, is now a private house.

There are three ways of reaching the western shores of Loch Awe: one is by taking the road from Ford. It is narrow, winding, and rough, but it goes to Dalavich and eventually to Kilchrenan;

the second is from Kilmelford at the head of Loch Melfort, by way of Loch Avich, and the third is the B845 from Taynuilt, down Glen Nant to Kilchrenan. This will be described later in connection with Taynuilt.

This side of the loch is heavily afforested; Inverliever Forest was bought by the Forestry Commission from the Malcolms of Poltalloch in 1908, Dalavich was created for the forestry workers in 1952, and nowadays there are over 63 miles of forest roads, open to the public and all walkable. The Forestry Commission office in Dalavich will supply maps and details. You can go to New York from Dalavich. Just walk past the old church, along the shore for a mile or so, and there it is: a little drystone jetty. It was named after the York Building Company of the eighteenth century, which supplied charcoal for the iron-smelting furnaces at Bonawe on Loch Etive and Furnace on Loch Fyne. The charcoal was ferried across Loch Awe to Portinnisherrich on the eastern shore, thence to Loch Fyneside.

The glaciers that created Loch Awe carved their way through the Eurach Gorge and scoured out a channel on their way to the sea. When that opening became blocked with glacial deposit and the frozen waters turned instead to the Pass of Brander, the channel remained. Along it flowed a stream, and a mile or so downstream at Kilmartin, the valley opened up to the great plain which is the birthplace of the first kingdom of Scotland.

The road from Loch Awe and Ford, B840, emerges into the deep green valley of the Kilmartin Burn opposite the remains of Carnasserie Castle, a ruin which perches high on the hillside, surveying the length of the lovely, wooded, fertile glen. There is a good car park where the burn burbles by, and a metalled track that winds its way up to the castle.

It was never intended to be a defensible castle: it was built in 1565, ostensibly for the 5th Earl of Argyll, by John Carswell, Superintendent of the Reformed Church and subsequently Bishop of the Isles, and clearly intended as his own residence. In deference to the earl, Carswell had the Campbell coat-of-arms inscribed in stone over the doorway; Carswell's own Gaelic scholarship is revealed in the wording, *Dia le na nduibhne*, 'God be with O'Duine', referring to the Campbells' ancestor. The castle takes the form of a tower-house with a hall and a staircase-tower, it is in good order with strategically placed explanatory plaques, and is looked after by the Secretary of State for Scotland — or, perhaps, by one or two lads who do it for him. Carswell used his Gaelic erudition to good effect when he translated John Knox's *Book of Common Order*, the first book ever to be printed entirely in Gaelic.

Kilmartin village is perched on one of the shelves of land left by the retreating glacier: these can be traced on both sides of the glen, like the famous 'parallel roads' of Glen Roy. It is not large, just a small cluster of cottages, a church, an hotel, a restaurant, one or two shops, a wood-carver's workshop with craft-shop attached, and an old watch-tower. The latter is known as Kilmartin Castle: it stands on the north side of the village and was probably built in the sixteenth century by John Carswell when he was Rector of Kilmartin. It became Campbell property, and a somewhat vague story is told of an attack on it by unnamed aggressors at an unspecified time. It was set on fire, and its tenant, one Colin Campbell known as 'Wonderful Colin', escaped through a burning outbuilding; his armour was red-hot from the fire so he leapt into a pool of the Kilmartin Burn called the *Linnhe Lurach* to cool it and himself. The Cairn Restaurant nearby probably still has Steamed Colin on its menu.

The church was built in 1835 on the site of several pre-decessors; it is in the simple Church of Scotland style and houses three ancient carved crosses which formerly stood in the churchyard. All are battered and broken, one is fifteenth-century, another sixteenth, but the third, a column carved with delicately interlaced Celtic patterns, is said to be from the ninth century. This is the Kilmartin Cross. One of the others has a figure of Christ crucified: the arms of the cross are broken, but have been fixed back on. One arm used to lie beside the column in the churchyard, the other features in a story told by Joan Pearson in *Kilmartin: the Stones of History*.

'I hear from the Reverend Turner, who was formerly minister at Kilmartin, that when the council workmen were digging near the bridge over the Kilmartin Burn not long ago one of them was just about to split a piece of stone with his pick when he stopped.

'Officials from the Department of the Environment were soon on the scene and, as Rev. Turner put it, "With the piece of stone in the back of their van they rushed to Kilmartin graveyard and tried it on top of the broken column." One can imagine their delight and excitement when they found that it fitted exactly'.

There is a remarkable collection of carved grave-slabs in the churchyard. Some are in a roofed mausoleum, others lie flat in a stone surround. They show warriors in armour, swords, and galleys. The *claidheamh mor*, the great sword or claymore, was originally the mighty two-handed sword carried by mediaeval Highland clansmen: these are the swords carved on the stone slabs, all from the celebrated Loch Awe workshops and dating from the fourteenth and fifteenth centuries. Some were collected by a Malcolm of Poltalloch, who had the name Poltalloch incised on each one. Some of them may have been brought from *Eilean Righ* in nearby Loch Craignish: its name, Island of the King, indicates that it might have been a burial-place for the early kings of Dalriada.

The church is at the apex of a line of cairns. Cairns are chambered burial vaults, and there are no less than six of them south of the church. The early Christians used existing pagan places of worship for their churches, and the evidence points strongly to some kind of religious significance in the line of cairns, which date from Neolithic to Bronze Age: a linear Necropolis. This plain was accessible and fertile, two good reasons for early settlers to make their homes there. Nether Largie South, the fourth in line from Kilmartin, is the earliest with a twenty-foot-long chamber, divided into four sections. In it were found burnt and unburnt bones, and a Neolithic bowl which is now in the British Museum. Bronze Age beakers and evidence of interment were found there too, so the cairn was in use for a long time. The other cairns are all from the Bronze Age (1700–300 BC) and are called, from the south, Nether Largie Mid, Nether Largie North, and Glebe Cairns, the latter being that nearest Kilmartin itself. The other two are Ri-Cruin, on the Poltalloch Estate, and Dunchraigaig, to the east of it on the far side of the A816, the main road.

Interspersed with these cairns are some standing stones, also Neolithic. One group stands just south of Nether Largie South Cairn, consisting of an outlier and three pairs, in the shape of an X. The central stone is nine feet tall and is engraved with curious cup markings. Another semi-circle is at Temple Wood, and another a mile south, just off the road, at Ballymeanoch: these stand in two rows, four in front, two in the back, with a fallen outlier. Another mile south and there are seven more in groups of three, two and three, but three are fallen. Their markings, of the cup-and-ring sort, have never been satisfactorily explained, since unlike the Secretary of State for Scotland, the people who put them there did not leave helpful information on plaques. All of these ancient sites are accessible, two of the cairns, Nether Largie North and South, may be entered, and the Temple Wood stone circle (to the west of the line of cairns) has an information board and site-plan.

There are also remains hereabouts of more recent habitations, the various mansions built and demolished by sundry Campbells and Malcolms: Kilmarton House, Old Poltalloch, and New Poltalloch. The Malcolms, the local landowning family, eventually resided at Duntrune Castle which they bought from the Campbells of Duntrune in 1785. The castle, standing on a rocky promontory overlooking Loch Crinan, was built in the thirteenth century; as it is still a private residence neither it nor its access road are available for public scrutiny. In 1644 the

Campbell castellans were besieged by Montrose's valiant general Sir Alasdair MacDonald. A piper was despatched to spy out the castle's strength, and while he was doing so he became aware of a plan by the Campbells to trap MacDonald's men. In trying to extricate himself to warn his chief, he was caught. The Campbells cut both his hands off, then buried him alive beneath the floor of the keep, where he died, slowly. When building work was in train during the nineteenth century, they dug up a skeleton with no hands: they buried it beneath a four-foot standing stone, now called 'The Piper's Grave', near the shore half a mile east of the castle. Just north of this, up on the hill, is the original Duntrune, *Dun an t-Sroine*, Fortress of the Promontory, an Iron Age hill-fort. Celtic myth abounds with stories, and one of them concerns the sons of Uisneach; young Naoise MacUisneach, lover of the beautiful Deirdre of Glen Etive, came to Duntrune and flirted with the daughter of its lord, but the story of Deirdre of the Sorrows ought to wait for its proper setting, Glen Etive.

Three more ancient forts are sited on the promontory of Ardifuir, and below them is Scodaig Point. This name recalls the beginnings of the Scottish nation, because it is named after Queen Scotia, mother of the whole race of the Scotti. Here, legend has it, she landed from her gold-bright galley, on her god-given horse, which left behind a trail of hoofprints. They are still there, and you can see them etched deeply on the shining surface of the wave-splashed rocks.

The later Roman historian Ammianus Marcellinus says that in 364 AD 'the Picts, Saxons, Scotti and Attacotti were harassing the Britons with constant disasters.' This is the first written reference to the Scotti. By this time the early settlers of Dalriada had consolidated their hold on the area, ousting the indigenous Picts from the rock of Dunadd and using it as their capital. The sons of King Erc of the Irish Dalriada, Fergus, Angus and Lorn, with all their followers, arrived in Loch Crinan and sailed up the winding Add, in 498 AD. Tradition says that they brought with them the legendary *Lia Fail*, the Stone of Destiny, a block of red sandstone held for many years in Cashel Cathedral. It was reputed to be the stone used by Jacob as a pillow. 'And Jacob rose up early in the morning, and took the stone that he had put for his pillows, and set it up for a pillar, and poured oil upon the top of it.' (*Genesis, 29.18*) How this stone found its way from Bethel to Ireland is not entirely clear (but no doubt the Irish have a cogent explanation), but it was regarded with great reverence by the Scots, who brought with them also the memory of a prophecy that wherever the stone rested, the race of Scotia would prevail. Fergus was the first king of Dalriada to be crowned, seated upon the stone, up on the rock of Dunadd.

Between the low coastal hills on whose promontories Duntrune and the other old forts were built, and the hills of the ridge between Loch Awe and Loch Fyne, the River Add, augmented with the waters of the Kilmartin Burn, meanders through the Great Moss to Loch Crinan and the sea. The Add rises in the Leacan Muir, that bleak wilderness; its progress across the Moss is slow. *Moine Mhor*, the Great Moss, is a huge expanse of fenland which once was a tidal lagoon, inlet from the sea. The rock of Dunadd rears up from it like an island in the ocean, so obviously defensible that long before the Scots came, the Picts (or whatever they were called) had used it.

From the A816, travelling towards Lochgilphead, there is a track on the right, making straight for the hill. It is a vile, pot-holed, stony and rutted track, and it ends in a clearing by a farmhouse. From the clearing one may ascend the rock, and people do so all the time, although it is hard going. The entrance to the fort is between two huge slabs of rock, a natural cleft, which leads to a terrace where there was a hut-settlement. You climb steeply to another terrace, and then to the top. The higher of the two knobbly humps is Summit Fort, the lower is where the ceremony of the coronation took place. There is a carved outline of a foot in the rock, and nearby the faintly incised figure of a wild boar, symbol of courage. The candidate for coronation, clothed no doubt in white and bearing the wand of justice in one hand and the sword of kingship in the other (since justice and defence were the two principal duties of mediaeval kings), would place his foot in the imprint and swear a sacred oath to follow in the foot-steps of his predecessors. When seated on the Stone of Destiny, he would then be crowned king.

St Columba himself crowned one of the kings, Aedann mac Gabhran, in 574; as St Columba and his Christian missionaries brought literacy along with their faith, this was the first recorded coronation. On the lower terrace, covered with a slab of rock, there is a well dedicated to him.

From Summit Fort look out over the plain: you can see for miles all around, to the low coastal hills to the west, to Loch Crinan south of them, nearly to Lochgilphead southward, to the Argyll hills to the east, and a long way up the plain towards Kilmartin. Directly below, the Add winds its silvery way across the Great Moss. No wonder that Dunadd remained the Dalriadic capital until Kenneth MacAlpine made himself king of all Scotland in 843 and moved his capital (and the Stone of Destiny) to Scone. Legend says that for a while the stone was kept in Dunstaffnage Castle, in Lorn, but if so it was in the Dalriadic fort which preceded it. Successive Scottish kings were crowned while seated on it at Scone until Edward I of England lifted it, took it south, and installed it under the coronation chair in Westminster Abbey, where save for one brief interlude, it has been ever since. Perhaps it was the stone Jacob used as a pillow at Bethel; but it was at Scone for over 450 years, and as John Prebble says in *The Lion in the North*, 'Geologists say it is Lower Old Red Sandstone, and quarried nearby.'

When MacAlpine conquered the Picts and moved his capital away, the name Dalriada fell into disuse, substituted by the name Argyll. But Dunadd is still venerated by modern Scots, which is why there is a constant stream of visitors to it. It was early April when I climbed the rock, and it was slippery with mud, yet there were people of all ages, from small children to the fairly elderly, reaching the summit. They were pilgrims to the cradle of the Scottish nation.

5

Knapdale and Kintyre

The long peninsular extending south from *Moine Mhor* is nearly bisected by West Loch Tarbert; the first section is Knapdale, the second and larger, ending in the rocky headland called the Mull, is Kintyre. The island of Gigha lies off Kintyre's west coast. The peninsula consists of a chain of low hills, none over 2,000 feet, and barren wilderness in the centre, and fertile farmland and settlements along the coasts. Very few of the roads cross it. It is fifty-four miles long, and never more than ten wide.

The name Knapdale means hill and dale: a knap is a sharp-pointed hill, of which there are plenty. Its east coast, from Lochgilphead, along which the A83 runs to Tarbert, fronting Loch Fyne, is attractive but not very exciting; its west coast, deeply indented and beset by rocky islands, is both.

The entire peninsula is severed at its northern extremity by the Crinan Canal. The reason for its construction was to enable sailors wishing to go from the west coast to Loch Fyne or Clydeside to obviate the need to negotiate the entire length of the peninsula. Sir John Rennie initiated the survey, and work began in 1794; the canal opened in 1801, but capital was short and it was not properly finished: in 1805 seventy yards of its bank were destroyed by flooding and it had to close. It was reopened in 1809 but was still unsatisfactory, so in 1816 the

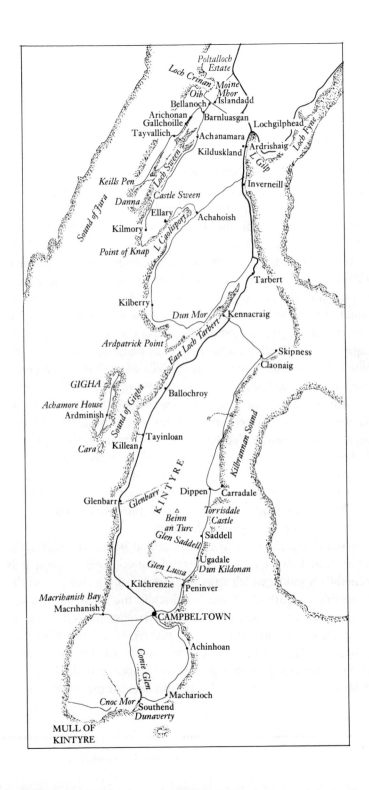

Poltalloch
Estate
Loch Crinan
Moine
Oib
Mhor
Bellanoch
Islandadd
Barnluasgan
Arichonan
Gallchoille
Achanamara
Lochgilphead
Tayvallich
Kilduskland
Ardrishaig
Loch Sween
L. Gilp
Keills Pen
Inverneill
Danna
Castle Sween
Ellary
Achahoish
Kilmory
L. Caolisport
Point of Knap
Sound of Jura
Tarbert
Kilberry
Dun Mor
Kennacraig
Ardpatrick Point
East Loch Tarbert
Skipness
Claonaig
GIGHA
Ballochroy
Achamore House
Sound of Gigha
Ardminish
Kilbrannan Sound
Tayinloan
Cara
Killean
KINTYRE
Glenbarr
Dippen
Carradale
Glenbarr
Torrisdale
Beinn
Castle
an Turc
Glen Saddell
Saddell
Glen Lussa
Ugadale
Dun Kildonan
Kilchrenzie
Peninver
Macrihanish Bay
Macrihanish
CAMPBELTOWN
Achinhoan
Conie Glen
Cnoc Mor
Macharioch
Southend
Dunaverty
MULL OF
KINTYRE

great Thomas Telford came and inspected its length and breadth; the vital improvements were made, and by 1817 it was more or less as it is today. It runs from Loch Crinan along the base of the Knapdale hills, above *Moine Mhor*, to Ardrishaig on Loch Fyne. There are fifteen locks, giving a rise of sixty-four feet. In 1847 Queen Victoria was drawn along it in a barge by three horses, each ridden by a postilion in scarlet livery. It is used now principally by pleasure-boats, which in the dry summer of 1989 faced the problem of shallow water. Nothing large could be admitted.

At Crinan there is a large basin controlled by a lock which lowers boats into Loch Crinan. There are some houses, a shop or two, and the imposing white castellar frontage of the Crinan Hotel. The view from its terrace on a warm sunny morning (if you can drag your attention away from a refreshing pint) is superb. Immaculately snow-white gulls plane across the shining blue loch, beyond which the green hills of the Poltalloch estate rise above rocky headlands; the roofs and windows of grey Duntrune Castle can clearly be seen. Away to your right the flatlands of *Moine Mhor* stretch to the Argyll hills, hazy shapes beyond the winking lighthouse at the canal lock's entrance. Thirsty weekend sailors come up from their boats in the basin to throng the terrace, waiting for the lock-keeper to return from his lunch: the view holds their attention, as if amazed to find that the West Highlands can easily rival the Mediterranean for warmth, colour, and spectacular scenery.

A road runs alongside the canal, and at Islandadd, where the River Add flows into the lagoon of Inner Loch Crinan, it is joined by another which runs in a dead straight line across the Moss to just south of Kilmartin. Much of the Moss was drained in the nineteenth-century by the Malcolms of Poltalloch, to make use of its wonderful fertility, and crossing it is reminiscent of other fenlands, like those of East Anglia, or Romney Marsh, or the Camargue, with intersecting sluices and ditches, vast fields of grain, myriad wild birds, and over all the great bowl of sky giving that uniquely luminous quality.

The canal road, B841, joins the A816 at Cairnbaan, where there is an hotel, and on the south bank of the canal its eponymous cairn. Beyond Cairnbaan the canal follows the contour of the hills, and is raised above the road until it reaches Ardrishaig on Loch Gilp. This extension was necessary because Loch Gilp is very shallow, and dries out completely at low tide. Necessary or not, it appears to have disturbed the former inmates of a long-vanished friary at Kilduskland, behind Ardrishaig, because phantom White Friars have been seen gliding noiselessly along the canal bank there. Mind you, they might only become visible to human eye after a session in the nearby bar of the Royal Ardrishaig Hotel.

The northern part of Knapdale, immediately south of the Crinan Canal, is called the Oib, from *ob*, inlet. It is very heavily afforested, and riven by innumerable little lochans and the headwaters of Loch Sween. There are only two roads which penetrate it, but plenty of paths and tracks: the energetic are likely to be best rewarded. The first road, B8025, leads off the canal road at Bellanoch, sharply at an angle and up into the hills, and the other forks from it at Barnluasgan, a mile farther on. The tracks through the woods and glens of the Oib are marked on the large-scale Ordnance Survey maps, and they are vitally necessary, a *sine qua non*, or perhaps a *sine qua* get lost. Dreadful things might happen to forlorn and hapless wanderers, especially in *Gleann na Beiste*, for in one of its lochans nearby there lives a monster. It once came charging after Ewan Bacach, the famous Knapdale archer, who only managed to evade the serpentine creature's clutches by flinging his plaid over a standing stone; the monster saw the stone wearing the plaid, thought it was Ewen, and coiled itself so tightly round it that the stone was wrenched from the ground and split in two, and there it still lies. You have to be a bit careful in the Oib.

From Barnluasgan the B8025 does a double hairpin and curls around an old hill-fort, Dun Arichonan. At the most southerly point of this zig-zag, on a low terrace on the south side of the road and usually hidden in the bracken, are the Barnluasgan Stones. They constitute a sixty-five-foot oval of boulders, put there by early inhabitants for no fathomable reason, unless it was a monster-trap.

Houses are few, and only sad, derelict settlements now brood over the secret waters of Caol Scotnish at Arichonan and Gallchoille. Caol Scotnish is the northernmost creek of Loch Sween, widening at its southern end to form little *Loch a'Bhealaich*. On its banks lies the lovely village of Tayvallich (*Tigh a'Bhealaich*, the House of the Pass), where visitors mingle with the yacht-owners at the tables of the inn's patio, bright with parasols, sip their drinks and enjoy the serene beauty of the sequestered loch. Swallows and martins dive and swoop above the water among the white boats at anchor, waterfowl glide across the still surface, breaking the mirrored reflections, creating tiny V-shaped wakes. There are shops here too, a camping and caravan site, and one of the best-kept public conveniences in the West Highlands, where standards are high. A private house opposite the village store is the original *Tigh a'Bhealaich*, a drovers' inn.

The pass that gave the house its name is in the low hills, used now by a small road that runs from the village to Carsaig Bay, from which there is a fine view across the Sound of the island of Jura. From this favourite picnic-place a Forestry Commission track leads off northward along the coast to isolated settlements so lonely that the poet Thomas Campbell, staying at the house of Dounie in 1796 as tutor to the children of General Napier, could stand very little of it before he craved to return to the fleshpots.

From Tayvallich the B8025 runs inland until it finds the western bank of the long, silent, silvery *Linnhe Mhuirich*. Its far side is another peninsula, with *Linnhe Mhuirich* on one side and Loch Sween on the other; it is managed by the Scottish Nature Conservancy Council, because it still has a fine spread of old oak woodland, interspersed with moss, marsh and fen, and as cars are forbidden to enter there is a wealth of wild-life, of fish, fowl, and good Red Admiral. Taynish House is on the tip of this wonderfully unsullied tongue of land, overlooking the tortuous entrance to *Linnhe Mhuirich*, where its waters gurgle and slide and bubble over jagged reefs of rock, and fierce tide-rips swirl around the dozens of tiny islets where herons lurk. Despite these hazards there was a slate quarry at the northern end of the Linnhe, and the barge-skippers had to brave the terrors of the entrance. The quarry, now flooded, can still be seen, and a mile farther on, so can the massive ramparts of *Dun Mhuirich*, another ancient fort. As the little quiet road ventures farther along the shore of the Linnhe, past a rare farmhouse, the woodland thins and gives way to a bare and windswept land-scape, ablaze with gorse-yellow. Where the road skirts the marshy end of the Linnhe, many years ago a packman was violently assaulted and murdered. If you travel this way by night you may be followed by a queer, white, hazy light: it is his unhappy spirit.

Near the end of the Keills peninsula a track goes off to the island of Danna which is accessible by a causeway over the tidal flats. Then along the road there is a cottage with a gate, past which a muddy track skirts the shore of *Loch na Cille*. A tiny chapel and a stone cross stand up on the low hill to your right. This is Keills Chapel, dedicated to St Cormaig. There is an island in the mouth of Loch Sween, some way beyond Danna, called *Eilean Mor Mac Cormaig*, where there is also a chapel and a cross, and the plural form of Keills seems to indicate that the two chapels were parts of a religious teaching school. Keills Chapel is re-roofed and contains, in addition to some mediaeval carved grave-slabs, the eight-century Cross of Keills, which used to stand where its modern replacement does now. One of the grave-slabs has a hole in one end, and is reputed to have marked the burial of Ewen Bacach Graeme (Lame Hugh), the Knapdale archer who was chased by the monster. He wanted the hole in the gravestone so that even when dead he could see his favourite hunting ground, Cruach Lussa, on the far side of Loch Sween. Ewen would seem to have been better at archery than logic.

The muddy track continues to the point, where sharp jagged rocks spike the air like dragon's teeth. There is an old stone jetty on the foreshore, where cattle used to be brought ashore from Islay and Jura: they were driven along the western shore to Carsaig Bay, then across the pass and down to Tayvallich for a rest at the House of the Pass.

To explore the eastern shore of Loch Sween you must return to Barnluasgan, at the northern end of *Loch Coille Bharr*, from which tracks disappear into yet more remote and unheard-of little farmsteads, and woods and islands known only to their inhabitants. The road dives through thick woods, crosses the eastern side of *Loch Coille Bharr* then makes for Achnamara, a village of wooden houses created by the Forestry Commission for their foresters. Then you are down by the shore of Loch Sween, and at Ashfield there is a delightful view across the gleaming loch to the white dots of Tayvallich's houses at the head of *Loch a'Bhealaich*.

The way to Castle Sween is long, narrow, and highly satisfying; there are the usual passing-places, not much traffic, and still fewer houses. At last, opposite the island of Danna, is a sign pointing to Castle Sween Caravan site. This is a well-organised establishment with a shop, restaurant and bar, and its caravans sited close to the foreshore of the loch. Beyond it, on a rocky headland commanding the loch's entrance, is Castle Sween.

Considering that it is the oldest stone castle in Scotland, it is in excellent condition, its walls still formidably high. It was the first of the Norman-style square keeps, with a tower at each corner, and was originally roofed. A round-tower was added to the northern corner for sanitary purposes in the thirteenth century, and in the fourteenth century a large tower-house was

Castle Sween

attached to the eastern corner.

In about 1130 the famous Somerled succeeded his father as King of Argyll (or Lord: the written word is *Regulus*, ruler) and waged war against the Norsemen, who held all of Kintyre from West Loch Tarbert southward. Castle Sween was built, probably between 1130 and 1135, to guard the first safe harbour north of West Loch Tarbert. Somerled's Castle Claig in Fraoch Eilean in the Sound of Islay (between Islay and Jura), built in 1154, is similar. This castle was held for him by the Lord of Knapdale, MacSuidhne Ruadh (Son of the Red Warrior). Its name, *Caisteal Suidhean* or *Suidhne*, means either Castle of the Warriors, or Castle of Suidhne; the pun might be intentional, as a complement to the worthy and reliable Lord of Knapdale.

After Somerled's successful campaigns, Knapdale and Kintyre were ruled for 300 years by Clan Donald, Somerled's descendants. Between the fourteenth and sixteenth centuries, the MacNeils of Gigha acted as constables of the castle, then the MacMillans. When the MacDonald Lords of the Isles declined and fell in the late fifteenth century it was first claimed by the Crown, then granted, with all Knapdale, to the 1st Earl of Argyll, It was still held by the Campbells in 1644 when Sir Alasdair MacColla Ciotach MacDonald besieged it for Montrose and the King, and burnt them out. After much repair and consolidation, the castle is now open to visitors at all times, without charge.

Stand on the wooden platform up on the battlements and look out, towards the open sea at the loch-mouth; see the still water shining like glass reflecting perfectly the white yachts, a solitary fishing boat making a fishtail wake as it moves slowly out to the Sound of Jura, the pale sea-birds mewing and wheeling about the ancient turrets and down by the water, swallows and martins darting back and forth to their nests in the old walls' many crevices; feel, in a place built for warfare, the sense of hallowed peace, its quietness broken only by the earth's natural sounds – until a child in the caravan park squeals, and a dog barks, and a car engine intrudes.

A few more miles along the lochside will bring you to Kilmory, where there is a chapel dedicated to St Maolrubha (pronounced Maree, as in Loch Maree, named after him), and a fourteenth-century Celtic cross called MacMillan's Cross. According to W. H. Murray, both of them are in 'the ugliest farm in Argyll': as he wrote that in 1967 there has certainly been time to beautify it.

The Point of Knap is the southernmost tip of this peninsula, on the far side of which is Loch Caolisport. The road stops, so you have to go all the way back along Loch Sweenside, down to the canal road, and along the A816 to Ardrishaig. South of Ardrishaig on Loch Gilp there is a right turning at Inverneill called B8024, the only road that crosses Knapdale. It climbs to 634 feet, at first through the dark battalions of the Forestry Commission's coniferous armies, then to a bald, bare, rugged and stark landscape; right at the top is a high, windswept freshwater pool called Loch Arail. The road takes you gently down to the head of Loch Caolisport at Achahoish, where a track leaves to serve Ellary, on the western side of the loch not far from the fore-mentioned ill-favoured farm at Kilmory. Achahoish shelters under the slopes of a hill called *An Torr*, 613 feet, on whose summit once stood *Caisteal Torr*, but since the castle has been treated as a stone-quarry there is not much of it left. It was once the stronghold of Conall, the 5th King of Dalriada. According to Adamnan, Abbot of Iona in the seventh century, Conall ruled Dalriada between 560 and 574, and as St Columba arrived on the scene in 563, Conall would have been the local authority, and it may have been he who gave Iona to Columba. There is a tradition that St Columba sometimes used a cave on the western shore of Loch Caolisport, about three miles from Achahoish, facing the first bay; the island at the mouth of the bay is called *Eilean na h'Uamhaidh*, Island of the Cave. Seton Gordon says that the saint celebrated the Sacrament in the cave, and 'the old altar remains; in the rock near it are two circular hollows, one small, the other larger. The holy water was kept in the smaller hollow; the larger was for the washing of the pilgrims' feet. On the wall of the cave above the altar is carved a small cross, thick, sturdy, and shapely — the work of master hands.'

The B8024 road, running mostly along the clifftops now, gives you splendid views of Jura and Islay across the Sound of Jura. Another Iron Age fort crowns a promontory on the north side of Miller's Bay, in which there is a camping and caravan site, and a little farther on at Kilberry Head is the site of *Cill Bhearaigh* itself, a monastery named after St Berach, who visited St Columba at Iona. Kilberry Castle, a comparatively modern house, has a collection of carved stones and a Celtic cross from the monastery.

This western Knapdale coast is both cultivated and pastoral, with sheep everywhere (including in the road, a frequent Highland hazard). Inland the hills rise, screening from view their intractable wildness. It is worth simply standing by the roadside and sniffing the clean, healing air, and gazing down at the ever-changing, polychrome sea, all its greens, blues and greys mingling, merging with the green-brown islands on its horizon.

Due south of Kilberry the road turns sharply left, dropping steeply to the head of little Loch Stornoway, then strikes off inland to cut off Ardpatrick Point. The landscape here is predominantly green and lush, forested with old oak, sycamore, rowan and ash, and studded with outcropping rough crags, towering behind you. Sparkling water gleams through the trees again as you go down to West Loch Tarbert at Dunmore, where a derelict castellar mansion vegetates in the trees and there is another old fort, *Dun mor*. Near it a large stone marks the reputed grave of the Irish hero Diarmid, the stories of whose hunting of the boar and tragic death were brought to Scotland and associated with a good many localities.

From the pier at Kennacraig on the far shore of the long, narrow loch, the steamers ply to and from Islay; the western shore road passes through beautiful woodland, the tree-hung hills to your left, the gleaming loch on the other hand. Barely a mile separates the two lochs of West and East Tarbert, and as at the Tarbet on Loch Lomondside, the name denotes an isthmus.

In 1098 King Magnus Bare-leg of Norway came to the Isles to put down a revolt by the Gaels against his deputies, which he achieved with maximum cruelty. Further ambition impelled him to challenge King Edgar of Scotland and threaten to invade mainland Scotland. Edgar allowed him any island circumnavigable in a sea-going vessel. Kintyre, Magnus knew, had a coastal strip more fertile than most of the islands, so he caused his longship, under full sail and with himself at the steering-oar to be hauled across the little isthmus between the two lochs Tarbert, so that he could claim to have the 'island' of Kintyre: and was granted it. King Robert Bruce repeated this extraordinary feat with his whole fleet, apparently to fulfil a local prophecy: 'Scotland will prevail against all, when a ship in full sail rides over the Moss of Kilcalmonell', which was then the isthmus's name. Scotland certainly did not prevail when King Magnus did it.

Vessels were quite often dragged across the isthmus, in fact, to avoid the long voyage round the Mull. In the canal-fever days of the late eighteenth-century, a Tarbert canal was suggested.

James Watt, in 1770, thought it feasible, in 1776 Henry Bell estimated a cost of £90,000 for the project, and Parliament sanctioned it; but fifteen years went by, nothing had been done, the costs doubled, and by that time the Crinan Canal had opened instead.

Bruce also built the castle at Tarbert in 1326, on a 100-foot hillock. There had been a fort in so obviously strategic a spot, commanding the approaches up the East Loch to Tarbert and the isthmus, and it is recorded that King Selbach of Lorn burnt it in 712. In the thirteenth-century the walls enclosed a space of 120 square feet. Bruce's new building was augmented with a keep in the fifteenth-century, and it is the broken-down wreck of this tower that today moulders away above the busy little port.

East Loch Tarbert is a perfect haven, three miles long. It is still the centre of a thriving fishing business, which gives what would otherwise have appeared a mere holiday resort a sense of urgency. The fishing-boats moor at South Quay at some remove from the head of the harbour where the roads run alongside rows of attractive colour-washed houses, shops and inns, small boats lie at anchor and a multitude of gulls feed off the fishermen's scraps. There are times when the entire harbour is filled with pleasure craft, at a stage or the end of one of the periodic races in Loch Fyne and the Firth of Clyde, and the Tarbert inn-keepers think it's Christmas. Boating obviously features strongly in Tarbert's holiday attractions, boat-hire firms offer sailing and cruising, fishing licences are available, and if these maritime activities pall, there is a nine-hole golf course.

Two miles north of Tarbert on the Lochgilphead road there is a large nineteenth-century mansion called Stonefield Castle, now an hotel. Its builder, Sir Joseph Dalton Hooker, was the man who introduced into Scotland the first large-leaved rhodo-dendron from the Himalayas. The mild, moist climate of the West Highlands enabled it to thrive, and thereby caused Sir Joseph's name to be execrated by the keepers of such as Brodick

Castle, and all other gardens where rhododendrons are
regarded as pernicious weeds.

Throughout the length of Kintyre, there are only two roads
which cross it. Like Knapdale, the coastal belt is grassy and
fertile, but the interior is high, bleak moorland and mountain.
The first of the crossing roads is at Kennacraig, where a minor
road winds across the hills to connect with the Arran ferry at
Claonaig. The other is the main road itself, A83, which cuts in
eastward from the west coast to Campbeltown. This A83 is an
excellent road, and the temptation to speed along it must be
resisted, as there is much to see (unless, of course, you are late
for the Gigha ferry at Tayinloan). The east coast road is much
narrower and twistier, and altogether more entertaining.

As the A83 clears West Loch Tarbert and takes you along
Kintyre's west coast, the landscape becomes open, windy, and
sheep-infested; the blue Atlantic thunders below you, and out to
sea the island of Gigha can clearly be seen, beyond it the hazier
outline of Islay. Guarding the entrance to West Loch Tarbert is
Dun Skeig, said to be one of the most completely preserved
vitrifed forts in Scotland. Iron Age fort-builders would raise a
stone wall and strengthen it by lacing great baulks of timber in it
and across it; this form of criss-cross timber within a stone wall
is known as *murus gallicus* and is common in Continental sites.
Many of them, when excavated, were found to have been burnt,
and the timbers, burning fiercely, had vitrified the stone walls.
There is debate among archaeologists as to whether this was
done on purpose, to reinforce the walls, or was a result of
accident or of enemy attack.

The bay below Dun Skeig has a caravan and camping site,
and nearby is the village of Clachan (the Gaelic word for any
village or township) which is thought to be the oldest surviving
settlement in northern Kintyre. Its church, built on the site of a
thirteenth-century predecessor in 1760, is dedicated to St
Colman-Eala, Colman of the Swans, which gives the entire and
very extensive parish of Kilcalmonell its name. Farther on down

the road, between it and the sea, there is a Bronze Age cairn at Corriechrevie, and at Ballochroy some standing stones.

South of Ballochroy the land projects towards Gigha in a low-lying sandy triangle called Rhunahaorine Point: here in 1647 Argyll had his revenge for Inverlochy.

Montrose and Sir Alasdair MacDonald had sacked Inveraray and trounced the 1st Marquis of Argyll and his Campbells at Inverlochy. Thereafter, although he beat the Campbells again and the Covenanters too, Charles I's defeat at Naseby did Montrose no good and he lost support. The promised sack of Glasgow never materialised, and MacDonald took his Irish MacDonells on the homeward path, by way of Kintyre: this was Campbell country and had once been Clan Donald's, so a vengeful raid was contemplated. Sir Alasdair MacDonald, of giant build, cropped black hair and the bearing of a hero, was the son of a Colonsay chief called Colla Ciotach MacDonald: Coll the Left-handed. Alasdair was therefore known as Mac-Colla Ciotach, generally shortened by his lowland enemies to Colkitto. Argyll and his men had taken several fearful thrashings from MacDonald's wild hillmen, steered by the military genius of Montrose, and they were now out in force, believing that at last their time was come. At Rhunahaorine they fell upon the MacDonalds suddenly and with overwhelming numbers; the fight was short and sharp and very soon the MacDonalds, totally outnumbered, had to retreat. Sir Alasdair managed to escape across the water to Ireland, while the survivors of the battle marched south to the stronghold of Dunaverty, on the Mull of Kintyre. Every year, Rhunahaorine Point is bright with the blooms of thousands of tiny crimson wild roses: local tradition insists that they grow from the MacDonald blood shed at Colkitto's last stand. Modern occupants of the camping and caravan site there may reflect on it as they fry their breakfast bacon, enjoying the view.

On the higher ground of Rhunahaorine Point there used to be a stronghold of the MacDonalds of Largie, but their current residence, three castles later, is the house not far away at Ballure. Beyond the ferry terminal at Tayinloan, on the right of the road, there stands the ruined church of Killean, abandoned since its roof fell in during a service in 1770. It still contains the family vault of the MacDonalds of Largie; in the overgrown churchyard, within a stone's throw of the sea, with Gigha a few miles offshore, gulls mewing overhead, butterflies settling on the wildflowers, whose scents mingle with the tangy sea-odours, old stones protrude from the greenery recording many a MacMillan and MacCallum of Killean and other villages and crofts of West Kintyre.

The ferry linking Tayinloan with Gigha is the same kind as that which runs from Claonaig to Lochranza: a landing-craft with a ramp at one end and engine, cabins and wheelhouse at the other. It accommodates about six cars and a surprising number of foot passengers, and takes twenty minutes to cross to Ardminish Bay. We did so in a flat calm, on a still, warm, hazy morning; the water was translucent as glass, we could see the bottom for some way out, and then shoals of fish, and a huge jellyfish beneath the surface. A cormorant flapped along fifteen yards of water, dived, reappeared somewhere else; a seal surfaced, played to the gallery of oohs and aahs from admiring passengers before going about its business; over to the south the little islands Cara and Gigalum hung indistinctly in space as sea and sky fused in the opaline mist. The ferry-boat clanked into the concrete slipway and we landed in Gigha.

The island is six miles long and a mile and a half at its widest. It has a rocky spine running down its centre, its flanks on both sides green and fertile, visited by mild rain-clouds and washed by the Gulf Stream. Its name is the Gaelic version of the Norse *Gudey*, which means either Good, or God Island. There are so many associations with not just the Christian God but also with ancient mystic gods that people still call it Isle of Gods.

The cluster of houses comprising the village of Ardminish stands at the top of the hill above the bay; the ferry collects its passengers for the return journey, smart yachts lie tranquilly at anchor, children play on the white sand along the rocky shore; always, the sea-birds' evocative cries fill the placid air. The parish church is at the top of the village, and opposite the churchyard is the post office and general store, which is also a guest-house. This is run by J. and M. McSporran, and Mr McSporran, in addition to being the postmaster, is also the delivering postman, the policeman, the coastguard, the registrar, piermaster, and firemaster. We saw him, as we were drifting slowly back to the pier in late afternoon, wearing a straw sombrero and organizing the primary school's athletic games: a close tussle was developing for the high-jump and we stayed and watched as two little girls battled it out with one boy. Most of the island's 160 inhabitants seemed to be there, from the six farms and thirty-nine cottages; they live mainly from the land and fishing, but in the season tourists bring in some extra business.

The little church, standing in a spacious churchyard, is plain and dignified in the usual Church of Scotland fashion, and has several memorial windows, one to Lieut.-Col. Sir James Horlick, late of the Coldstream Guards, who died in 1972 aged 86. It was he who created the gardens at his Achamore House, a little way south of Ardminish. You simply walk down the village road past the inn, which is large and white with a modern extension; a palm tree shades the garden, where you can sip your beer and enjoy the fine view of the Kintyre hills across the blue water, perhaps listening to the strains of an accordionist playing Scottish airs in the bar. The lane is lined with cottages whose hedges are crimson and purple fuchsia, their gardens full of roses.

Achamore House lies on the gentle hillside, screened from westerly winds by thick woodland and the ridge. Sir James Horlick laid out the gardens in 1945, planting the kinds of trees and shrubs that you see in other Highland gardens like Crarae and Brodick; great trees, flowering bushes like azaleas and rhododendrons, a walled garden, cool glades with benches for the foot-weary. By a flowing pool there is a little wooden summer-house, given to Sir James by the Gigha people on his eightieth birthday. Two recommended routes are blazed with green arrows for a two-hour walk, blue for half an hour. The ferry passengers might have made a bee-line for the gardens, but the shady walks soon swallow them up and allow them to enjoy the blissful garden peace.

South of the gardens, on a low green knoll below Achamore Farm, there stand the 'Old Ones' of Gigha. They are two odd-shaped stones, standing as if on watch over the island, known as the *Bodach* and the *Cailleach*, the Old Man and the Old Woman. No-one is known to have put them there, they have just always been there, so they have been endowed with an atavistic sanctity; they have guaranteed fertility and prosperity throughout the ages, from immemorial days of sun-worship and earth-beliefs; even past conversion to Christianity, people would place offerings of milk and meal before them, hoping for a good harvest, or bountiful proclivity for their cattle or themselves. They stand gazing over the lovely Ardlamey Bay, towards the green hills of Islay and the rolling waves: they have a knowing air, for they have seen it all before.

In the south of the island, on the east of the peninsula called Leim, the road runs between fields of barley and ends at a jetty where there is a fuel store and some fishing-boats; lobster-pots lie in heaps outside a row of nearby cottages and on the pier, the sun gleams on the glassy water and the sea-birds rise in their hundreds from the little islands offshore. One of these is Gigalum, the largest is Cara which is named like Gigha from a Norse word, *Karoe*, Coffin Island. There are two buildings on Cara, both in ruins: a fifteenth-century chapel, and an eighteenth-century house built by MacDonald of Largie, but there are no inhabitants save for a brownie, which used to attend to all the household chores left undone overnight, and give a sharp thump to whichever neglectful person had caused it needless work. The household might have long since departed, but the brownie is still there, so they say.

To the north of Achamore House lie the ruins of Kilchattan, the thirteenth-century chapel of St Cathan. The simple quadrangle of stone walls is roofless and the gravestones are surrounded by high grass and wild-flowers, but here were buried the old MacNeil barons of Gigha, and here too lies Sir James Horlick, their successor. Bees, humming about the luxuriant fuchsia bushes in brilliant bloom, are your companions in the silent sanctuary, as you turn from the lichened stones to contemplate the rich green fields tumbling down to the blue Sound, where white-sailed boats move slowly before a backdrop of the green hills of Kintyre, hiding their heads in misty cloud.

North of Ardminish the landscape is almost treeless; there is a nine-hole golf course on the hills, occasional crofts, and a wide panorama from almost anywhere. The road runs straight as a die past *Dun Chiofaich* and *Creag Bhan*, the island's highest hill at 331 feet. *Dun Chiofaich* is a hill-fort which figures in one of the ancient Celtic legends about the hero Diarmid: he brought to Gigha the beautiful but faithless Grania, wife of Fionn Mac-Coul, who even then proceeded to tempt the local chieftain Chiofaich (or Kifi) in his hill-fort lair. Diarmid fought him over it, beat him, and hurled him down its southern slopes, where there is a tiny stone enclosure called 'Kifi's Grave'.

There is another Tarbert in northern Gigha, where the island narrows to about half a mile; on the eastern side, on the slopes of the hill Cnoc Largie, there is a well called *Tobar Mor*, the Great Well, in which there lived a female *direach*, a guardian, who for an offering of silver would control the wind. The MacNeils of Gigha would go there when they wanted a favourable wind to carry their galleys abroad: the silver having been offered, the stone cover of the well would be removed, the waters stirred with a white clamshell three times sunwise while incantations were recited, then three shellfuls of the sacred water would be thrown high in the direction the wind was wished to come from; before the day was out, the wind would change.

There have been of late several new Barons of Gigha, since the island's ownership has been fluctuating. When it was up for sale in 1989, Mr Malcolm Potier of Brasted Chart in Kent, a financier, bought it for six million pounds. According to a report in the Daily Telegraph; his offer was reported not to be the highest, but Mr David Landale, then Secretary to the Duchy of Cornwall, chose Mr Potier's rather than certain Middle-Eastern offers. Unfortunately Mr Potier became a victim of the economic recession of the 1990s and Gigha is now owned by the Holt family of Inverkip Marina in Wemyss Bay, Ayrshire.

The passengers gather again by the jetty, wrenching their children away from the beach, watching the ferry leave Tayinloan and chug towards them. It is the last ferry, and practically everyone who was on the morning one will leave by this one, plus others who came earlier or later. The Holy Island, its beaches, sea-birds, bright flowers, its plenitude of ancient cairns, stones and hills, its indefinable air of confident serenity, recedes into the western haze.

From Killean on the mainland of Kintyre the A83 winds its inexorable way southward and across the Barr Water at Glenbarr, which has another Bruce association. Many are the stories about Bruce's wanderings between 1306 and 1307, before and after his retirement to his arachnid cave: this story does not agree with the one in which he arrived in Arran with 300 men and a fleet of galleys, as it was James Douglas who came to Kintyre, crossed it, then went to Arran. Probably no-one will ever know the entire truth, for so many contest it.

According to this tale, Bruce landed hereabouts in 1307 after his sojourn in Rathlin, and met a tenant farmer, Gilchrist MacKay of Kilmaluag. MacKay conducted Bruce across the wilderness of the interior, over the shoulder of *Beinn an Turc* and down to Ugadale on the east coast, whence he took ship to Arran. While waiting for a boat, Bruce gave MacKay a great jewelled brooch as a reward, and promised that when he was again recognised as King of Scotland, he would give him all the crown lands of Arnicle in Glenbarr, and Ugadale. He duly honoured his promise, and the Brooch of Ugadale is still kept by the MacNeils of Ugadale and Lossit, who are descendants of Gilchrist MacKay, at Lossit House near Macrihanish.

Bellochantuy Bay is open and exposed to the fierce Atlantic weather, which sends the seas rolling and crashing against the foot of the high cliffs. Its name is from *Bealach an t-Suidhe*, the Pass of Resting: not much resting for the cottagers on the bay. A few miles farther south, on the verge of Macrihanish Bay, the road at last turns left to run inland, across the flat and fertile plain called the Laggan, to Campbeltown. On the way it goes through Kilchenzie: there is a ruined twelfth-century chapel dedicated to St Kenneth, who is buried in the offshore island of Mull called Inchkenneth. The Laggan, four-and-a-half miles wide, was once a peat-moss but was reclaimed by drainage; through it the Macrihanish water drains to the four-mile-long bay. In 1876 the famous golf course was opened that makes use of the belt of machair behind the beach: a true links course. There is also an airport there at Macrihanish Bay, and a large number of grass-covered mounds belonging to the Royal Air Force, because here are stored nuclear depth bombs for the Nimrod anti-submarine aircraft, in sufficient quantities to be allotted to allied aircraft in the event of hostilities. Macrihanish is the front line for any attack from the Atlantic.

The Laggan separates Kintyre from the Mull so thoroughly that it was probably once under water, making the Mull an island. The A83 finally comes to an end south of Campbeltown, where a right fork goes to Macrihanish, and the left will take you the ten miles to Southend, on the Mull. It passes through Conie Glen, following the Conieglen water. The land is arable and pastoral, and the bare green hills and isolated farmhouses make it look more like Yorkshire or Derbyshire than a part of the Highlands. At the glen's entrance the road passes between *Beinn*

Ghuilean on the left and Tirfergus Hill on the right; Tirfergus means land of Fergus, the first king of Dalriada. Some of his followers, settling here, brought with them earth from the glens of Antrim, because it would be imbued with St Patrick's gift of freedom from snakes. You need not worry about monsters in Tirfergus.

At the southern end of Conie Glen, on the summit of *Cnoc Mor*, is a huge hill-fort believed to be the chief stronghold of the original Pictish inhabitants of Kintyre, called the Epidii, 'People of the Horse'. Southend is the village at the first of the three bays, Brunerican, of this southern knob of land. Its unprotected houses have a weather-worn appearance but its inn is warmly hospitable. The golf course there has 18 holes; there is a caravan site looking out to Sanda Island, which has a lighthouse built in 1950 and the ruins of St Ninian's Chapel; at the foot of the cliffs above the sea-shore there stands the tall white Keil Hotel, whose 1930s architecture looks alien to this windy coast; nearby are the ruins of Keil School, burnt down in 1924. Behind both hotel and school ruins looms the towering Rock of Dunaverty, whose name has been taken for the golf course: it has memories far grimmer than those connected with golf.

On the site of an earlier fort, at the top of the Rock are the scattered remains of a once-great MacDonald stronghold, dating from the thirteenth-century, second in rank only to Dunyvaig, headquarters of the Lord of the Isles in Islay. In 1306 Angus MacDonald, Lord of the Isles, sheltered Bruce there on his way to Rathlin, one jump ahead of Edward I's English fleet. The English unsuccessfully besieged the castle, a hard nut to crack. Early in the sixteenth century James IV, most popular of all the Stewart Kings and a Gaelic speaker, tried to assert his rule over Kintyre. He rebuilt the castle at Tarbert, then moved south and garrisoned Dunaverty. Sir John MacDonald by then had been stripped of his lordship of the Isles, but he was not going to condone this insult to his pride: his MacDonalds stormed and recaptured the castle. In full view of the king who was out in the bay in his ship, they hanged his castellan from the battlements.

The most gruesome of all the castle's horrors, though, occurred in 1647. MacColla Ciotach had lost the battle at Rhunahaorine Point and escaped to Ireland; some of his men had sought refuge in Dunaverty, still held by their clansmen, swelling the garrison to about 300. David Leslie and his army of Covenanters (those who supported the Presbyterian cause) closed in, and the siege was on. Dunaverty's strength was its source of water, a natural spring: its weakness was that the spring was outside the walls, and although concealed, it was discovered by the besiegers. Deprived of water, the garrison was forced by thirst to offer terms of surrender. The Covenanters' Presbyterian minister, John Neave, however, would take no Catholic prisoners. There were no terms: all 300 captives were either run through on the spot, or hurled off the clifftop to the cruel rocks below. All were killed. The Rock of Dunaverty is encrusted with a crimson lichen called *Fuil nam Sluagh*, Blood of the Hosts, and it may be this that gives it the name Rock of Blood, or it may be the memory of that pitiless massacre.

In 1685 the Marquis of Atholl came, clearing up after Argyll's abortive rebellion on behalf of the Duke of Monmouth: Dunaverty was by then Campbell property, so it was completely demolished.

West of Dunaverty another great cliff rears high above the sea: Keil Point, its name from the thirteenth-century chapel *Cille Columcille*. Its remains lie within a cemetery on the right of the road, where there is very little space between cliff, road and sea. St Columba is said to have landed there, before he went on to Iona, and to prove it there are his very footprints, incised marmoreally on a nearby slab of sandstone! One of these is reckoned to be of ancient origin, like that on the rock of Dunadd, but the other is of comparatively recent design. Between the knoll and the chapel there is a large overhanging boulder, with the faint outline of a cross marked on it, and beneath it St Columba's Well.

There are vast and complex caves in the bluff of Keil Point, used by hermits in one age and smugglers in another; past the cliff the road turns suddenly right and heads up Glen Breack-erie. If you want to go and see the lighthouse on the Mull, you must turn left off this road past Carskiey House and follow the five-mile route through the wild, rugged, sheep-dotted and heathery hinterland, up into the high hills. Violent corners threaten to hurl you from the dizzy heights, but if you stop at one of the passing-places (not for long, since they are often in use by other visitors) you may see spectacular views of the sea, and Sanda, and even the crouching bulk of Ailsa Craig, way out in the far distance. At the point where you reckon that one more 360-degree corner will cause a terminal accident, you reach a wider stretch, intended as a car park, with a notice admonishing you that cars may go no farther. The road continues, however, in a series of wonderfully sharp zig-zags, down a steep cliff to the lighthouse, which can be seen from above. You have already climbed to 1,150 feet, the drop from car park to lighthouse is 850 feet, and the lighthouse is the remaining 300 feet above the sea: on a clear day you can see from any of these lofty stages all the way to the Antrim coast and Rathlin Island too, dim, smudgy, purple shapes on a hazy horizon; the sea between is all colours from pale opal to deep indigo, with a multitude in between of the blues and greens that most artists despair of mixing.

The lighthouse was built in 1788 and repaired in 1820 by Robert Stevenson; its light is visible for twenty-four miles. This is the Mull of Kintyre, the most southerly point of the West Highlands.

To begin the journey north you must return to Southend; if you survive the perilous five miles back to Carskiey House, you can take a road over the hills to Conie Glen, and from Southend you can head for the east coast at Macharioch and Polliwilline Bay, where there is a good view of Sanda, then follow the cliff-tops. The road dips and rises in a hair-raising fashion and the scenery is spectacular. At Balnabraid, on the north bank of a river, there is a huge Bronze Age cairn with eleven stone cists, found to contain the bones of at least four adults and two children. At Achinhoan the cliffs are full of caves, one of which was used by St Ciaran. It can only be reached at low tide, which must have satisfactorily isolated it for the saint's retreat. St Ciaran was a predecessor of St Columba: in fact he died aged thirty-three when Columba was only eighteen. He founded a chapel on the south shore of the Campbeltown Loch, the first on the mainland of Scotland, and then went on to see the King of Dalriada at Dunadd. He subsequently founded another chapel on the Rhinns of Islay, called Kilchiaran.

From Kildalloig Head, high on the cliffs, you can see Davaar Island, at the entrance to Campbeltown Loch. Massive sheer cliffs rise straight up from the water, making even the landing of sheep for grazing difficult, although it is accessible at low water over a shingle bank near Kildalloig Head. Davaar is famous for its caves on the south side, one of which has a much-visited mural painting of 1887 by Alexander MacKinnon, of Christ Crucified.

The road along the southern shore of the Campbeltown Loch, 2½ miles long, is called the Kilkerran road: the mouldering remains of Kilkerran Castle, built by James IV in 1498, can be seen on the shore opposite the town cemetery. The name recalls the original name of the town: situated at the head of St Ciaran's Loch, it was called Kinloch Kilkerran. From the number of hill-forts in the vicinity it is clear that Kintyre as a whole was well-populated in the Pictish age, but the first Scots to arrive were some of those who followed Cairbre Ruadh from Antrim in 258. Their settlement was known as Dalruadhan after their leader; the name changed after St Ciaran's ministry to its inhabitants in the sixth-century. Then in the late eleventh-century, following the treaty between Magnus Bare-leg and King Edgar it came under Norse rule. Somerled's campaign in the twelfth-century changed that, and his descendants of Clan Donald made it one of their strongholds. When they lost the Lordship of the Isles and the Campbells rose in power, the transfer was only gradual: it was not until 1593 that James VI granted Kintyre to Argyll, and the 7th Earl made the little town, then called Lochhead, a burgh in 1609. The year of 1647 brought not only the battles and crimes of the Civil War, but also a terrible plague, which ravaged and practically depopulated the peninsula. Accordingly the 1st Marquis began to import into it lowlanders from Ayrshire, who with their industrious ways settled peaceably, intermarried with the surviving Highlanders, and re-established a thriving and prosperous community.

In 1667 Lochhead received its first charter and a new name, Campbeltown; in 1700 it was promoted to the status of a Royal burgh. Trade then began to prosper mightily, reaching an acme around the turn of the present century when, according to an article in *The Campbeltown Courier* of 10 March, 1989, it had a fishing fleet of 600 boats, a shipyard capable of turning out vessels of 4,000 tons displacement, and thirty-four distilleries (there are now only two). In 1887 Alfred Barnard toured the whisky distilleries of the whole United Kingdom, and survived, strong-headed enough even to write a book about them. He sailed from Gourock to Tarbert, then travelled by coach for six hours to Campbeltown. He stayed for a fortnight, visiting each of the twenty-one distilleries then in existence. He visited Scotia Distillery (now re-opened as Glen Scotia) when 'the morning gave promise of a very hot day, which fortunately for us was fulfilled. We walked by way of the sea-shore and Kinloch Park, on our way encountering many hardy fish women with sunburnt faces, selling fresh herrings which glistened like silver in the sunshine.' He found the distillery 'at the end of a subway in the High Street, hidden away out of sight, as if the art of making whisky was bound to be kept a dark secret.' Its annual output was 85,000 gallons, while Springbank, which still survives (a tremendously strong malt, to be taken with caution and much water) was 145,000 gallons. The old smuggling days were still fondly remembered in Barnard's day, as he tells a story of one old woman who was up before the sheriff for illicit distilling and smuggling. The Sheriff seemed inclined to be lenient: 'I dare say, my poor woman, it is not often you have been guilty of this fault?' 'Deed no, Sheriff,' she replied, 'I havena made a drap since yon wee keg I sent to yerself.'

Campbeltown's regular, pleasantly-styled 18th-century houses and public buildings lie back from the head of the loch behind Kinloch Park, twenty-four acres of gardens created in the nineteenth-century. Behind the Old Quay is the Campbeltown Cross, a carved fifteenth-century Celtic cross. The town's distilleries may be down to two, but it still has a strong fishing fleet, and a creamery, and it is the metropolis for all southern Kintyre's farming community. Its Museum in Hall Street displays evidence of its geology and archaeology, together with such items as the tools and clothes and weapons of its people. Campbeltown also has steamer cruises, and sailing, and other aquatic activities, and two golf courses, both of a high standard and within ten miles.

On the north side of the town is a hill-fort called Cnoc Scalbert, and farther along the B842 road you can see, down by the water's edge, the ruined chapel of Cille Couslan, dedicated to St Constantine, with carved grave-slabs in the churchyard. Just to the north of it on a promontory miscalled Island Muller there are remains of a tower-house castle called Smerby, built and held by the MacDonalds in their halcyon days. Heading north now, the road dips sharply to Ardnacross Bay, the pretty sea-shore village Peninver, where there is a caravan site, and a minor track that runs up the lovely Glen Lussa; high above the glen, on the thickly wooded slopes of *Maol a'Chuir* is a massive Bronze Age cairn called *Gort na h-Ulaidhe*, Enclosure of the Treasure. The excavators found hundreds of human bones in its five chambers, and a quantity of gold, which unaccountably seems to have disappeared. Because of the woods, the cairn is difficult to find.

On the road, beyond Black Bay and south of Ugadale Point, you will see on a promontory in Kildonald Bay an extremely well-preserved fort called Dun Kildonan: a stile in the roadside wall gives you access. It still has its original stone stairway leading to the wall-head, and a paved passage-entrance with door-bar holes. It is thought that this dun was occupied as early as the second century AD, and continued in use until the fourteenth century.

On Ugadale Point is Bruce's Seat, an old quern-stone on which the king is said to have rested while waiting for a boat to Arran. This is where he gave his brooch and promises to Gilchrist MacKay. A few more twists, turns, and glimpses of the sea between the trees, and then you are down in Saddell; if you turn off to the left at the bottom of the hill you will find a track that leads up into the wooded Glen Saddell, and there you will find the remains of a Cistercian Abbey, thought to have been founded in the twelfth-century by either Somerled himself or his son Reginald (Ranald). Not much remains, but in the chancel of its chapel, one of the carved tombstones is said to be that of Somerled. He died at Renfrew in 1164, but his body was brought to Saddell. The abbey was never extensive but was important and influential as the stronghold of religious power on the Argyll mainland until its dissolution by James IV in 1507. Its lands were then given to David Hamilton, Bishop of Argyll, who built Saddell Castle in 1508 on the site of Somerled's earlier fortress, constructed to command the lower reaches of the Kilbrannan Sound. It is a tower-house with corbelled turrets and machicolated parapets (machicolations are holes through which to drop things on assailants). The Abbey ruins are of course haunted, apparently by a great black hand which once pursued the village tailor at midnight right down to the castle, to which he bolted in panic. A set of finger-prints, known as 'The Devil's Handprint', is on the left side of the main door to this day. What the tailor was doing at the Abbey ruins at midnight is still not clear.

The Saddell Glen leads up to the flanks of *Beinn an Turc*, 1491 feet, which means Hill of the Boar. This is quite definitely where Diarmid O'Duibhne, the Fingalian hero and ancestor of Clan Campbell, hunted the boar and met his death. There were still boars in Scotland until the end of the seventeenth-century.

From Saddell to Carradale the road resumes its corrugated progress; at Torrisdale you will see on the left a large castellated Georgian mansion called Torrisdale Castle, then after a couple more ups and downs you reach Carradale Bay, where the Carradale water joins the sea. Here is the best beach on Kintyre's east coast, three-quarters of a mile long with a belt of machair behind it: there is a camping and caravan site there, and access to the rocky peninsula that encloses the bay, projecting south from Carradale village. On the end of this peninsula is a well-preserved vitrified fort. Those who say that the vitrification was deliberate, that the mixture of peat, kelp and wood, in which sand and soda is present, was burned in the siliceous rock-rubble within the stone walls, in a strong cross-wind, to create a fusion into a sort of cement, can point to the number of such forts (around fifty) in Scotland. If they were all burnt by accident or attack, then their garrisons were either uninsurably careless or militarily incompetent, since the sites of the forts are usually strategically immaculate.

Farther along the peninsula there are the remains of a mediaeval castle called Airds, again best reached from the bay. Carradale itself lies at the end of a turning at the hamlet of Dippen, and it is a very pleasant little fishing port which has turned into a holiday resort. There are two hotels, the Carradale and the Ashbank, several guest-houses, and practically every house advertises bed-and-breakfast; the Carradale Hotel is the bigger, with squash-courts backing on to the golf course's club-house, sundry other leisure facilities and sauna baths. The Ashbank is much smaller, a stone two-storey house with a bar, restaurant and six or seven rooms, and is cosy and comfortable with the best of Highland hospitality, which is odd because the owners are English.

The nine-hole golf course is on the sandy hills behind the village, on the far side of which is a little bay called Port Righ with a small, secluded beach and a good-looking guest-house. Carradale's main function is as a fishing port: it has a new harbour, built in 1959, from which boats sally forth into the Kilbrannan Sound for herring and mackerel, and away to Ailsa Craig for whitefish. On the quayside, where the sun-browned sailors gather for a cigarette and a discussion about the price of fish, there is a remarkable shop in a single-storey building, which appears to stock everything and has not sold much of it since around 1939.

Carradale is an excellent holiday-centre because it has something for most tastes (except fun-fairs, disco-halls and bright lights); there is the bay for sand-castles, swimming and sun-bathing; boating is possible, and fishing, and pony-trekking from a stables in the village. For those who prefer other forms of exercise, the Forestry Commission, which owns the nearest afforested hill called *Cnoc an Gabhar*, have organised a series of trails through its wooded slopes. They start from the Forest Office near Dippen, they are of 1, 2, 4½, or 7 miles length, all marked by coloured signs, and they give nature-lovers the chance to enjoy the quiet of the woods and perhaps to see some of its wild-life, for here be roe-deer, fox and otter, eagles, kestrels, harriers, buzzards and blackgame. The longest walk goes down by the sea-shore, where you might see the occasional seal or even a basking shark, and undoubtedly flocks of all kinds of sea-birds.

As far as Carradale the road, irrespective of its erratic behaviour, is fine and wide: after it there is just a single-track with passing places, and progress becomes more dilatory. At Brackley near the little cemetery there are the remains of a cairn called the Sanctuary Stones, the tallest of which is known as the 'Toothie Stane' and has iron nails and pins hammered into a crack in one side: if you oblige it with one of these metal articles, it can still cure you of the toothache, or the rheumatics, or whatever. The road stays close to the sea-shore for most of the way now, through tiny Grogport, where there is a sheepskin tannery and a caravan park (on the beach), and Crossaig: habitations are uncommon. After what seems to be a great deal of this very attractive but otherwise uneventful journey, you come to the ferry terminal at Claonaig, where the ferry goes to Lochranza. It is not quite the same as Dover, nor even Kennacraig or Tayinloan. There is one tiny hut, a car park, and the concrete slipway; it only runs from April to October, so what is the point of expense?

The beach road is now called B8001 and goes first to the ferry, then eastward through a series of diagonally slanting rocks on the foreshore to Skipness. Throughout the whole of this thirty-mile journey from Campbeltown you can see across the Sound to the coasts, hills, white-dotted villages and great mountains of Arran (provided they are not obscured by the customary rain-clouds). Skipness (from the Norse *Skipa-nes*, the Ship-point) is quite a long row of cottages situated on the landward side of the Skipness Burn where it runs down a steep glen, turns west and flows parallel with the beach before reaching the sea. It is a surprisingly large village considering that the road goes no farther except to the scattered crofts. At its end you go over a little hump-backed bridge and find a lodge-house with huge wrought-iron gates to your right, and a car park on your left. Skipness House lies beyond the gates, in gardens bright with rhododendrons and, in April, carpeted with daffo-dils; walk through and you will come to Skipness Castle.

Built mainly of Arran red sandstone, it stands impressively high and commands the head of Kilbrannan Sound, with the Sound of Bute, the mouth of Loch Fyne, and the Firth of Clyde all in conjunction to the east. It was built four-square, with a hall-house in the north-west corner, in about 1220 when Donald MacDonald of Islay was King of the Isles and Kintyre.

Its first recorded holder was one Dufgal in 1247, since it was he who gave the adjacent chapel of St Columba to Paisley Abbey. When the chapel was demolished and one of its walls re-used when the castle's curtain walls were built, in 1261 the little St Brendan's Chapel was built down by the shore to compensate Paisley. The tower-house at the castle's north-eastern corner was built early in the sixteenth century, when the MacDonalds had lost their power and the castle passed into Campbell hands. There is a fence around the castle, and notices warning visitors off because the structure is dangerous. The little roofless chapel of Kilbrannan (St Brendan) looks forlornly towards the Arran mountains: it has no Celtic crosses, nor carved slabs, just windswept solitude on the edge of the sea, where the gulls and terns glide above, mewing their echo of the long-dead congregation's prayers. It has not been used since 1692.

The road from Claonaig winds its lonely way back to the main A83 near Kennacraig, where Caledonian MacBrayne have built a somewhat more imposing terminal than at Claonaig, for here you may go aboard a ferry to Islay.

6

Islay, Jura, and Nether Lorn

Every day of the week, Caledonian MacBrayne Ltd run a ferry service from Kennacraig to Islay, and back. Sometimes it goes to and from Port Askaig, in the north of the island, sometimes to Port Ellen, in the south. On Mondays and Wednesdays they run a boat from Kennacraig to Port Askaig, then to the island of Colonsay, then to Oban.

Kennacraig is on West Loch Tarbert, an offshore island connected by causeway to the mainland, with a pier and a terminal building. Occasionally, you may be delayed by the necessity of finding space for a couple of container-lorries, or one loaded with huge empty wooden casks, returning to one of the distilleries. The boat sails, the wooded shores of West Loch Tarbert slide past, a zig-zag course at the loch-mouth clears the jagged reefs, and we are in the open sea, heading for Port Askaig. To our left are the soft green hills of Gigha; ahead, to our right, the high mountains of Jura, and south of them the lower, mellower outline of Islay. The sea is empty save for our ferry-boat, a few yachts and a couple of fishing-boats. As we draw nearer to the Sound of Islay separating the two islands, we can see bird-life in plenty: there are dozens of white gannets with great yellow bills, gliding, then dropping like a bomb into the water after fish. There are grebes, and divers, little petrels that skim the water inches above the surface, then still in tight formation, turn as one. Suddenly, there is a commotion in the sea, and excitement among the watchers. 'Did you see that?' 'Yes, it was a shark'. 'No, no, it was a porpoise'. 'I saw it, it was definitely a shark'. Probably it was just another monster, they are everywhere in the West Highlands.

The water is smoother in the Sound of Islay, protected by the high green cliffs of Islay and the gaunt, bare slopes of Jura, but is curiously agitated by currents, with swirling eddies and dappling rapids. The Islay hills look green and soft, like Velcro cut-outs; ahead we can see the red Jura ferry running to and fro crabwise, battling against the strong current. Near Port Askaig a fine red sandstone house stands high on the cliffs, surrounded by great gaudy splashes of purple rhododendrons.

Port Askaig nestles at the foot of the sheer cliffs, a cluster of houses with a good-looking inn, a shop, the harbour buildings, and a lifeboat station with the boat poised on its slipway ready to plunge into the tumultuous water. The Jura ferry, starting from the far side, is pushed quite a distance down the Sound, its engine roaring and the bow-wave foaming white over its ramp as it fights its way across the seething current.

A sharp winding road climbs abruptly through the rhododendrons out of Port Askaig, up into a wide-open, windy, green plain; part is moorland, most is pasture for cattle and sheep, and houses are few. Ballygrant is the only settlement before we are down among the trees again to Bridgend and the tidal sand-flats at the head of Lochindaal. The gardens and hedgerows are bright with roses and rhododendrons, the trees' foliage is fresh spring green and there are still misty bluebells beneath them. Islay's fertility is proverbial; cattle prosper on the grazing, cattle and sheep are everywhere, and cheese is a salient product. At one time Islay was famous for its horses, and there is an old saying in Gaelic to the effect that an Islay man would carry his saddle and bridle a mile so that he could ride half a mile. There are still horses, but the ineluctable motor car has prevailed.

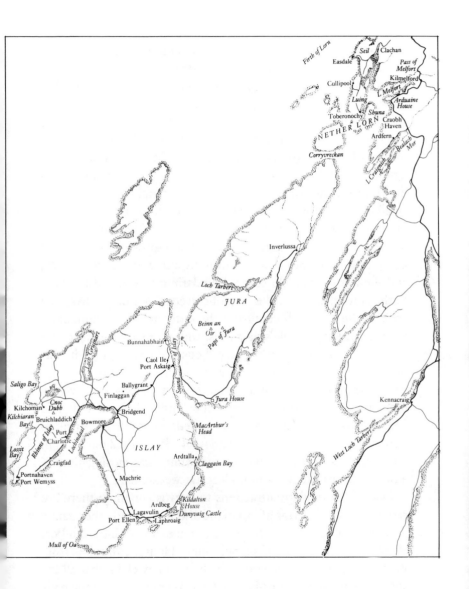

117

The name Islay is pronounced Eye'la. As in Inveraray, the final y is not used. Quite a large area of the island surrounds the long and wide sea-loch called Lochindaal, and the good two-way road from Bridgend runs down its western shore, which is a peninsula called the Rhinns of Islay. Bruichladdich on this loch-side road consists of a distillery and not much else, but it is not far to one of the island's three main townships, Port Charlotte. It is a harbour town, and its neatly kept, fresh-painted white cottages, touched with colours at windows and doors, stand at differing levels down to the water's edge. There is a stone pier, a lighthouse, and two hotels. There is also a museum: approaching from this northern direction, you turn right just opposite a small car park, then sharp left. The museum is housed in what used to be a church, built in 1843 by the Port Charlotte men and women themselves, when the Free Church broke away from the Church of Scotland. It was converted into a museum in 1977, and the adjacent single-storey Lapidarium was added in 1983. In the latter there is a collection of carved stones dating from the sixth to the sixteenth centuries; the old church accommodates relics from Islay people's past lives, with room settings from the Victorian period, an old black house showing how it was designed and thatched, there is a loom, spinning-wheel and winder, and of course much reference to Islay's vital whisky industry. There is also a library full of further information. The Museum of Islay Life, as it is called, opens from April to September from 10 am to 5 pm on week-days, and 2 pm to 5 pm on Saturdays and Sundays. In the winter the closing-time is 4.30 pm on weekdays, and it closes at weekends.

One of the modern attractions to Islay is shooting: there are red deer in the interior of moorland and forest, and other game. A company called A & C Sporting Services, operating from Port Wemyss and using the Craigfad Guest-House, two miles from Port Charlotte, offers shooting facilities. They claim that all the shooting on their estates is managed, keepered and personally supervised by themselves. Their telephone number is Port

Wemyss is 0496 86 296, if anyone is interested.

The A847 after Port Charlotte is single-track: a short way past Craigfad between it and the sea there is a cemetery on a knoll called Nereabolls with a ruined chapel. The road comes to an end at the tip of the peninsula with the two little harbours of Port Wemyss and Portnahaven. The latter is delightfully unspoilt, with old terraced cottages on three steep sides of its little natural harbour. The road from here to the western shore of the Rhinns of Islay is narrow, has very few passing places, and simply serves the scattered farmsteads. The landscape is green, treeless and windswept, with occasional glimpses of the sea at Lossit Bay and Kilchiaran Bay. Up the road from the latter, in a field behind a stone wall, is Kilchiaran Chapel, a roofless stone shell. There is an ancient undecorated stone font, and several carved grave-slabs, one with a figure of a praying man; ogival arches above his head indicate a fifteenth-century date, but the chapel itself is earlier. All these derelict chapels date from the later Middle Ages, and all seem to replace earlier structures. St Ciaran is credited with having founded this one, in addition to the other by the Campbeltown Loch. Little is known about him, except that he should not be confused with two other Irish saints called Ciaran, neither of whom left Ireland; one was the founder of the famous monastery at Clonmacnoise.

The narrow lane returns across the Rhinns to Port Charlotte, and for another excursion into this western area of the island and a visit to another ancient Christian site, you must return along the A847 and the shores of Lochindaal, through Bruichladdich, and turn left on B8018. The north-western corner of Islay is again treeless and predominantly green: bright sedgy fields full of sheep in endless succession down to the head of distant Loch Gruinart. You leave the road at a left fork just where you can see *Loch Gorm*, the Blue Loch: a flash of sparkling blue in a basin of the low green hills. South of it, sheltering under the steep cliffs of *Cnoc Dubh* and visible for miles because of the absence of tree cover, is the church of

Kilchoman. A rough lane leads up to it, by a couple of cottages and a new burial ground by the churchyard wall. Kilchoman Church is derelict, with broken windows, notices warning of danger, and a fence all around it; but the churchyard has the interest. Behind the church there stands a Celtic cross of unknown antiquity, made of local stone and called the Kilchoman Cross. Very tall, it is carved on both sides with the characteristic interlacing pattern, and on one side of the head, the Crucifixion. On the ground on one side of the cross there is a hollowed out basin in the stone, with a spherical stone in it. When you offer a prayer at the cross, you must turn the stone sunwise; without a hint of scriptural or canonical authority for this custom, we must assume it was simply always done, like the deference to the Old Ones of Gigha.

Sir Lachlan MacLean is buried in this churchyard, following a battle on the shores of Loch Gruinart. He was MacLean of Duart, in Mull, and in 1598 he landed with a large force in Loch Gruinart and the intention of invading and seizing all Islay. The MacDonalds of Islay may have lost their Lordship of the Isles, but they were not going to submit to such an indignity: they fell upon the MacLeans as they landed and slaughtered them in droves. There are many carved grave-slabs in Kilchoman churchyard, and one of them is Sir Lachlan's.

A circuit of Loch Gorm by the same very minor lane, serving only the isolated crofts, takes you first north to Saligo Bay, then back to B8018; if you then turn left you will arrive at the lovely bay of Sanaigmore, a farm perched on the edge of a beautiful sandy beach. It was here that Seton Gordon says that he and his wife pitched their tent, their first night on Islay. It is a place, he says, 'of free, vital air, where fulmars, razorbills, and guillemots have their home on the rocks. Oyster-catchers bathe in the sandy bays, and proud mother eider ducks shepherd their small families through breaking seas. At night sunset and afterglow redden the northen sky and the two rhythmic flashes of light from Dubh Hirteach lighthouse pierce the twilight. Before sunrise the hills of Mull rise dark on the rosy horizon and beyond them is the country of Morvern and Ardgour, scarcely mounting above the sea horizon. On days of great clearness the twin tops of Cruachan rise, ethereal and very faint, to the blue of the distant sky.'

This sounds like exaggeration, but the atmosphere of the northern isles is so clear that on one of these magical days when all of a sudden the mists disperse, the clouds vanish, and the sun beautifies the whole world of water, rock and mountain, visibility can be up to fifty miles.

From the head of little Loch Gorm you can take a route by B8017, skirting the tidal flats of Loch Gruinart where that gory battle was fought, over another stretch of the hills, back south to Lochindaal's main road, and then follow it around by way of Bridgend, where there is a woollen mill, by the expansive sand-flats where sheep graze, to Bowmore on the southern shore. A neat little town, Bowmore consists of a central street rising from the harbour pier straight up to the parish church on the hilltop, and other streets, also lined with solid stone houses, running off at right angles. Commerce centres strongly around the distillery, which has an excellent visitors' bar and lounge, where very persuasive young ladies will offer a taste of the product and sell you anything from a bottle of it (or more) to a woollen jumper emblazoned with the firm's trade-mark. Tours of the works are available, and it is strongly recommended that no visitor should drive anywhere after leaving, except home to his hotel: the whisky is excellent.

There are six distilleries in Islay. Bowmore and Bruichladdich have been mentioned; the others are Laphroaig and Lagavulin in the south of the island, and Caol Ile and Bunna-habhain in the north, near Port Askaig (although Bunnahabhain is not really near anything, it is on an extremely remote part of the coast). Much depends on the traditional methods of malting and peat smoking, and of course the water.

Bowmore Church is distinctive, because it is circular, rather in the Byzantine style. It was built in 1767, and local legend says that its rotundity was intended to confuse the Devil, who would find no corners to hide in. The ploy worked well, for Islay people are kindness itself, which this minor story illustrates. The windscreen-wipers of our car had become defective, and we stopped a young man in a van, in the wide main street of Bowmore, to enquire where there was a garage. He told us, but also asked what was wrong, so we explained. We had parked in the wide street centre, and he returned in a few minutes with a set of spanners. He corrected the fault, invited me to try it out, and saw that it worked perfectly; I had to chase him across the road to press on him some reward, so reluctant was he to accept it.

You will find kindness too in the persons of Islay's three post-bus drivers. Scotland's Post-Bus system celebrated in 1989 its first twenty-one years of service. The idea is that if the postman has to carry mail, he might as well carry passengers too, which means a great deal to rural communities where an ordinary bus service is economically impracticable. Throughout Scotland there are now 142 routes, covering more than 3,000 miles a day; each year they carry 100,000 passengers. They do make a small profit, but it is their social role that is important. They may carry doctors' prescriptions, milk, bread, and newspapers as well as mail, and their timetables are adjusted to suit the communities they serve. There are two Islay routes, based at Bowmore, one to Port Ellen and Ardbeg, the other to Portnahaven and Port Askaig. The drivers need to be tourist guides in the summer, pointing out places of interest. 'You've just got to help them the best you can,' says one of them. They must also be fluent Gaelic speakers, since to the older islanders it is still their first language.

South of Bowmore the A846 road wriggles round the church and cuts across the southern point enclosing Lochindaal. It then runs, straight as a die, across seven miles of flat peat-bog; after descending from the eastern hills, countless streams meander through it down to Laggan Bay. At the farther end there is an airport, which bears the same kind of relationship to Heathrow as Claonaig does to Dover, but runs a regular service to Glasgow. A man staying at the Craigfad Guest-House with his family told us that he often comes to Islay for the shooting, and can get from one of the outer London airports to Glasgow and from Glasgow to Islay rather more quickly than he can drive into London from Essex. Not far from the airport at Machrie there is an 18-hole golf course, with the Machrie Hotel nearby to offer refreshment, comfort, and solace for those whose handicap refuses to diminish.

Where the Kintra river flows into the bay, the peat-bog flats come to an end and a bluff of hills rises to replace them, a knob of land projecting south-westward from the island, called the Oa. The farthest point is the Mull of Oa, rising 430 feet sheer above the sea, and it is crowned by a tall tower commemorating a disaster of 1918.

Somewhere off this point the liner *Tuscania* went down, taking with it 266 American soldiers, on their way to France. A worse shore for a wreck can scarcely be imagined, as the sea crashes angrily on jagged rocks under huge overhanging precipices. The ship's lifeboats stood no chance, they were simply lifted by the sea and dashed to pieces on this murderous lee-shore. The American Red Cross gave the memorial to their soldiers and to the British seamen who lost their lives.

The A846 does a sharp left and right turn as it joins the almost parallel B8016 from Bridgend, and enters Port Ellen (*Port Eilean*), past its maltings as they work hard to supply the distilleries. The stone-built township lies at the head of a sheltered bay, the third of the island's largest communities. There is a pier for the Kennacraig ferries, a huge ugly warehouse standing nearby, a quayside piled high with lobster-pots for the fishing-boats, and dozens of moorings for yachts. Low, white-washed cottages fringe the bay, and in the main street there are banks, hotels, shops, and a church for every denomination (but the 'Wee Freeze' is not a chapel of the breakaway sect from the Church of Scotland, it is a frozen-food store). Carraig Fhada Farm, by the lighthouse, has a collection of animals like pygmy goats and rabbits, species of birds such as guinea-fowl, duck, pheasant, and an indoor aviary containing finches and budgerigars. It opens from 10 am to 8 pm throughout the summer season.

The best part of the island now stretches before you; great green-leaved trees grow luxuriantly here, rhododendrons purple the hillsides, bright grassy pastures are filled with livestock. By the shore there appear little secret bays, sealed in by guardian rocks, white sands gleaming. The distilleries of Laphroaig and Lagavulin face the sea, and from the latter you can see a stark ruin on a rock in the bay called *Dun Naomhaig*, Dunyvaig Castle, once a stronghold of the MacDonald Lords of the Isles. It contains fragments of a twelfth-century predecessor, and masonry of the fourteenth and sixteenth centuries superimposed, all grafted on to the naked rock, standing out on the eastern side of Lagavulin Bay where an eye could be kept on the anchorage on one hand, and the approaches from Kintyre and Ireland on the other.

On the loss of power of the Lords of the Isles, in the late fifteenth century, it passed to the MacDonalds of Dunyvaig and the Glens, who held it for more or less a hundred years, as it was taken from them occasionally by Campbell forces on behalf of the king. There were two major sieges, in 1615 when it was bombarded by Campbell guns (and subsequently repaired) and in 1647 when the MacDonalds held it for the Stewart cause against a Cromwellian army, and actually managed to surrender on reasonable terms which were not immediately betrayed. It was abandoned in 1677 and its ruin dates from then, the effect of centuries of disuse and neglect.

After Ardbeg the road becomes single-track, and the landscape more Arcadian than ever; Kildalton House lies among rainbow-coloured rhododendrons, and beyond it a little bay so perfect it cannot exist. Bearing north-eastward now in a straight line for a change, through this lush, idyllic countryside, you see a sign pointing to the right up a lane to Kildalton Chapel, which is sited on the landward side of the low coastal hills. The chapel is a roofless ruin, but in the churchyard stands the Kildalton Cross, the only surviving complete Celtic High Cross in Scotland. It is thought that a sculptor from Iona carved it, in about 800 AD, from the local blue stone. The carvings are of a Virgin and a Child on the front, and various animals and plants on the back. Within the chapel walls there are some grave-slabs showing grim old warriors carrying their two-handed swords.

The little road reaches Ardtalla only, on Claggain Bay facing east towards Kintyre, and thereafter there are neither roads nor habitations, except for the lighthouse at MacArthur's Head, all the twenty miles to Port Askaig. The hills are only 1,500 to 1,600 feet high, but it is all wilderness. So the motorist must return through Port Ellen and, perhaps as a change, use the B8016 across the peat-flats to Bridgend. There are minor roads which cross the northern part of this eastern no-man's-land, and one of them passes near Dun Nosebridge, a large fort said to be of Norse origin. This road emerges at Ballygrant, on the A846 road to Port Askaig, but before heading back for the ferry you might take a side road to the north, signposted Finlaggan Castle, and an appallingly rough track from that. You can park your car under the trees by a house, but then you must walk down a short track towards Loch Finlaggan. At the end of the track there is a cottage which by now will have been completed as an interpretive centre by the Finlaggan Trust. Beyond it grassy meadows lead down to the lochside (it is a freshwater loch in the green hills) and to the two islands that are of enormous importance to Clan Donald. There is hardly anything left of the castle that stood on the larger island, nor its chapel, just overgrown hummocks of stone: the dilapidation is complete. Yet these islands, the larger called *Eilean Mor*, the smaller *Eilean na Comhairle*, constitute the 'Cradle of Clan Donald'.

Somerled, who conquered the Norsemen and became ruler of the Isles as well as ruler of Argyll, Mull, Tiree and Coll, had three sons: Dugall, who inherited Argyll and founded Clan MacDougall, Angus, and Reginald. Angus received Bute and part of Arran, but he and his three sons were killed, and his land was claimed by Reginald, who had been given Kintyre and Islay. Reginald had two sons, Donald, founder of Clan Donald, and Ruairi; Clan Donald held Kintyre, Morvern, Ardnamurchan, and Islay, while Clan Ruairi became Lords of Gamoran, which included Moidart, Knoydart, and the islands Eigg, Rhum, Barra, Uist and St Kilda. Clan Dugall's opposition to Robert Bruce cost them their power and land, but John of Islay increased his by marrying the heiress of Clan Ruairi and claiming all their land. He then divorced her and married Margaret, daughter of the heir to the throne. John was the first Lord of the Isles, *Tighearna nan Eilean*. When he died in 1387, he was master of all the Hebrides from Lewis to Islay, except for Skye, and of all the western mainland from Kintyre to Knoydart.

Eilean na Comhairle, Council Isle, was the chosen site for the election of a new Lord. The inauguration ceremony is described by Hugh MacDonald of Sleat, the clan's historian: 'At this the Bishop of Argyll, the Bishop of the Isles, and seven priests were present. . . There was a square stone, seven or eight feet long and the tract of a man's foot cut thereon, upon which he stood, denoting that he should walk in the footsteps and uprightness of his predecessors. . . He was clothed in a white habit to show his innocence and integrity of heart, that he would be a light to his people and maintain the true religion. . . . Then he was to receive a white rod in his hand, intimating that he had the power to rule, not with tyranny and partiality, but with discretion and sincerity. Then he received his father's sword, or some other sword, signifying that his duty was to protect and defend them from the incursions of their enemies in peace and war. . .' Any similarity here to the coronation of the ancient kings of Dalriada at Dunadd is probably not coincidental.

The islands are small, the ruins so fragmentary, that it is difficult to imagine a great castle and so much human activity and ritual taking place on them. A breeze ruffles the loch-water, orchestrating all the reeds and grasses of the islands and shore to bend in harmony; anglers wait patiently at the water's edge, and a family of ducks make little V-wakes in the shallows; martins and swallows swoop to the surface, extinguishing the brief lives of minute insects. Finlaggan has many secrets, mostly hidden beneath the grass: what the Trust is trying to do is to prevent further deterioration, excavate the site and perhaps discover some of the secrets.

The other principal MacDonald castle belonging to the Lords of the Isles was Claig Castle on Fraoch Eilean, in the Sound of Islay close to Jura's shore. Its name means Heather Island: the words, *Fraoch Eilean*, were shouted as a war-cry by MacDonald warriors, and the clan's badge is *Fraoch gorm*, common (blue) heath. Claig Castle usually served as a repository for the Lord of the Isles's most important prisoners, since even if you managed to crawl out of the dungeon, you would not be going very far, as no-one could swim against the Sound's currents. The MacDonalds used to own the whole of Jura at the height of their power, subsequently shared it with the MacLeans of Mull, and eventually lost it by royal charter, in 1690, inevitably to the Earl of Argyll.

Jura is quite different from Islay: the latter is fertile, fairly low-lying, populous, while Jura is comparatively barren, extremely mountainous, and has few villages and no towns. In shape it is like a Stone Age flint axe-head, but nearly cut in half by a long sea-loch from the west called, from the connecting isthmus (naturally) Loch Tarbert. The greatest of the mountains is *Beinn an Oir*, 2,576 feet, the higher of the two Paps of Jura. The female anatomy often seems to come to Highland minds when naming mountains: the two summits of Beinn Cruchan are sometimes given the title Paps, and there is, for instance, a mountain in Arran called *Cioch na h-Oighe*, the Maiden's Breast.

What roads there are, serving what settlements there are, run along the southern and eastern shores of Jura; the western shore has steep cliffs for much of the way, no roads and no human homes whatever. Sir James Turner in 1646 said that Jura (even then, when the population was far greater) was 'a horrid ile and a habitation fit for deere and wild beasts.' Even its name is thought to be derived from the Norse *Dyrey*, Deer Island, and today deer and goats heavily outnumber humans. There is, nevertheless, a distillery producing the famous Jura Malt, and the grounds and walled gardens of Jura House, in the south not far from Fraoch Eilean, are now open to the public. 'The listed walled garden,' says its blurb, 'offers spectacular views and wide varieties of local plants and shrubs peculiar to the protected West Coast climate.' The gardens are open at Easter, and thereafter from May 1st to October 1st, Monday to Saturday, 10 am to 5 pm.

Jura is certainly peaceful, and that strange, unhappy man Eric Blair, better known by his *nom-de-plume* George Orwell, came here in the late 1940s. He was already tubercular, and succumbed to it in 1950, but Jura offered a cottage, rest, and tranquillity. He wrote at least some of *Nineteen Eighty Four*, published in 1949, in the island. The climate failed to cure him, but in the past at least it seems to have had properties to guarantee longevity, judging by the tombstone that Seton Gordon says he found in the burial-ground at Inverlussa, where the island's single-track road, titled A846, deteriorates into a track. The inscription runs:

Mary MacCrain, died 1856, aged 128.
Descendant of Gillour MacCrain,
who kept 180 Christmases in his own house
and who died in the reign of Charles I.

There are even more red deer in the island of Scarba to the north of Jura, and in the narrow channel between the two islands there occurs the notorious whirlpool known as Corryvreckan

(*Coire Bhreacain*). Here the incoming tide, noticeably strong in the Sound of Islay, reaches eight knots or more, and when a westerly gale hits a spring flood there is such a boiling of the water that its uncanny roar can be heard as far away as Crinan. Martin Martin, an early writer quoted by Ronald Faux in his yachting guide *The West*, says: 'The sea begins to boil and ferment with the tide of flood and resembles the boiling of a pot; and then increases gradually until it appears in many whirpools, which form themselves in sort of pyramids and immediately spout up as high as the mast of a little vessel, and at the same time make a loud report.' Large ships, unwary enough to venture near, have been caught and overwhelmed by it, and small craft stand no chance. There is, it seems, a submerged pyramid of rock which causes the upsurge in the centre of so many racing currents.

Tide-races and currents are a feature of the mainland coastline too, where hundreds of little islands and rocks, sea-lochs, long fingers of land, and rivers issuing from the inland glens meet in a confused jumble. The yachting marinas of Ardfern in Loch Craignish, and Loch Melfort, and Craobh Haven, are always full of craft, but their owners need likewise to be full of craft: they need a wealth of sailing and navigating experience to cope with these waters. On those Highland days when the sea is so innocuously still and crystal-clear, the hills exultant in colour and a light breeze from the west, the whole business may seem so easy; but the weather can change in a few minutes and utter disaster may be the result of indifference to the perils.

The name of this region is Nether Lorn, beginning in the south where the A816 road climbs out of the lush valley of the Kilmartin Burn, reaches a height of 546 feet at *Bealach Mor*, the Great Pass, and all of a sudden, there below you is Loch Craignish. The loch is six miles long, full of islands and rocky reefs, and it issues at a point opposite the north-eastern end of Jura to one side, and Loch Crinan to the other, for its eastern side constitutes the low hills that enclose the Kilmartin valley and plain.

The road from *Bealach Mor* descends quickly to the head of
the loch, and from it the lane B8002 serves the western side.
First it arrives at the Ardfern yachting centre, where there is a
safe anchorage behind one of the islands, boat-repair sheds and
much activity, with boats out of the water and plenty of
hammering, sanding, varnishing and painting; overall there is
that boats-and-water smell that enthrals any addict of 'messing
about in boats'. There is also an inn called 'The Galley of Lorn'
which has a petrol pump and a clientele of boat-people, with
their tales of fine cruises, near-misses, and no doubt the sighting
of many a monster.

The lane skirts the loch for a few miles, then suddenly you
find that there is another loch on your right, with a track that
leads to Craignish Castle. An inhabited tower-house, it stands at
the head of the little loch, a sea-inlet on the western side of
Craignish Point; like most West Highland castles, it replaces
two or three earlier forts, one of the twelfth century which is
only recorded back to 1414. The present keep dates from the
sixteenth century but has more modern alterations such as
windows, chimneys, television aerials and for all I know, central
heating. Seton Gordon says it was a seat of the MacEacherns,
W. H. Murray thinks it was originally a MacDougall stronghold,
and both agree that the Campbells of Craignish held it for
centuries. This would be the reason why MacColla Ciotach
besieged it in 1647 on his ill-fated march south; after a
prolonged siege he was obliged to give up and move on. It is
divided into apartments now, and has a garden laid out by the
famous Osgood MacKenzie of Inverewe. There are no intrusive
sounds here apart from the ever-present and even companion-
able plaints of the sea-birds, and the lapping of the loch-water
'with small sounds by the shore' as Yeats put it; there is the
smell of the earth, the trees and the sea, and even Orwell might
have been content to live here (probably in the gardener's hut
rather than the castle).

From the head of Loch Craignish the main road crosses the Craignish peninsula in a series of tortuous hairpins and arrives on the shores of Loch Melfort. A side-road leads to the yachting centre of Craobh Haven, and the main road curves round the head of a bay formed by a promontory into the loch. On this is Arduaine House, once the seat of the Campbells of Arduaine, but is now the Loch Melfort Hotel, whose fine gardens are owned and administered by the National Trust for Scotland. In the bay there is a pier from which small ferry-boats ply to the islands of Shuna, just opposite, and Luing on its seaward side. It is more usual, and more convenient, to reach Luing (pronounced Ling) by the Cuan Ferry from Seil, to its north: that is how the writer Leslie Thomas landed one day, when he got lost. Told by the ferry-man to take 'a wee fork to the right' to get to Cullipool, he took a track into the hills instead and crawled back to Cuan through a peat-bog, at some detriment to his clothing. The next day he came back and tried again, but this time took a 'wee track' to the left: 'It was about the same width and the same contortion as the one the day before. The mud was about the same consistency.

'But this time it was the right thing to do. At the highest point of its rise I turned and, to the west, through a shallow gap in the hills, I saw a stretch of the wildest blue sea, bitten into short pieces by the wind. It swept and leaped between Luing and the Isle of Belnahua, flying white as soapsuds over skerries and around a lighthouse beleaguered on a cap of rocks. It was a seascape to make the heart leap, to excite the eyes; a bright blue and white violence that only those who live in the wild places know.'

It was on the skerries off Belnahua, one terrible, storm-wracked night in October, 1936, that a small Latvian cargo ship called *Helena Faulraums* struck: the savage wind and pitiless seas smashed the vessel to pieces, and the crew were thrown into the seething icy waters, the life crushed out of them. The people of Luing found some of the bodies washed up on the shore the next morning, and fishermen went out to look for survivors, but

131

all they found were a few more bodies. They were all buried in a
cemetery at an old, isolated church in the middle of the island;
relatives in Latvia sent headstones and memorials, and one of
them, noticed by Leslie Thomas, commemorated a young radio
officer on his first voyage. The fractured English of the
inscription, beneath a framed photograph of the young man,
adds to its poignancy:

Radiote Legrath Albert Sultcs.
Died Oct. 26th 1936
Was storm — Tore blossoms.
Destroyed dreams of
Happyness.

In 1989 fifty Latvians visited Luing, the latest of several
calls they have made over the years, to ensure that the graves are
cared for. There was a memorial service in the churchyard,
during which two Latvian ladies in their national dress laid
wreaths on the graves. Then the islanders took them in boats to
Belnahua so that they could lay other wreaths on the water
where the ship went down. The Latvians gave the people of
Luing carved wooden plates in gratitude for their part in this
rare, sympathetic, fifty-year-old liaison.

Cullipool, in the north-west of the island (the only other
village is Toberonochy in the south-east) once made its living
from its slate quarry, the most important in the West Highlands,
which once employed 150 men and produced 15,000 slates per
week. When Iona Abbery was being rebuilt, its roof was slated
from Luing's quarry, as it had been in the first place. Leslie
Thomas met John Brown, the man who quarried and cut them:
' "They said they had to be good slates. They had to last for a
thousand years. I cut the slates, down there see, by the water's
edge, and sent them off and they put them on the roof of the
abbey."

"Will they last a thousand years?" I asked. We were walking
up his field towards the road.

"Aye," he said quietly. "I said if they didna they could bring them back."

The quarry closed in 1965, the year when they completed work on Iona Abbey, and Cullipool lost its living.

Loch Melfort is almost entirely enclosed, with Shuna and Luing across its entrance and the hills all around, so it makes a quiet anchorage. At its head, the village of Kilmelford has a shop, post office and hotel, and from it a minor road goes off to Loch Avich and Loch Awe. There are plenty of hill-lochs in the untroubled country between the main road and Loch Awe, like Lochs Tralaig and Scammadale, but Loch Avich is the biggest. All, I am told, are full of fish. Kilmelford looks the same as it has for years, but according to a newspaper report of December, 1988, it is on the western verge of a potential gold-mining area that stretches fifty miles north-eastward to Aberfeldy in Perthshire. In 1988 the Dublin-based Ennex Mineral Exploration Corporation found gold in quantities at Tyndrum, and a Canadian firm found it at Aberfeldy. They forecast that the zone will produce five tonnes of gold per year, which would put Scotland on equal terms with France — but not quite up to the South African level of 500 tonnes per year. There is little danger, fortunately, of Kilmelford or any of the other villages in the area turning into Boom Towns on the Klondyke pattern complete with their own Dangerous Dan McGrews, because the gold is way underground and costs millions to get to the surface.

The A816 wriggles up the Pass of Melfort, with fine views back down the loch, then down to the deep and lovely Oude glen, which has been dammed as a reservoir; a heavily forested hill-country leads you then to Glen Euchar, where the Euchar river flows down from Loch Scammadale, and a little farther on a road leads to Kilninver on the left, then by way of a pleasant lane by a little lochan, steeply down to Clachan at the bottom, Seil Sound, and the Bridge over the Atlantic.

Seil Island is separated from the mainland at this point by only seventy feet of water (whether you call it Seil Sound, the

Firth of Lorn or the Atlantic Ocean is immaterial, they are all connected) and the great Thomas Telford, in his wisdom, built in 1792 a bridge, a single span forty feet above the bottom of the Sound, for the greater comfort and convenience of travellers. It was some time before the marine inhabitants of the Sound tumbled to the new snags of swimming through the gap: at low tide the water tends to be shallow, and in 1835 a seventy-eight foot whale got stuck. In 1837 a whole school of 192 little pilot whales were stranded. The bridge is narrow for road traffic, and you cannot see what is coming from the other side, but it is also graceful and beautiful when flowers purple the lichened stones and reflect in the water.

The first house on the Seil shore is the hotel *Tigh an Truise*, the House of the Trousers. In the years following 1746, when as a punishment for some Highlanders having supported the Jacobite rising, all Highlanders were forbidden to carry weapons or to wear clan tartans, the kilt, or any other form of Highland dress, they not unnaturally resented it. Neil Munro has his Baron of Doom, in *Doom Castle*, for example, wear his full Highland regalia in secret, in the safety of his own castle. The men of Seil, before Telford built the bridge, invariably disregarded the law and wore the dress of their ancestors. If they needed to go to to the mainland, however, they dared not, so at *Tigh an Truise* they changed into trousers and left their plaids under lock and key.

The inn is plain, simple and good, and it is delightful on a sunny afternoon to sit outside it with your beer on a table, on its little terrace, and watch the martins and swifts swooping and diving under the old bridge, above the waters of the Sound, and up to their nests in the inn's eaves.

The islands of Seil, Luing and Shuna, and the smaller islets in the group, are composed of pre-Cambrian rock which is too old even for fossils, but it splits into good slate for roofing. Like those in Luing, the slate-quarries of Seil brought prosperity from the eighteenth to the twentieth centuries; when the demand for slates disappeared, one by one the quarries closed, Luing in 1965, Balvicar, the only one in Seil after Easdale flooded, in 1968.

Easdale is the name for the little offshore island and the village on the Seil shore, which is celebrated for its multiplicity of craft shops. The biggest is the Highland Art and Craft Centre, a capacious single-storey emporium stocking a wide variety of (fairly) local products. Many of these are the work of its owner, C. John Taylor, who exhibits his paintings, sells his poems, and plays tapes of his music. Tastes differ, but we find that the best product by far of this establishment is its Highland Butter Tablet.

7

Lorn

North of Kilninver the Euchar river discharges into the long and narrow Loch Feochan. On its south side the good A816 can convey you rapidly past the pleasure of its scenery and past the elegant Knipoch Hotel. At its head, by Kilmore, the waters of two glens meet and pour into it: from Glen Feochan in the south and Loch Nell in the north, both in the wild and hilly hinterland between the coast and Loch Awe. In the river-flats at the head of Loch Feochan there are several burial-chamber cairns in nearly as much profusion as in the Kilmartin plain. More cairns, a stone circle and standing stones are at the northern end of Loch Nell, too, which gives some indication of the Lorn population in the Bronze Age.

Lorn was one of the brothers who according to legend led the Scots settlers into the West Highlands in 498. Fergus was the brother with most authority, and it is quite possible that they were not brothers at all, merely associated followers of King Erc of Irish Dalriada, or 'brother adventurers-in-arms'. Fergus certainly took the lion's share, but Lorn's part was extensive enough, from Loch Craignish in the south to the shores of Loch Leven and Loch Linnhe in the north, and the whole district still bears his name.

Loch Nell of the cairns is a very pretty little fresh-water loch which supplies Oban with drinking water; it is accessible from Kilmore, Oban or Connel, but these are only minor roads and there is none on the eastern side, so generally the only forms of life you see there are the local farmers and crofters, anglers, the numerous species of duck, geese and swans on its surface, and the sea and moor birds that fly over it. Its steep banks are well-grassed, white-dotted with sheep and in spring ablaze with golden gorse-bloom. On the lane that goes north from it to Connel is Barranrioch Farm, which nowadays is the Oban Rare Breeds Farm Park. It has only been running for a couple of years and is already popular among visitors. What the owners have done is to turn a thirty-acre croft into a home for survivors of almost extinct breeds of domestic animals, not confined to those from Scotland. There are many breeds of sheep, for example, which are not required by modern breeders, there are pigs like the Gloucester Old Spot and the Berkshire, and among cattle there are specimens of the ancient Longhorn, the British White, the tiny Dexter, the Scottish Belted Galloway and the Highland. Highland cattle are not that rare, you can see quite a number of herds in Argyll alone, but no Highland animal park would be complete without some. Red and roe deer are present too, and visitors may follow a trail along a burn into woodland, where they may be glimpsed. There is a Pets' Corner intended for children, where sundry assorted creatures suffer themselves to be stroked and fed. This might be something of a relief if you happened to be one of them and had been burdened with a name like 'Jimmy Wong, the Vietnamese Pot-bellied Pig.' The park has won the approval of the Rare Breeds Survival Trust, the first in Scotland to have done so. It is open every day from 10 am until sundown.

From the A816 at the head of Loch Feochan another minor road goes off in the opposite direction, to the loch's north coast and Kilbride, where a side-track will take you to a holiday village and what is styled 'a Real Country Pub' called the Barn at Cologin, then to Lerags and Ardoran, where there is a yacht

Dunollie Castle

marina. The hills behind this shore are not particularly high, but they descend in cliffs to the western sea-board, crowned with a surprising number of ancient forts, the biggest of which is Dun Ormidale, a vast tribal centre. This western shore of Lorn, south of Oban, is protected from the westerly winds by the island of Kerrera (accent on the first syllable), whose northern end also protects Oban harbour. There are no roads on Kerrera, and few houses. There is a passenger ferry from the Gallanach road along the coast, which has to be summoned by the passengers. There are farm tracks, plenty of open green space and solitude, wildflowers and birds, with cairns, forts and caves for the archaeologists.

At the far northern tip of Kerrera there is a tall stone obelisk, well-known to anyone who takes ferries out of Oban: it is a monument to David Hutcheson, who founded a little steamer company which later merged with another run by David MacBrayne, and one day grew up to be Caledonian MacBrayne Ltd. At the southern end is Gylen Castle, a tower-house built in 1582 by Duncan MacDougall of Dunollie on a sheer cliff, to command the southern approaches to Oban harbour. Leslie's Covenanters wrecked it in 1647, and at the insistence of the minister John Neave, the same who had the garrison of Dunaverty murdered, the MacDougall defenders were slaughtered to a man. They were Catholics, and they were loyal to the king. In the fire they lit to burn the castle the famous Brooch of Lorn was believed lost: this was the brooch pulled from Bruce's cloak in 1306 and kept by the MacDougalls. Later, however, it turned up in Campbell possession and was held by various branches of the clan until 1822 when Campbell of Lochnell very civilly gave it back to the MacDougalls at a dinner at Inveraray. Gylen castle is open, without charge, at all times.

From the top of the hill of Soroba the road plunges down to Glen Sheileach and you are in the town of Oban, a name that means 'a small creek'. It was on Glen Sheileach's flats where the little river enters the sea that the township first developed. By

English standards it has a very recent history as a town, since the first documentary reference to it is in 1637, as 'Obane in Glenshellach'. However important a landing-place it had by then become, it was most likely not much more than a group of small thatched houses. On the other hand, there is evidence of rather earlier occupation: when they were clearing some low cliffs away in the nineteenth century, to make way for George Street, they found some caves and evidence in them of their use by Azilian Man, who did so in about 6,000 BC. These were Middle Stone Age, or Mesolithic, people, who were hunters and had migrated from Europe.

Oban was still not large in 1773, when Dr Johnson and Boswell set sail from Lochbuie in Mull: 'We had a good day and a fine passage, and in the evening landed at Oban, where we found a tolerable inn.' Development came swiftly, however, and in the early nineteenth century the population increased from 600 to 1,500. Fishing, farming, and ship-building were the main sources of income, sufficient for promotion to the status of burgh in 1811. The coming of steam-boats in about 1850 helped, and town-planning and development began: this was when Azilian Man came to light after 8,000 years. It was the railway, in 1880, that turned the little port into a holiday resort and the virtual capital of the West Highlands.

The resident population is now about 7,000, but since there are plenty of hotels and guest-houses, and practically every house advertises bed-and-breakfast, you can reckon on about five times that number for five months of every year. The fishing fleet is still an important source of out-of-season income, there are the ferries, there is a distillery, and there is an industrial estate, but the products of the latter go mainly to supply the tourist industry. The Oban Craft Co-operative produces woollen goods, local forms of jewellery and pottery, and there is glass-ware from one of the estate's factories.

From the top of the hill, Oban Bay presents an eminently photographable picture: a pool of still, gleaming harbour water, fringed by green hills, alive with moving, gliding, brilliant white gulls; fishing boats at one quay, the red funnels of a ferry alongside another, yachts riding at anchor, constant activity on the water, on the quaysides, in the air. Tall, elegant hotels fringe the waterfront, houses peer over one another's roofs up the hillsides, and up on the clifftop at the rear of the whole scene, that extraordinary neo-Colosseum, McCaig's Folly.

In 1890 an Oban banker, John Stuart McCaig, decided to build a memorial to his family on the grand scale; it gave employment to local people at a hard time, it used local granite, and it rose impressively above the town. McCaig planned to incorporate in it a museum, an art gallery, and an observation tower 100 feet high. But he ran out of money, and it was never finished. Stone once put in place, generally stays there, and McCaig's Folly stood for years, its interior an overgrown wilderness, and to some discerning visitors it was an eyesore. Tourism saved it, since although totally alien to everything Highland, it had an endearing eccentricity and was certainly a landmark. Work was undertaken to tidy up the inside, and in 1983 an observation platform was built on the seaward side. In season it is floodlit at night, just like a castle or cathedral, which means that it is now an accepted, integral part of Oban.

Behind the Folly, behind the town's hills, in an old quarry is the Glencruitten Golf Course, a full 18 holes of such complexity that compared with links courses like Macrihanish or Dunaverty it is like playing half-way up Beinn Cruachan. The railway runs at a height along one side, on its tortuous and ingeniously engineered way to Connel. On the harbour-front, on the esplanade past the stately hotels, past the Corran Halls where celebrated entertainers give pleasure to visitors every summer, on the Ganavan road past the pink granite St Columba's Cathedral (designed by Sir Giles Gilbert Scott) of the Roman Catholic diocese of Argyll and the Isles, the road curves round the rocky cliffs that fringe the northern side of Oban Bay.

Dunollie Castle stands high above road and bay, on its own rocky pinnacle. To reach it, stop in a lay-by on the road below in a grove of trees: there is a gate, and a steep stony path that zig-zags up to the castle. There are a few tumbled walls on the perimeter of a small level space, and a plain square ivy-covered tower. The view from this height is superb: all of Oban Bay and harbour to the south, across the wide Firth of Lorn to the shores of Mull, and beyond it the hills of Morvern, with the long finger of Lismore Island in the right background. There is no question of the value of this site for a castle.

So clearly strategic a situation carried many a fortress before the present masonry was even carried up the hill. A fort called Dun Ollaigh occupied the site in 686 and was mentioned four more times in the annals of Ulster between that date and 734 — three of the times because it was burnt. The present ruins probably date from the twelfth century and may have been built by Somerled's son Dugall, who inherited most of Argyll, and Mull, Jura and Lismore, and founded Clan Dougall and its mediaeval power. The family title, Lord of Lorn, was assumed at this time, and so was its badge the Galley of Lorn, taken from the Great Seal of Somerled. King Alexander II in 1229 recognised the growth of MacDougall power by granting Duncan, son of Dugall, the title *de Ergadia*, meaning of Argyll, and he passed it on to his son Ewan at his death in 1247. Ewan augmented the clan's power and added to Dunollie. He also built another stronghold on the site of Dunstaffnage, another early fort. Successive MacDougall chiefs lived in Dunollie, even after the disaster of opposing Robert Bruce, and the loss of their land and power. Dunollie's strength held out against Leslie's malevolent Covenanters in 1647, and in 1715, for the pretender James VIII (III of England), MacDougall's wife successfully fended off the Argyll Militia. Their lands were forfeited because of this Jacobite support, but were returned to them in 1745.

Clan Dougall did not rise again under Prince Charles Edward's leadership, and so kept their land. In 1746 MacDougall, perhaps heartily glad of escape from the malicious persecution following the slaughter of Culloden, built a mansion in the glen behind the castle, using some of its stones for the purpose. The clan chiefs have lived there ever since, in Dunollie House, as does the present Chief, Mrs Morag MacDougall, and they still keep there the Brooch of Lorne. It is a huge thing, 4½ inches in diameter, of ornamented filigree silver, shaped to a dome in the centre and crowned with a mighty rock-crystal; it is circled by eight jewelled obelisk-like projections. The dome is unscrewable, which means that it was intended as a reliquary, the inner cavity to contain some holy relic. Such times, many without doubt spurious, were greatly treasured in the Middle Ages.

Beyond Dunollie the road terminates at Ganavan Beach, where there are fine sands and the Ganavan Pavilion, which has recently been refurbished by a local company to accommodate not only a bar, but also a restaurant where almost any kind of meal can be ordered, and a shop and a games room; there is also nearby a children's play area, so the whole family can be absorbed by it. There is a caravan site at the back of the beach, and if you want to go windsurfing you can even do that on Ganavan sands, with someone to teach you.

There is no way of cutting through the hills to the A85 road north of Oban from Ganavan, you simply have to go back into the town and turn left by the Corran Halls. A few miles along the A85 at Dunbeg a lane turns off left to Dunstaffnage Castle, which stands, beyond a research establishment, at the head of a promontory jutting out into the Firth of Lorn and enclosing a little bay. Two islands, *Eilean Mor* and *Eilean Beag* (Great and Little), lie off the head, and the significance of the site is that it commands the entrance to Loch Etive to the east, the wide sweep of Ardmucknish Bay north, and the Lynn of Lorn, the sound between Lismore and the mainland, not to mention the wide firth over to Mull westward. The existing castle was built on an outcrop of Old Red Conglomerate by either Duncan MacDougall or his son Ewan in about 1230, but the military strength of the site had long been recognised. A fort of uncertain antiquity called *Sean Dun*, the Old Fort, was located on a knoll at the head of the bay; it was earlier known as *Dun a'Mhonaidh* (pronounced Dunavona), a prominent Pictish stronghold in Roman days, and was taken over by the recently arrived Scots under Lorn. Precisely when the *Lia Fail*, the Stone of Destiny, was moved there from Dunadd is open to debate, but legend connects it with *Dun a'Mhonaidh* until the time in the mid-ninth century when Kenneth MacAlpine overcame the Picts and transferred it to his palace at Scone. Legends are plentiful in early Scottish history, facts and dates less easy to come by.

The MacDougall castle was forfeited when Bruce beat John, Lord of Lorn, in 1308; he besieged and captured Dunstaffnage, and in the early 1320s gave it to the Campbells. However, a royal charter of 1388, issued by Robert II, gave it and the Lordship of Lorn to John Stewart of Innermeath, which was hardly surprising since he was a member of Robert II's family.

1463 brought the Dunstaffnage murder story. A later Sir John Stewart's family consisted only of daughters, all three of whom had married Campbells; Stewart's only son was illegitimate, born to his mistress. When Lady Stewart died, he realised that his inheritance was likely to pass to the Campbells when he followed her, so he arranged to marry his mistress and legitimize Dugald, his son. This, of course, was anathema to the Campbells and likewise to the MacDougalls, who still insisted that the Lordship was rightfully theirs. A plot was hatched between the two interested parties. The Campbells were in the wedding party, Alan MacDougall was there as a servant to them. As Sir John and his bride walked from the castle to the chapel, which lies a short distance to the west, and just as they approached its porch, Alan MacDougall leapt forward and stabbed Sir John, who fell, dying. MacDougall escaped in the confusion. The priest, sensing the plot and its injustice, raised Sir John's spirits sufficiently for him to say the important sentences of the wedding rites, and with his last strength slip the ring on his bride's finger. Dugald was legitimized, the plot foiled, and the mistress made bride, widow, and dowager within the space of minutes.

Despite the drama and romance, however, there was no happy ending. Soon the MacDougalls attacked and captured the castle, and a royal expedition in 1464 was despatched to recover it; in 1469 Dugald Stewart resigned his lordship and the castle to the crown, and in the following year James III granted it to Colin Campbell, the first Earl of Argyll. By staying close to the authorities the Campbells, as usual, got their own way in the end. They appointed a Campbell as hereditary Captain of Dunstaffnage with orders to make the place available to the Chief whenever he wanted it.

Under Campbell captaincy the castle received plenty of attention during the sporadic royal attempts to keep the Mac-Donalds, MacLeods and Camerons under control, and in that tragic year for the MacDonalds of 1647, old Coll Ciotach of Islay, father of Montrose's famous Sir Alasdair, was captured by the Covenanters in their usual treacherous fashion, as if word of honour did not apply to Catholics, and taken to Dunstaffnage. Near the present house of Saulmore across the little bay, they wedged the mast of Coll's own galley across a cleft in the rock and hanged the old man 'amid their fiendish yells'. Despite the Campbell vicissitudes in the seventeenth century, the castle continued in their ownership to the present day, when Mr Michael Campbell, 23rd Captain of Dunstaffnage, retains his right of residence there. One notable resident, for a short time and against her will, was Flora MacDonald in 1746, on her way to trial in London.

Versions of Dunstaffnage's name's derivation differ: one is *Dun Stamh Neas*, Fort of the Seaweed Point: there is certainly plenty of it about, especially at low tide. The castle consists of a curtain wall, conforming to the area of the natural rock on which it stands, with round towers at the corners. The gatehouse on the southern side is accessible from a stone staircase with a gap between it and the door: the modern wooden bridge replaces a drawbridge. The gatehouse was altered and a tall tower-house added in the late sixteenth century, and this is the only habitable part of the castle, where Mr Campbell's apartment is kept ready for him. A dwelling-house was built against the north wall in 1725, but it is roofless now. Wooden staircases give visitors access to the ramparts, from which the castle's strategic position may be fully appreciated: westward you can see across the Firth of Lorn to Mull; looking north you see the rocky islands off southern Lismore; farther round, eastward, there are the beaches of Ardmucknish Bay, Ledaig, and Ben Lora, while farthest east there is the Connel Bridge at the entrance to Loch Etive. To the south, there is the little bay full of anchored yachts, and the mainland hills.

The castle's chapel, a short walk westward, is regarded as a 'Masterpiece in Miniature', because enough of it remains to show the best in thirteenth-century church architecture. It was the transition period from the Romanesque of the Mediterranean world, with its round-headed arches, dog-tooth decoration and skilful ornamentation, to what has since been called Gothic, with characteristic pointed-arched lancet windows. 'It is astonishing,' says the Dunstaffnage guide-book, 'to find, in this remote part of Scotland, a little building in the highest style of the first glorious flowering of Gothic art — worthy in all respects, save that of mere size, to take its place alongside the noblest ecclesiastical monuments of contemporary France or Britain.' Its builder, whether Duncan or Ewan of Lorn, also founded the priory of Ardchattan, on the northern shore of Loch Etive, and there are marked similarities, so possibly the same architect designed both. The Captain of Dunstaffnage in 1740 added a Campbell mausoleum to the chapel's eastern end, with a classical portico and on it inscribed a dedication to the Saints Fiacre, Margaret, and Louis. The chapel itself is thought to have been dedicated to the French St Fiacre, who sounds as if he should be the patron of taxi-cabs, and the Campbells, in their modesty, claimed descent from the other two. If the day of your visit is warm and sunny, bees humming about the flowers along the chapel walls, butterflies settling on them, woodpigeons calling from the tall trees around it, gulls crying overhead and nothing else to disturb the somnolent peace, you will find it very hard to picture the scene of that vile murder in 1463.

The castle is open to the public (with an entrance charge) on Monday, Tuesday, Wednesday and Saturday from 9.30 am to 7 pm (and from October to March to 4 pm), and on Sunday from 2 pm to 7 pm with the same closing hour during the winter as the weekdays. It closes on Thursday at noon, and remains closed all day Friday.

The Connel Bridge is visible from the battlements of Dunstaffnage, and because it is on the cantilever principle, its high angular metal-work can be seen from many other distant points in the vicinity. It crosses the entrance to Loch Etive and there is no other way of crossing, since the ferries here at Connel and at Bonawe have ceased to function. It was built in 1903 to carry a branch of the railway north and along the shores of Appin to Ballachulish. The line was axed in 1966 (its ghost can still be traced, and the bridge at the Loch Creran narrows still stands), but such a valuable link could not be dispensed with, so it turned into a road bridge, controlled at each end by traffic lights. There was a period when it was used by both the trains and the road-traffic, but not at the same time.

The former Connel ferry had to contend with the hazardous and treacherous waters of the Falls of Lora. A ridge of rock stretches part of the way across the entrance to Loch Etive, which causes violent disturbance to the water as the tide flows in and out, so that you have the weirdest phenomenon, a two-way fall: inward towards the loch at flood tide, outward to sea at the ebb.

The falls, and Ben Lora in Benderloch to the north, are

named after *Laoghaire*, one of the legendary heroes called the *Fianna*, or Fingalians, a band of warriors led by the colossal Fionn Mac Cumhail, or Fingal, whose exploits abound in West Highland folk-tales. The legends are Irish, but so were the Dalriadic Scots who brought them. The name of Connel is simpler, from *conghail*, a tumultuous flood, a reasonable description of what goes on at the foot of the village, its church, railway station, and the Falls of Lora Hotel. Both road and railway skirt the loch on their way east, until they cross one another near Achnacloich, a mansion in the Scottish baronial style which has woodland gardens overlooking the loch, and is now open to the public daily from March to June and from August to October. From here the road passes through Fearnoch Forest, while the railway sticks to the lochside until they unite again to run down to Taynuilt.

The cottages and houses of Taynuilt lie on and off the main road, down its high street and along the lochside, over a fairly wide area, and the village's chief fame resides in the Bonawe Iron Furnace, situated between Taynuilt and the lochside jetty, which used to be the southern landing-place of the Bonawe ferry. The furnace was established in 1752 by the English Richard Ford and Company, which operated in Ulverston in Furness. They leased wood rights and the site for an ironworks from Sir Duncan Campbell of Lochnell, and further wood rights from the Earl of Breadalbane: iron-smelting began in 1753. The ore was generally imported from Furness, because the important ingredient was the abundant supply of Highland timber, which came from all the neighbouring forests within the leases, usually by pack-horse after being converted to charcoal. Quantities of charcoal were tipped into the funnel of the furnace along with the iron ore and a flux, and the chimney widened in a way that ensured that the mixture was continuously but slowly descending; the limestone flux helped to remove impurities, and the chemical reactions were maintained by an upward blast of air from a massive pair of water-powered bellows. The metal trickled down to the hearth and was then drawn off as pig-iron.

The families of the furnace workers, many of whom were English, were provided with housing, a church, and a school, and a fine big house was built for the manager. The quayside, where iron-ore was unloaded from the sailing brigs, and the pig-iron returned, soon found its uses for the local populace. George Knott, an associate of the firm and son-in-law of Richard Ford's son William, complained to his agent in 1781 that it had become an outlet for smuggling, and wanted it stopped. 'Put a stop, if possible,' he added, 'to that confounded drinking in general, and by your shewing the example it may be more easily done, for I believe there is not such another drunken hole in the Kingdom.'

By 1876 charcoal blast-furnaces were rare, and Bonawe closed. Its buildings have been rescued from decay, refurbished, and set up as a monument to the fairly recent industrial past by Historic Buildings and Monuments, under the care of the Secretary of State for Scotland. Its exhibition, with explanatory information, is superb, with life-size figures in the key working areas. It is open to the public every day.

The Furnace is not the only reason for a closer look at Taynuilt: there is, for example, the earliest of all monuments to Lord Nelson, which the Bonawe workmen erected in 1805; there is an 18-hole golf course, opened by Mr Michael Bonallack in June, 1991; there is also the Inverawe Smokery on the far side of the River Awe, near its issue into Loch Etive. You have to go on towards the Pass of Brander and turn sharp left, under the railway, returning westward along the wooded slopes of Beinn Cruachan. Inverawe House is the home of Mr and Mrs Campbell-Preston, who set up the smokery in 1979. Visitors may view the smoke-house, which works in the traditional way with old-style smoke-boxes and local oak chips; the fish are brined with a mixture of salt and sugar, then hung in the smoke-box. The process takes two days, and the products include smoked salmon, Loch Etive trout, eel,

The Pass of Glencoe, from Rannoch Moor.

Loch Morar in the Spring – from Bracara.

Glenfinnon – the monument to the Jacobite Rebellion of 1745, at the head of Loch Shiel.

The Five Sisters of Kintail at sunset.

Eilean Donan Castle, Loch Duich.

The Lochalsh Hotel, Kyle of Lochalsh.

Black Cuillins, Isle of Skye (general view).

Eas Mor (the Great Falls) in the Black Cuillins, Isle of Skye.

Black Houses (crofters' cottages) in the Isle of Skye Museum.

The Old Man of Storr, Isle of Skye.

The River Ewe at Poolewe, Wester Ross.

Ullapool, Loch Brown.

Ardvreck Castle, Loch Assynt.

The Old Man of Stoer, Sutherland.

Balnakeil Bay, near Durness.

cod's roe, kippers, halibut, and various patés; smoked venison is also offered, and all are available in the smokery's shop, strongly recommended by these customers.

Bonawe is really the village on the northern side of the loch; beyond it, and beyond the smokery on the southern side, Loch Etiveside is completely roadless. W. H. Murray says that there were plans in 1968 for a road along ten miles of the northern shore, but fortunately these have never matured. There are tracks and Forestry Commission roads, but the best way for a visitor to see one of the loveliest lochs in the West highlands is to board a boat at the jetty near the Iron Furnace. Loch Etive Cruises operate twice daily in the summer season, at 10.30 am and 2 pm, their boat holds up to 125 passengers, and the cruise lasts for three hours. The boat glides gently from the jetty beneath the cables strung between two gigantic pylons, one on either side of the loch, and then you pass among the things of nature only. The mountains tower above the loch's placid surface, first the mighty Cruachan, then *Monadh Liath* and Ben Starav, riven by the passes of Glen Noe and Glen Kinglass. On rocks by Inverliver Bay you may see the seals flopped out indolently in the sunshine; you might, with luck, catch sight of the red deer on one of the mountain-sides, or perhaps a golden eagle circling high above the peaks. You cruise all the thirteen miles up the loch to the mouth of Glen Etive, where the beautiful Deirdre of the Sorrows lived in the legendary past, until you are carried back to Taynuilt. An informed commentary points out all points of interest, including birds and beasts that might otherwise escape untutored notice.

Another river that joins the loch at Taynuilt is the Nant, and a road that dog-legs sharply uphill from the A85 just across the river-bridge follows its course up the narrow, thickly wooded, deep glen. There is a spot on the Nant by a modern picnic-site which is called Tailor's Leap: the said tailor had an illicit still at the nearby burn, where it falls over a forty-foot drop into the Nant; when hotly pursued by the excisemen he broke the long-jump record to get across the Nant and away. A short way on from here, on the right of the road and near where the Nant descends from the hills into the glen, the Forestry Commission have laid out a superb Nature Trail through some of the old deciduous forest still remaining, for much of this forest fed the Bonawe Furnace. Along the way they have reconstructed a charcoal-burning kiln, where billets of wood were heaped beneath a covering of turf and heather and smoked to dry the sap from them, converting them into charcoal.

Leaving Glen Nant, the road continues over the hills, then follows the Kilchrenan Burn down to Kilchrenan and Loch Awe.

The village of Bonawe, across the Loch Etive narrows from Taynuilt, was created for the nearby quarries, which at one time employed around 300 men. Production is much diminished, and a large tenement building stands derelict. Redundant houses in the Highlands are seldom demolished, they just stand until they fall down, and as most of them are stone-built, they seldom do. A few miles farther west along the northern shore, beyond Inveresragan, is a fine house attached to the ruins of a once-prosperous priory. Ardchattan was founded, it is thought, in 1230 by Duncan MacDougall, Lord of Lorn, or his son Ewan; either of them may also have built Dunstaffnage Castle and its chapel. Its monks were of a most unusual order, the Valliscaulian, whose mother abbey was at *Val des Choux*, Valley of Kale or Cabbage, in Burgundy. Its rule was based on a combination of the Carthusian and Cistercian, embodying the most rigorous points of both. For example, there was silence at all times, no meat or gravy, hair-shirts worn all round the clock, sleeping fully clothed with no mattress. There were only three houses outside France, and they were all in Scotland — there was no connection with England. They were all dedicated to St Mary and St John the Baptist, and their monks wore the white Cistercian habit. Scottish monasteries were not dissolved all at once, as in England, they dwindled; a 16th-century prior was a

Campbell who founded a dynasty, which inherited the Ardchattan land when the last of the monks died.

The house is based on the original refectory of the priory.
Bruce is said to have held a council in it during the course of his
mainland campaigns in 1308. It was the last royal council to be
conducted in Gaelic. The priory church and the rest of the
buildings are in ruins, but enough remains to note the similarity
of ornament to the Dunstaffnage chapel, except that throughout
Ardchattan use is made of a kale-leaf decoration, from the
order's name.

Some famous people are buried at Ardchattan: one, under the
floor of the house's smoking-room, is Bishop Carswell of
Carnasserie; another is Colin Campbell of Glenure, victim of
the notorious Appin murder. The house is open, with a guided
tour, at certain selected times during the summer; its lochside
gardens are open for inspection of herbaceous borders and
shrub roses every day from April to October, from 8 am to 7 pm.

The curious knob of land partly closing in the entrance of
Loch Etive is a high plateau dipping steeply down to the
lochside. The flat top is the Achnacree Moss, a wild, eery
swamp of peat-cuttings, little lochans, gorse and sedge, inhabited by more rabbits than the entire human population of the
West Highlands. The Moss Road that runs in a dead straight
line across its northern end is full of honeysuckle and wild rose,
its hawthorn bushes full of finches, and its air full of a multitude
of sweet scents. Curlews call to each other across the Moss,
flying low over the yellow gorse; here too are two of the biggest
chambered cairns of all. One, Cairn Ban, is called Ossian's
Grave because it was believed that this son of Fingal was buried
there; the other, a little farther east, is a great twin-chambered
cairn called Achnacree Beag. Both of course are haunted.

On the Moss's eastern side, the ribbon of houses along the
cliff-top road, called North Connel, have one of the finest views
in Lorn, from Achnacree Bay towards Bonawe. At the narrows
the loch bends northward, so the twin peaks of Beinn Cruachan

fill the background of this picture, the other hills plunging their wooded sides down into the still loch-water, which mirrors the whole in perfect reflection. There are times, it must be admitted, when the clouds hang right down the hillsides to the water, and Cruachan disappears from view, and the water is as grey and ruffled as the sea at Herne Bay on a bad day. On the western side of the Moss there is a small airstrip down by the water, where gliding is taught. North of that is the North Ledaig caravan site whose serried ranks can be seen from Dunstaffnage, and over it all looms the modest height of Ben Lora.

The district of Ben Lora, including all the lower land around it, is called Benderloch, the name given in particular to the village at the foot of Ben Lora's steep scarp side. *Beinn eadar da loch* means Hill between two lochs, which aptly describes Ben Lora with Lochs Etive on one side and Creran on the other. There is a splendid archaeologically interesting site at Benderloch whose legends unite Loch Etive with Ulster. It is an outcrop of rock jutting into Ardmucknish Bay on which are traces of two vitrified forts and a later dun: as a Pictish stronghold, it was called *Barr nan Gobhainn*, 'Fort of the Ridge of the Armourers'. Some writers chose to confuse this name with a Latinised version Beregonium, for no known reason since the Roman influence never reached this far. Its other name is *Dun Mhic Uisneachan*, Fort of the Sons of Uisneach, which connects it with the story of Deirdre of the Sorrows.

Deirdre *Nic Cruithnigh*, Daughter of the Picts, was the daughter of one particular Pict, a first-century King of the Picts. When very young she was betrothed to Conchobar, King of Ulster, who received permission to come to Alban (the old name for Scotland) and fetch her when she arrived at the age of eighteen. She spent her girlhood on the shores of Loch Etive in company with the three sons of Uisneach, Naoise, Ainnle, and Ardan; they grew up together as if she were a sister, in innocence and happy friendship, and mutual love. Deirdre's closest friend of the three was Naoise, the eldest. The Pictish

154

Royal House kept them under strict supervision, but within these bounds they were left to roam freely, and the boys hunted and fished and brought their catch to Deirdre. She built her *grianan*, sunny bower, on the banks of the Etive river near Dalness, and there they lived an idyllic life for ten years.

Then King Conchobar's men came to fetch her: she refused to leave without the three boys, and so they were taken to Ulster too. On the voyage Deirdre composed and sang her 'Farewell to Alban', expressing her deep, heart-rending sorrow at leaving her home and the joyful life in Glen Etive. When they arrived in Ulster, Deirdre still declining to be parted from the three, they were lodged in a house and an explanation was brought to Conchobar. Assuming a carnal interpretation of her attachment, the king became furiously jealous and launched an attack on their house. The brothers resisted, but were all captured, and the king in his fury had them all beheaded at once. Rosemary Sutcliff, in *The Hound of Ulster*, describes the scene that followed: 'And all the Red Branch Warriors let out three heavy shouts above them. And Deirdre broke free of the men who held her, and she tore her bright hair and cast herself upon the three headless bodies and cried out to them as though they could still hear her. "Long will be the days without you, O sons of Uisneach, the days that were never wearisome in your company. The High King of Ulster, my first betrothed, I forsook for the love of Naoise, and sorrow is to me and those that loved me. The sons of Uisneach fell in the fight like three branches that were growing straight and strong; their birth was beautiful and their blossoming, and now they are cut down.

' "O young men, digging the new grave, do not make it narrow, leave space there for me that follow after, for I am Deirdre without gladness, and my life at its end!"

'And as they would have dragged her away from Naoise's body, she snatched a little sharp knife from the belt of one of the men who held her, and with a last desolate cry, drove the blade home into her breast, and the life of her was gone from between their hands like a bird from its broken cage.'

It is not entirely clear what all this has to do with a Pictish fort at Benderloch: legends do have a habit of attaching themselves to places.

Lochnell House, of the Campbells of Lochnell, stands across the bay on a green-forested finger of land; above the shores of Loch Creran, where it bends to make its narrow entrance to meet the Lynn of Lorn, there rises Barcaldine Castle, known locally as the Black Castle. A tall tower-house, it was built in 1609 by Sir Duncan Campbell of Glenorchy, and granted in 1699 to Alexander Campbell, whose family occupied it until they built Barcaldine House in 1724. The tower fell into ruin through neglect, but was restored by Sir Duncan Campbell in 1896. It opens to the public at certain fixed times or by appointment, but occasionally in the great hall they hold that peculiarly Highland event called a *ceilidh*: impromptu singing, dancing, and piping, story-telling or poetry-reciting, or whatever else the assembled company wants.

It was here, in that abominable winter of 1691–92, on the 31 December, that MacIain, the Glencoe MacDonalds' old Chief, having journeyed to Fort William to make his sworn oath of loyalty to King William III and been told that he had to do so before the Sheriff in Inveraray, was detained by Captain Thomas Drummond. Says John Prebble: 'He told his men to put MacIain's gillies in a hole beneath the castle. The Chief was locked in a narrow *garde-robe*, where he stayed for twenty-four hours in what must have been cruel agony for a man of his size and age. . . The old year was gone when he finally released the MacDonalds.' Sheer malice had motivated Drummond, but all around him, MacIain's enemies were laying their plans for his and his clan's ultimate destruction.

It seems inapt, after these old Highland tales of sorrow and tragedy in the classic mould, to move abruptly to the modern reign of King Mammon. On Loch Creranside, at 'St Columba's Bay' (not marked on the O.S. map) there is to take place 'Phase

1 — 1989 Construction Programme', in which there will arise Lochside Time Share Lodges, Holiday Homes for Sale or Investment and Residential and Business Units. What will Phase 2 bring forth: Disneyland and a Multi-Leisure Complex, perhaps? The site cannot be far from the Sea-Life Centre, which is also on the lochside and has been established since 1979. A highly ingenious method of bringing marine life to the public's attention involves the use of huge glass-sided tanks, so that you can stand and be surrounded by fish of all kinds, from conger eels to octopus and vast shoals of herring: all of these creatures, it is pointed out, are to be found, and all have been caught, off the shores of Scotland. Seals are the favourites, and pools have been designed for them so that they can slide from one to another down chutes. There is also a restaurant, where you can eat some of the exhibits. 140,000 visitors, we are told, witnessed the watery wonders in 1988, and even more in the Centre's jubilee year of 1989. It opens in mid-February, from 9 am to 6 pm every day, and until 7 pm in July and August, until the end of November.

The hillsides along the whole length of this part of Loch Creranside are planted with Forestry Commission conifers, through the middle of which runs the road across Glen Salach, B845, to Loch Etiveside. A high and lonely road, although very lovely, it was taken by poor old MacIain, after his release by the spiteful Drummond from Barcaldine, on his slow and painful way to the Bonawe ferry and the long road to Inveraray. It was 1 January, the weather was foul, and it would not be surprising if he was disinclined to appreciate the scenery.

The Forestry Commission has marked out an area of *Gleann Dubh*, the Black Glen, east of Glen Salach and the Barcaldine caravan park, with a number of trails. Each has a coloured sign to follow, and in case visitors might be put off by the dour-sounding name they have called it Sutherland's Grove. Through the middle of it the *Abhainn Teithi* thunders down in a series of cascades; there are all the wonders of spring flowers, birds, butterflies and insects to admire, and you can spend many a happy hour walking the tracks.

Loch Creran is nine miles long, and narrows, as most of the West Highland sea-lochs do, to a point only 150 yards wide, crossed by the old railway bridge. This one has not been converted for road use, so you have to travel all the way round the head of the loch; this is no penance, for you can enjoy the beauty of sylvan slopes dipping to the placid loch-waters. When you come to Invercreran at loch-head you are in the country of Appin.

8

Appin and Lismore

The railway bridge at the Loch Creran narrows was built in 1903; there has been no rail since the closure of the line in 1966, but if you are not prone to vertigo you can still walk across, over the swirling waters. Creran is from the Gaelic *criathar*, pronounced 'crearar', meaning a sieve. Looking down from the bridge, it is easy to understand this name, because at flood-tide the water forces through the narrows with the action of a riddle, a great volume rushing through a constricting neck. As at Connel, there used to be a ferry, braving the perils of the currents, rapids and eddies, plying to and fro between the Creagan Inn on the north shore, and a stone building on the south shore which was once a storehouse and is now a restaurant called the Butterchurn.

Appin is the mountainous region between Loch Creran and Loch Linnhe; some of its mountains exceed 3,000 feet, like *Beinn a'Bheithir, Sgurr na h-Ulaidh,* and *Beinn Fhionnlaidh.* There is only one road, the A828, from Invercreran to Ballachulish, a few lanes in the south-western corner, and otherwise just tracks to serve the farmsteads in the glens. The traffic mainly goes through, on its way to Fort William or to Oban, and Appin keeps its secrets.

One of the minor roads runs from the loch-head beside the

Creran river past the fine, luxurious Invercreran Country House Hotel, to the cottages and church of Invercreran, then along to Fasnacloich and eventually to Elleric, deep in the hills where Glen Creran meets Glen Ure. There is some Appin history there, but it can wait.

The main road runs under the shoulders of *Beinn Churalain*, passes the northern end of the old railway bridge and goes through Creagan, where boats can moor conveniently near the inn. Then leaving Loch Creran you enter Strath Appin, passing over the river *An Iola*, which runs down *Gleann na h-Iola* to Invernahyle (which is how you pronounce the latter part of the name). A lane leads off left, one of three that penetrate the south-western verge of Appin. This country is different from the rest: it is low-lying, heavily wooded, pastoral, and very green. There is a profusion of little bays and'inlets from the loch. North Shian is the only hamlet, peaceful and beautiful itself, but from it there are delightful views of the little island of Eriska opposite and the entrance to Loch Creran: filled with rocks and skerries, it is white-flecked and fearsome when a sea is running, gold-edged when the water is still. You wind your way through this enchanted, Arcadian landscape, to a pretty village tucked under the low tree-hung cliffs called Port Appin, where the famous Airds Hotel overlooks the Lynn of Lorn, and the northern tip of long, lonely, lovely Lismore Island (accent on the second syllable). Through an archipelago of islands, rocks and skerries, past the point of Lismore, the expanse of Loch Linnhe shines blindingly bright in a shaft of sunlight; over the humble green crest of Lismore the great bald hills of Kingairloch loom hazily; all around, the eternal gulls and terns glide and cry, omnipresent reminders of the cruel sea's proximity, of the souls of long-drowned sailors, fishermen, Highlandmen.

At the head of the jetty at Port Appin the Ferry Inn provides a welcome refuge for those waiting for the ferry. The sailing times are at two-hourly intervals, starting at 8 am (except on Sundays when it starts at 10 am), but if you arrive just in time to see the

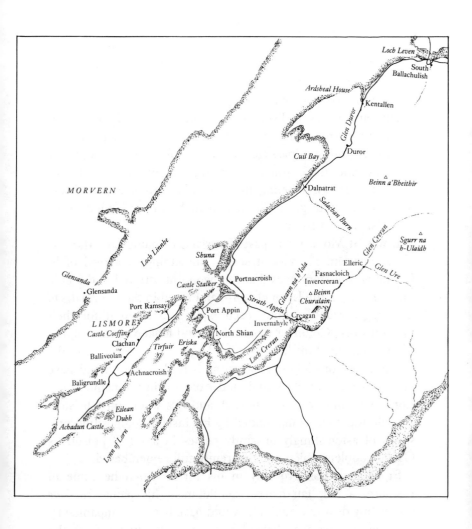

ferry on its way to the island, there is sometimes relief at hand. It happened to us, so we resorted to the inn, asked for some coffee, and explained our plight. The landlady said that someone from the island had just telephoned her to persuade the ferryman to run back immediately and pick her up, and perhaps if she talked to him he might take us over. She did, and he would: no coffee, we were on our way. The ferry-boat is small, with a saloon big enough to carry perhaps twenty passengers, but it has a powerful engine and needs it, because as elsewhere on this dangerous coast, the currents are strong and there are two skerries to be negotiated on the passage across. It only takes about five minutes, and there you are jumping out of the boat to the concrete slipway, meeting the lady who had telephoned and wants urgently to go to the mainland. You have landed in the Holy Island of Lismore.

It was St Moluag who gave the island its name *Lios Mor*, the Great Garden. He was, it seems, something of a rival of St Columba; the story goes that the two saints arrived at the little *Eilean Dubh*, in the Lynn of Lorn, and raced in their curraghs to the bigger island's shore, each hoping to claim it for their mission work. Columba was leading, and looked set to win, but Moluag chopped off his own little finger and threw it on to the beach ahead of Columba, shouting 'My flesh and blood have first possession of the island, and I bless it in the name of the Lord.' Columba was not amused, and this whole un-Christian episode was then compounded by his instant composition of a series of astonishingly unsaintly curses in a set of poisonous Gaelic couplets which are apparently still remembered.

St Moluag was probably in his forties when he came to Lismore, a tall, fair-haired, gentle man: his name *Mo-luag* means 'my dear fair one'. He would have been accompanied by a dozen acolytes who helped him set up his first cell on the beach called Port Moluag. The island is full of him and his works.

From the moment when you step off the jetty and begin to

162

walk along the island's only through road, you realise why St Moluag chose to call it a garden: there are flowers everywhere. We visited Lismore in July, and there were great, glorious bushes of fuchsia, growing wild and glowing with crimson and purple. At the farmhouse of Stronacroibh a side-lane departs westward to Port Ramsay in just half a mile, where there are the cottages and anchorage that served during the nineteenth century as port for Lismore's lime industry. Lismore is a limestone ridge (which helps to explain its fertility) and its lime was quarried and exported, to the profit of the islanders to whom it gave employment. The lime was burnt in kilns, some of which are still there, then was loaded into boats. The lime-workers had a few acres of land with their cottages so that they could keep animals and be self-sufficient. The closure of the lime industry killed Port Ramsay, and the cottages now are mostly holiday homes; but a granite quarry has opened in Glensanda, across Loch Linnhe in Morvern, and some of the islanders now work there, commuting daily across the loch in motor-boats.

Lismore is about 8½ miles long, but never more than 1½ miles wide, so the sea is always near at hand, bringing its wild tangy smells and the sound of the myriad sea-birds that rise in thousands from the rocky Appin shore, their cries mingling with the more prosaic bleating and lowing of the island animals, for the grassy pastures support plenty of sheep and beef-stock. Flowers splash the wayside with colour, yellow, blue, purple, pink, and the dark red of the fuchsia. From various parts of the road you can see the stump of Tirfuir standing on a grassy knoll high above the shore: a lane to the left past Achuaran will take you to within scrambling distance of it.

Tirfuir is a broch, which is, writes Peter Clayton in *Archaeological Sites of Britain*, a 'curious and distinctive structure peculiar to Iron Age Scotland, and generally dated around the beginning of the Christian era.' There are 500–600 known brochs, nearly all on the northern mainland and the northern and western isles, and they were tall stone towers, with a single entrance and often with passages and rooms within the walls. The courtyard area inside is small, and they cannot have been intended to withstand a long siege as hardly any have a source of water within them. Tirfuir, or *Tur a'foir*, Tower of refuge, is a name that gives the impression that it was not permanently inhabited. Certainly when intact it would have been around forty feet high and command views of the whole coastline. The Picts built it and used it, and it is quite possible that Tirfuir was their name for the island before the coming of St Moluag in 563. Just beyond the turning of the lane to Port Moluag and the broch, a sign on the right of the road indicates 'St Moluag's Chair'. There is no gate so you have to scramble over the stone wall, and there is no chair except for a seat in a rock, where the saint would often rest during his travels around the island. The 'chair' is high on the spine of the island, and he would have seen Loch Linnhe and the Kingairloch mountains on one side, and the Lynn of Lorn and as much of the Lorn coast as the weather permitted, on the other. With good highland clarity, he could have seen Ben Nevis to the north, Cruachan eastward, and maybe even the Paps of Jura away to the south-west. For centuries afterwards, people would come and recline in the 'chair' and pray for relief from their rheumatism. They would need it, because mild though the climate is, rain falls on Lismore in abundance.

The principal village in Lismore is Clachan, which is the Gaelic word for a village with a church. This one is called the Cathedral Church of St Moluag. For a small parish church in a thinly populated island, this might seem a grandiose title, but the present building is only the choir of the original cathedral, which extended westward with nave and tower. It was built when a new diocese of Argyll was founded in about 1200, and St Moluag's holy Lismore was thought appropriate for the bishop's seat. So insular a site was soon found to be inconvenient, and within fifty years the bishop moved away. His cathedral stood until the Reformation, when it was burnt.

The surviving choir section does duty as the parish church; sixty feet by twenty, it is solid, simple, and beautiful. The piscina and sedilia are still in place, and a couple of original doorways, now blocked up; you can see the fine archway at the west end which used to lead from the choir into the nave, and is now the rear wall. There is a gallery, from which you can see better a stained-glass window showing Saints Moluag and Columba. St Moluag founded his first church on this spot, and although no trace remains of it, there is beyond the west end of the churchyard a rough circle of about 250 yards in diameter which might indicate the line of earthwork forming his *lios mor*, the sacred enclosure itself.

St Moluag died in 592 while visiting one of his other foundations in Rosemarkie, and his body was brought back to Lismore and buried there: where exactly, no-one knows, but somewhere in that enclosure. His reputation was high, he was called 'Moluag the clear and brilliant, the sun of Lismore in Alba'. He had a pastoral staff, and after his death it was kept as a sacred relic. One family had the duty and right to keep it, and that family still keeps it. The staff was known as the *Bachuil Mor*; a thirteenth-century Bishop of Lismore granted the title of Baron of Bachuil to each successive head of the family, whose name is Livingstone, along with a small estate. The present Baron of Bachuil, Mr Alasdair Livingstone, showed us (by appointment) the *Bachuil Mor*, which is kept in a glass-fronted wall-safe in the living room of his home, Bachuil House. It is small, plain, with traces of metal ornamentation, and a crooked head, as simple a staff as you might expect of such a saint. The Baron also showed us a document of 1544 issued by the Earl of Argyll, confirming the family's rights to keep the staff and land, as had that particular baron's father, grandfather, great-grandfather and all predecessors. He told us of another, more recent and very curious tradition in his family, of fifty-year generations: his grandfather was born in 1815, his father in 1865, himself in 1914, and his son in 1964.

The manse, a handsome house near the church dated 1840, is now the Lismore Guest-house. A little south of it there is a track which leads to the western coast and the ruins of Castle Coeffin, clinging to the tip of a spur of land above the little bay, *Port a'Chaisteal*. The crumbled remains of a thirteenth-century hall-house are superimposed on an earlier fortress of Viking origins, the home of one Prince Caiffen who gave it his name.

At the farm of Killandrist on the main road a track goes off southward to the shores of Loch Balnagowan, and to the old mill of Balnagowan, which still has its mill-wheel but is now a farmhouse. From this you can follow a footpath down to the sea-shore, along the grassy ledge between sea and low cliffs, to Achnacroish, which has a pier where the car-ferry from Oban comes in (infrequently; twice most days, three times others). It also has the only café on the island, which turns out to be a converted caravan. The only post office on the island is at Balliveolan, on the main road between the track and the proper road to Achnacroish, and it is the only proper shop too.

The southern part of the island is even more sparsely populated, but there is a surprising number of Iron Age duns, and cairns, and there is Achadun Castle. Another minor road leaves the main road beyond the Achnacroish turning, at Baligrundle, and goes to Salen, where there is a little bay with a stone quay and a disused lime quarry. Derelict cottages, storehouses, and lime-kilns stand about the bay beneath the limestone cliffs, relics of the departed industry. Fishermen still use the quay, and the bay is the prettiest in the island. Its service road continues to Achinduin, and Achadun Castle stands above Achadun Bay. Like Coeffin, it is in a bad state, having been totally neglected since 1510. It was once a residence of the Bishops of Argyll, but they found it greatly more convenient to use Bishop Hamilton's Saddell Castle in Kintyre.

It does rain in Lismore, especially in the autumn, but it has the kind of blissful tranquillity that is hard to find. There is nothing that is so attractive to tourists that they come every day in their thousands, as they do to Iona, so the island remains unspoilt to the extent that its flowering waysides, green pastures full of sheep and cattle, widely-spaced crofts and teeming bird-life cannot have altered so very much since the days of St Moluag, and long may it remain so.

From Port Appin on the mainland the lane has to negotiate the southern shores of Loch Laich, a tidal inlet, before returning to the Strath Appin road; in the process there are splendid views of an old grey castle, standing in isolated seclusion in the middle of the bay. It is one of the most romantic-looking castles in the West Highlands, and could well have inspired many a 'Doom Castle' type of novel, but the facts about Castle Stalker are less exciting. *Stalcair* means Castle of the Hunter, and the name reveals its purpose; James V had it built in 1540 for his kinsmen the Stewarts of Appin, provided he could use it now and then for hunting expeditions. A hunting-lodge inaccessible except by boat might not appeal to some folk after a long day in the hills after the red deer, but Stewart kings had plenty of reasons for craving security: too many of them had been murdered. It had a seventeenth-century period of Camp-bell ownership, was regained by the Stewarts for four years, then lost again in 1690 when they championed the exiled James VII (II of England) instead of William III. It became a much-admired Victorian Romantic Ruin, but a Stewart acquired it again, completely restored it, and now lives in it. Except by appointment it is not open to the public.

The main road A828 skirts the northern shore of Loch Laich; when the tide is in and the sun is out, there is no more arresting view, of flashing, glittering water amid green hills, and Castle Stalker's grey stones gilded like an enchanted castle in some Arthurian legend. Cameras leap out of their cases, but there are not all that many places where a driver feels he can safely stop.

In the Episcopalian Church of Portnacroish, almost directly opposite the castle, there are reminders of the Stewarts' fighting past. Inside the church they kept a replica of the blue and yellow

Appin banner, the only Highland banner to have survived public burning after Culloden; outside it, on a tree-covered knoll in the churchyard, is an obelisk commemorating the Battle of Stalc, fought at the head of Loch Laich in 1468 in the contentious and turbulent days following the murder at Dunstaffnage of Sir John Stewart, Lord of Lorn. The Stewarts and their allies the MacLarens fought against a combination of Campbells, Mac-Farlanes and MacDougalls, and won. Dugald, Sir John's son, was confirmed in his Lordship: he gave it up the following year, but ruled Appin alone for thirty-four years.

Leaving Loch Laich the road follows the contours of the hills and bears round northward. Shuna Island with its little castle on its southern tip, shows green and bare to the left, and at Appin House you are again down at loch-level, running smoothly alongside what used to be the old railway. Past Dalnatrat where the Salachan Burn emerges from its afforested glen and plunges into the loch, down by the water is Keil Chapel in its burial-ground, which is the traditional last resting-place of the Stewarts of Appin. A small brass plate there records the interment of the remains of James Stewart, called James of the Glen; nearby in Cuil Bay the Duror Burn flows down from Glen Duror, where he lived. He is one of the central characters in the tragedy known as the Appin Mystery.

An unsolved mystery fascinates the human race, whether it be the fate of the *Marie Celeste*'s crew, or whether or not there is a monster in Loch Ness; an undetected murder comes top of the list.

The year was 1752, and the events of 1746 were still rebounding crushingly on the unhappy Highlanders. They were forbidden either to carry arms or to wear their traditional dress, the tartan plaid, in any visible form. Clan chiefs were in exile, on pain of death should they return, and rents were often collected from their clansmen to keep them in pocket. Their normal rents were also collected, so they were paying twice over. Stewart of Ardsheal took to the glens of Appin and evaded his pursuers for nearly six months, for some time hiding in an extraordinary hollow boulder on the south bank of the Creran river, still called 'Ardsheal's Stone'. King George II's government, shocked to the core by the fourth Jacobite rising within fifty-six years, turned on the Highlanders as a man lashes out at a bee that has stung him, crushing it. Clan Campbell, having as always stayed loyal to the government, continued to act for it. In 1748 Colin Campbell of Glenure was appointed Government Factor for Ardsheal's forfeited estates in Appin, and for Cameron of Lochiel's in Lochaber, which was awkward for him because his mother was a Cameron. Red Colin, as he was called from the colour of his hair, was a sensible man, reluctant to exacerbate further the bitterness of the Highlanders at their humiliation, and his relations with the leading Stewart, James of the Glen, were good.

James Stewart was the illegitimate half-brother of Ardsheal, an upright, straightforward, highly respected and responsible spokesman for his folk, conscious of Glenure's delicate position, and anxious that inflamed sentiments should be kept as soothed as possible, to avoid further pointless insurrection and its inevitable savage repression. The Highlanders had lost so much, they could not afford to lose more.

His superiors, however, were disturbed by Glenure's lenient attitude to the Stewart tenants and his Cameron relations, and gave him notice that he would lose his position if publicly accused of Jacobite sympathies; he had permitted a close relative of an attainted traitor to remain on the latter's forfeited estate. James Stewart knew Glenure's predicament, and feared far worse treatment of his kinsfolk from a harsher factor, so he voluntarily quitted his farm of Auchindarroch to become tenant of another Campbell friend at the much smaller Aucharn, not far away. Glenure therefore installed a new tenant in his place, but he was another Campbell, which placated his superiors but angered the younger kind of local dissidents, who could see nothing save in terms of black and white, good and bad.

One of these young firebrands was the ne'er-do-well foster-son of James of the Glen, Allan Breck Stewart (called *Breac*, speckled, because he had survived small-pox but not its effects); he had never achieved anything honourable himself but was a born agitator, and had often been heard in the Appin drinking-houses, dextrously poisoning the minds of other brainless young idiots with tirades against the government and threats to Glenure's life. Any sane man could see the appalling dangers of this kind of talk, if translated into action: a single act of violence might well destroy them all.

In the spring of 1752 Glenure, now painted with the colours of a hard-faced, treacherous tyrant, was obliged to evict some tenants and replace them with government sympathisers. These were incomers, not Stewarts, and James Stewart had accepted them on condition that they paid the double rent for Ardsheal's support. Despite Glenure's efforts to ensure the future well-being of those evicted, James protested, and after a visit to Edinburgh and some legal manoeuvres, he was told that he might yet save them by a Formal Protest made on the spot, on the day, and in the presence of a lawyer and witnesses. There was a fortnight to go to the day set for the evictions.

On the 14th May, the day before the evictions, Glenure was riding back from Lochaber, with three companions, towards Kentallon on the coast; they passed through the wood of Lettermore (Leitir Mhor) along the narrowing track, in single file. A shot rang out and Glenure slumped across his saddle. A man carrying a large gun was seen running off up the hillside, but all attention was on the dying Colin Campbell, and no-one gave chase.

Suspicion pointed to Allan Breck Stewart, but he was nowhere to be found; the authorities suspected a Jacobite plot and demanded instant retribution, with Clan Campbell cla-mouring for the honour of their name. A suit of clothes, belonging to James Stewart, was found at the known hide-out of Allan Breck, so James Stewart was arrested. He had been working in the fields at Aucharn at the time, with many witnesses, but what did that matter? He was a Stewart, he could be proved to be an accomplice, and a scapegoat had to be found.

For three months James was imprisoned in Maryburgh (the old name for Fort William), then taken to Inveraray for trial. Inveraray was still in the process of being dismantled and reconstructed, and the new Court House was not yet built, so the trial was held in the old church. There were three judges, one of whom was the Duke of Argyll; eleven of the fifteen jurymen were Campbells. Despite a complete lack of evidence, yet giving credence to some that was procured or perjured, James was found guilty and sentenced to death. He was hanged on 8 November at a knoll by the Ballachulish ferry called *Cnap a'Chaolais*. He was allowed to speak, and he told of his complete innocence, and asked God's pardon of those who had perjured him, several of whom he named; he recited Psalm 35, still called in those parts '*Salm Sheumais a'Ghlinne*', James of the Glen's psalm, and then mounted the scaffold. His body was hung in chains for three years, until at last his friends were allowed to gather the scraps and bury them at Keil. A monument, by the turning to the new Ballachulish Bridge, marks the place of the execution.

No-one ever discovered who killed Red Colin Campbell, although there were plenty of theories, and there still remains the belief that the murderer's identity is still held secret by certain Stewards of Appin. There seems no reason for this except perhaps family pride, since the murder was an act of incredible irresponsibility, atoned for by the sacrifice of a good man.

The modern Ardsheal House is built on the foundations of Charles Stewart of Ardsheal's old home, and is now a fine hotel, on a projection into Loch Linnhe. The road, cutting inland from Duror to Kentallen, reveals green pastoral country filled with sheep, and an abundance of craft-shops filled with their wool in various fabricated forms. The road returns to the lochside, fringing the woods of Lettermore: the old road still winds through the trees, higher up the hillside, and there is a plaque which marks the spot where Campbell of Glenure was shot dead.

The Ballachulish ferry used to ply across the Loch Leven narrows, but there is now a splendid new steel bridge. The alternative to the ferry was to drive all the twenty-five miles to Kinlochleven and back the other side. Ballachulish, *Baile a'Chaolais*, Village of the Narrows, is part of Appin but leans towards Glencoe, and shares in the enormous influx of tourists to that unhappy valley. Appin, its glens now thinly populated, keeps its secrets and stands aloof from the thronging crowds.

9

Mull and Iona

Mull is a big island, twenty-five miles by twenty. The ferries from Oban are the modern type of roll-on, roll-off, and they make the eight mile journey in about forty minutes, with four or five sailings a day. The nearest port is Craignure, and that is where most of the tourists go, whether with their cars or bicycles or to board coaches which will conduct them about the island. They go for the sake of Mull's scenery, and quite often for through passage to Iona, which attracts modern-day 'pilgrims' by the thousand.

The ferry-boat, drawing away from the south quayside, gives you a splendid view of Oban, its busy activity, shops and hotels along the waterfront, the great tower of St Columba's Cathedral and the white arches of McCaig's Folly atop the hill. As the boat nears the harbour entrance there is David Hutcheson's memorial on Kerrera to one side, the ivy-hung tower of Dunollie to the other. Then you are out beyond the clutches of land and heading into the Firth of Lorn towards the massively mountainous Mull.

The ferry steers between two lighthouses, the big white one of Lismore and the little one at Lady's Rock. The big one stands on Eilean Musdile, is now fully automated and was originally built in 1833 under the supervision of Robert Stevenson, father of the celebrated R.L.S. There are frightful currents hereabouts as the waters dash frenziedly over a treacherous skerry called *Liath Sgeir*, more commonly known as Lady's Rock, and this is marked by the second beacon. There is a story behind its English name (the Gaelic one just means grey rock).

Lachlan MacLean of Duart, in Mull, had married the Earl of Argyll's daughter, Lady Elizabeth Campbell; she had failed to provide him with a son, so in 1523 he planned to dispose of her in a way that would combine maximum success with minimum risk, and then inform her father of her illness and death in tones of grieving distress. The unhappy lady was dumped at low tide on the exposed rock of *Liath Sgeir*, because her husband knew it would be covered at high water and that she would be swept off and drowned. A scheme as vile as this deserves to miscarry, and this one did: some fishermen from Tayvallich, passing by in their boat, heard most piteous cries, saw the lady waving to them from the rock and rescued her. From Tayvallich she was taken up Loch Fyne to her father's castle in Inveraray.

MacLean saw in the morning that the rock was bare, assumed his plan had worked, and set off for Inveraray wearing deep black to tell his father-in-law of their mutual bereavement. A pitiful death-bed scene could easily be invented. He brought with him a coffin, carefully weighted, and a large band of retainers, and was received with courtesy and sympathy — at first. Then he was shown into the dining-hall, and it is not hard to imagine his state of mind when he saw Lady Elizabeth seated at the head of the table. The rules of Highland hospitality forbade Argyll to make any attempt to chastise the wretched Lachlan, and he was allowed to leave, but not long afterwards when he was in Edinburgh he was overtaken by certain other Highland rules, those which call for vengeance for a crime committed against a member of one's family. Lady Elizabeth's brother, Sir John Campbell of Calder, quietly and efficiently murdered him.

Craignure is a small port with a row of houses, an inn, a shop,

Mull and Iona

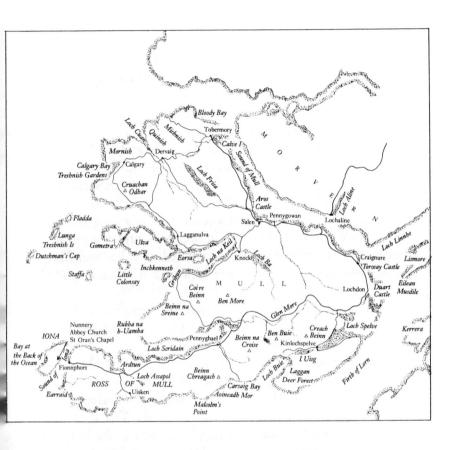

a nine-hole golf course, and the Mull and West Highland Narrow Gauge Railway, which runs along the coast, through the woodland, and down to Torosay Castle. It is the only passenger-carrying miniature railway in the West Highlands, and runs principally in the summer season. Torosay can also be reached quite easily from the main road, A849, going south. It is a Victorian baronial-style mansion, and its gardens are open to visitors from May onwards in the season.

Not far beyond Torosay's entrance, a lane leads off left to Duart Castle and reaches it after a long and spectacular tour of Duart Bay, with dramatic views of the castle and the Sound of Mull and the high Morvern hills beyond. The castle looks at its best when seen from the ferry: dark and menacing, it perches on its rocky crag like some predatory raptor. Duart, *Dubh Aird*, means Black Height: the first known fortifier of the site was MacDonald, Lord of the Isles, in the mid-thirteenth century, but in 1390 Donald MacDonald granted it to Lachlan Mac-Lean, who had married his sister. Lachlan therefore founded the MacLean House of Duart.

Clan MacLean claims that is descended from one *Gillean na Tuagh*, Gillean of the Battle-Axe, who is said to have dis-tinguished himself at the Battle of Largs in 1263 against King Haakon's Norsemen. The power of the MacLeans of Duart was broken when Sir John joined Dundee in his rising for James VII (II of England) in 1691, and lost. His lands were forfeited, but he tried again in the 1715 rising for James VIII (the 'Old Pretender'), and lost again. Duart was granted to the Duke of Argyll and was used as a barracks for troops, which did it little good. It fell into what the Victorians called 'romantic ruin' and was only rescued from decay by Sir Fitzroy MacLean, the Clan Chief, and restored in 1912. In that year he welcomed Mac-Leans from all over the world back to Duart once more, and the Chief's family have lived there ever since.

With great skill and a miracle or two, coach-drivers manage to drive along that narrow land round the bay, and at the castle there is plenty of parking space and other facilities for visitors. You enter the castle though the courtyard, then into the building by way of a kitchen, one of Sir Fitzroy's 1912 additions. No matter how indifferent the temperature outside, that passage-way from the kitchen strikes chill into the bones; it leads past the castle's well, a cell where a life-like prisoner lies in chains, and a dungeon with figures of Spanish officers captured when one of the Armada ships sheltered in Tobermory Bay in 1588. Although the dungeon looks less than luxurious, it was prefer-able for the officers to their ship, because Donald MacLean of Morvern blew it up, and himself as well. Steps lead up to the Sea-room, which has a glass-windowed panoramic view of nearly all the Firth of Lorn, and even of Ben Nevis on a good day; one of the cannons from the Spanish ship is there too. You enter the great keep through the massive thickness of the walls. That the entrance is on the seaward side is not coincidental, since castle-builders tended to site the most vulnerable point on the least vulnerable side.

The great hall of the keep, a lofty, cold, square room, contains portraits of past MacLeans, including Sir Fitzroy who lived until over 100; there is a collection of the family silver, some relics of the Crimean war, in which a MacLean took part, and family photographs: the present Lord MacLean used to be Lord Chamberlain to H.M. Queen Elizabeth II. A spiral stair in the thickness of the wall leads to the first floor and the state bedroom, which despite a vast four-poster bed is colder than ever. Lord MacLean used to be the Chief Scout, so the top floor is devoted to an exhibition which shows the development of Scouting from Baden-Powell's first experiments at Brownsea Island to the world-wide movement of today.

The view from the battlements is breathtaking; there is the Sound of Mull and Morvern, Lismore and Loch Linnhe, and across the Firth of Lorn to Oban: the shining water in the centre, the great dark hills fringing the entire scene, their heads communing with the heavens. A sentinel could give warning of an approaching fleet as soon as the sails of its galleys came into view (provided he could see anything at all with the weather the way it often is).

After the lane to Duart Castle, the main road soon drops down to Lochdon, a hamlet with a school at the head of Loch Don and a narrow lane that wriggles out to Grass Point on the loch's southern end. Soon after, crossing the head of Loch Spelve with the high hills rolling upwards to your right, there is a turning at Strathcoil which will take you to the Garden of Mull. On the corner of the turning there is a monument to the bard Dugald Macphail, who lived from 1818–1867, a stone pillar built from the broken walls of his home.

When you have crept around the base of the hill Cruach Ardura you are on the shore of Loch Spelve: an odd shape, it is almost land-locked, with a very narrow entrance. There are very few habitations, but sheep are everywhere, on the green hills, in the road and on the foreshore; so are the sea-birds, with noisy, red-billed oyster-catchers screaming in discord with the great white herring-gulls. Loch Spelve and Loch Uisg to its west form a valley between the mainland hills and a ridge which is almost an island, separated only by two half-mile necks of land. A lane from Kinlochspelve serves the very few houses on this long, hammer-shaped mass of hill and moorland by running along the southern shore of Loch Spelve, but otherwise it is a trackless wilderness, and the western end is the Laggan Deer Forest.

The steep wooded slopes of *Creach Bheinn Bheag* plunge precipitously down to Loch Uisg, streaked with colour like an artist's palette, with bright green foliage, bluebells and yellow gorse, and all the purples, pinks and reds of the wild rhododen-drons. This beautiful glen, known as the Garden of Mull, emerges at the head of Loch Buie. Behind the low shore-flats the *Abhainn a'Chaiginn Mhoir* hurtles down from a deep corrie between Ben Buie and Creach Bheinn, passing some ancient standing stones on its way to the hill-fringed sea-loch. There is green machair at the foreshore, a small caravan and camping site, and a post office into which it must be quite hard to fit a postage stamp. Nearby is the little church which is shared by the Church of Scotland and the Episcopalian Church, which prides itself on being the original pre-Reformation Scottish Church. A track along the foreshore leads to the graceful and elegant Lochbuie House; from the machair by the shore you can see the crumbling grey tower of Moy Castle.

Dr Johnson and Boswell stayed in Lochbuie House in 1773, and after Johnson had refused Lady Lochbuie's offer of cold sheep's-head for breakfast, they 'surveyed the old castle, in the pit or dungeon of which Lochbuie had some years before taken upon him to imprison several persons; and though he had been fined in a considerable sum by the Court of Justiciary, he was so little affected by it, that, while we were examining the dungeon, he said to me, with a smile, "Your father knows something of this"; (alluding to my father's having sat as one of the judges on his trial.) Sir Allan (MacLean) whispered me, that the laird could not be persuaded, that he had lost his heritable jurisdiction'.

The dungeon which Lochbuie had used so freely was no joke: it was a pit filled with nine feet of water, with one rounded stone in the centre, on which the prisoner was obliged to sit, or else swim, or drown. The castle was built in the fifteenth century by the then Laird of Lochbuie. The MacLeans of Lochbuie spell their name MacLaine, but they are a junior branch of the MacLean of Duart family (they say senior). There is a local legend, that if ever calamity threatens the MacLaines of Lochbuie, a phantom, headless horseman gallops around the old castle and the estate. It happened about fifty years ago when the last Chief to live in Lochbuie House died. The horseman is the ghost of Ewen MacLaine who was warned by a fairy not to go into battle: he fought nevertheless, was decapitated, and his horse carried him two miles before his body fell off. It served him right, you should always do what a fairy says.

Loch Buie, a bay of the sea, is utterly charming. *Buidhe* means yellow or golden, and is the name of Ben Buie, 2354 feet, perhaps because of the gorse flower on its sides. The south-facing, sheltered bay, accessible by that long, lonely, winding road, and none other, is full of colours, its luxuriant, brilliant hillsides blending with the bright water and the constantly changing light of a northern sea-shore.

From Strathcoil and Macphail's memorial the main road, when it has followed the Lussa river upstream and turned sharply, then enters Glen More, and here the contrast with Loch Buie could hardly be more striking. There is no cover of any kind: the hills are brown, bare, and deficient of any sort of human comfort. 'The most gloomy and desolate country I had ever beheld,' said Boswell; 'O, sir,' said Dr Johnson, 'a most dolorous country!' The new road, although good, is only single-track, but below it you can see sections of the old road twisting through the burns and peat-mosses, and sometimes holidaying walkers with rucksacks and waterproofs making use of it. Highland weather can change in a matter of minutes, blazing sunshine and clear skies exchanged for pitch-black clouds and slanting, chilling, spirit-lowering rain. 'The thought of the hills of Mull concealed in the grey mists strikes some primitive chord of terror in the mind', writes H. V. Morton. Conditions like these, he says, make it 'perfectly clear why Scotland invented whisky.'

The northern side of Ben Buie, not in the least golden, is responsible for some of this, but as the glen broadens out and the road follows the Coladoir river down to the head of Loch Scridain, there is green grass again for pastures, and trees, and the lochside brings the welcome relief of an altogether gentler landscape. Loch Scridain is a long sea-loch running in from the west; on its northern shore the flanks of huge Ben More, 3,171 feet, rise up from the water's edge, and from there stretch the wild craggy heights of Ardmeanach, with their three-mile strip of headland strewn with stone blocks fallen from the 1,200-foot-high cliffs to give the loch its name: loch of the screes. This rock is Tertiary basalt: on the southern cliff-face there is an ancient wonder, a fossil tree, forty feet tall. It was swallowed up by the lava-flow in the Miocene Age, fifty million years ago. To see it, unfortunately, you need either to be a rock-climbing expert or a bird.

If you can tear yourself away from the comforts of 'The Clansman', an excellent hotel-bar restaurant at Pennyghael on the southern shore of the loch, then you might take a side-road that leads off southward, following the deep glen of the Leidle river, whose steep eastern bank wears the Forestry Commission's pine-plantation pattern like a hall-mark. The lane winds mysteriously between *Beinn na Croise* and *Beinn Chreagach*, then without much warning tips you violently down a nearly sheer slope through the trees to Carsaig Bay. If you are unlucky you may have a parking problem, as there is only the lane-end, leading down to the quay, and there may be some cars there already. One gentleman when we arrived had left his Volvo too far down the track to the quay and was spinning his rear wheels trying to move away: it took three or four of us to push him clear. In point of fact, although the view from the bay is delightful, it is probably better to spend a day walking to see the wonders of Carsaig. There is a five-mile track along the shore from Loch Buie, for a start, but there are three more miles along the beach, under the dark towering cliffs of *Aoineadh Mor*, to Malcolm's Point and the Carsaig Arches. On the way you pass *Uamh nan Cailleach*, literally the Old Woman's Cave, but called the Nun's Cave, because in 1500 sandstone was quarried from it for additions (it is thought) to the nunnery in Iona.

The Carsaig Arches are the result of columnar basalt overlying weathered sandstone in the 700-foot cliffs. Erosion by the waves has caused the sixty-foot arch (in which a large colony of shags live), the deep sea-cauldron beyond it, and the 120-foot column of rock beyond that, which is pierced by a tall 'window', seventy-three feet high. Artists, at risk to life and limb, have for years been at pains to portray these geological wonders, and a summer-school at Carsaig tries to ensure that many more of them will continue to do so. One of their achievements hangs in the bar of 'The Clansman'.

The motorist has no alternative but to climb perilously up that zig-zag road to the top again: it is better to put on your walking-boots and go there another way. As you travel the length of this strange twenty-mile peninsula called on its south-western extremity the Ross of Mull, after a while the hills appear lower and the trees fewer. At Bunessan a lane leads off to the left to Loch Assapol, a lovely little fresh-water loch overlooked by the Assapol Guest House, which makes a splendid centre for fishing, walking in the hills and observing the wild-life, flora and fauna, or any other kind of activity that Mull can provide, like leaving it to visit Iona for a day.

Bunessan is at the head of an inlet from the sea — for the Ross of Mull extends farther than the rock-strewn head of Ardmeanach opposite — called *Loch na Lathaich*. Houses flank the bay, there is an inn, a post office-cum-general store which is full to overflowing with goods (and yet the infallibly courteous ladies running it know exactly where everything is), and like Assapol, it is a perfect base for exploring the island. The green, low-lying area between it and the mouth of Loch Scridain is called Ardtun. There is a monument to the composer Mary MacDonald, who lived here from 1789–1872, and wrote the carol 'Child in a Manger'. Bunessan's name means 'at the foot of the waterfall', which can be found in the hills, not far from a road which crosses the Ross (only the second to do so) to Uisken, a small crofting village with a wide expanse of sandy beach.

After Bunessan the road winds its way through craggy, treeless wastes, past *Loch Poit na h-I*, which means Iona's Pot: the abbey monks used to fish from it. Nowadays only the otters do and others who have a licence. There is an offshore island south-west of this barren point called Earraid, which Stevenson picked for his shipwreck of the brig 'Covenant' in his novel

Kidnapped. His young hero, David Balfour, is cast ashore and spends a most miserable three days in the rain, with no shelter, until he is rescued by a pair of grinning fishermen and at last realises that he could have walked ashore to the mainland at low tide, so near and so shallow is the intervening channel. He had fed on shell-fish until he hated them, had been drenched to the skin and become ill. 'I have seen wicked men and fools, a great many of both; and I believe they both get paid in the end; but the fools first.'

From anywhere on the high road through the Ross you can look northward, past Ardmeanach's point, *Rubha na h-Uamha*, and see the dark sea studded with islands. The nearest is Staffa, like a platform, then the Treshnish Isles, Dutchman's Cap with its great hump in the middle, Lunga and Fladda, Little Colonsay and Ulva. The nearest of all, five minutes' journey across the Sound from Fionnphort (pronounced Finnafort) is Iona.

A landing-craft type of ferry scurries back and forth cease-lessly from Fionnphort to Iona, and although it carries motor vehicles it will not do so for tourists. Only residents, or officials, like men from the Hydro Board or British Telecom, or the postman, may take their transport on the ferry. The island is small, just over three miles long by no more than a mile wide, so you can walk. The ferry lands you on a concrete slipway where the only village in the island faces the Sound. Cottages, inn, shop and restaurant cluster together, sheltered from the rough Atlantic gales by the low ridge of hills running down the spine.

Iona was never its name in the past. After Columba's time it was called *I-Chaluim-cille*, the Island of St Calum; Boswell refers to it as Icolmkill. In Columba's time it seems to have been called, variously, Hia, Io, Hi, and Hii. The early writers Bede and Adamnan called it Ioua. None of these was a Gaelic word, and its original might have been the Norse Hioe (pronounced Eea), meaning Den Island, since in those distant times there were plenty of brown bears in the Highlands. The name Ioua was then changed in error by some idle scribe to Iona, and it came into general use because the Hebrew Iona (Jonah) means the same as the Latin Columba, a dove, and no-one could resist such a fortuitous coincidence.

Although Iona owes its existence as an important Christian shrine to the mission centre established here by St Columba, there is nothing tangible connected with him. All the buildings, stones and crosses belong to later dates: yet none of them would exist without him. St Columba, or Columcille, was born in Donegal in 521 of the O'Neill clan, was related to the O'Neill High Kings, and became a presbyter of the church. At least in his early days his nature was not particularly saintly, in fact he seems to have been something of a firebrand. He left Ireland to escape the king's anger, and with twelve companions journeyed to Dalriada. They arrived first at the Mull of Kintyre, then went to Oronsay, the island south of Colonsay, and finally settled in Iona, which was eventually given to him by his relation the king of Dalriada. The Irish Church of the time was very loosely organised and permitted any priest or presbyter, monk or even novice, to wander off to some remote spot and set up a cell, pray and preach, and earn sanctity by example. Columba and his men constructed their living quarters, service buildings, and a tiny oratory, on the sheltered eastern side of the little island, and Columba set the pattern for their daily routine and their style of conduct.

A later abbot of Iona, Adamnan, wrote in about the year 800 a hagiography of Columba, describing him as angelic in appearance, graceful in speech and holy in work; he could not let an hour pass without prayer, or a day without fast or vigil. He set off frequently on evangelizing missions. In one he journeyed up the Great Glen to the fortress of the Pictish King Bridei, where he astonished everyone by causing the monster in Loch Ness to submerge at his command by reciting the 45th Psalm in a strong, loud voice; the Pictish pagan priests were thrown into confusion, especially when he opened the gates of the fortress at a touch. Bridei was sufficiently impressed, if not to submit to instant conversion, then at least to give Columba his protection among his people; Columba in return gave him a pebble from Iona which would protect him. It didn't, he was killed in battle later on.

Columba's community waxed with renown, augmented by many a Dalriadic Scot, Pict, Briton, and even an Anglo-Saxon or two; his missions and those of his followers gradually found their way into most parts of the Western Isles and the mainland, his reputation growing meanwhile, especially when in 574 he was called to choose a new king for Dalriada. He selected Aidan, from the house of Gabhran and Fergus Mac Erc, and proposed an insurance cover by laying his saintly hands on Aidan and saying, 'Believe firmly, O Aidan, that none of your enemies will be able to resist you unless you first deal falsely against me and my successors — or my relatives in Ireland.' Mixing politics with religion was quite commonplace even then: Columba had put his Christian Church under the protection of the king, for his own spiritual good. Thereafter it flourished, sending evangelizing missionaries even into the Northumbrian kingdom, and such was the status of Iona as its headquarters that the little monastery became paved with the gravestones of kings; whether Scottish, Pictish, or Norse, was immaterial.

The first of Iona's religious buildings, beginning from the quayside, is the Nunnery. The whole island, including its historic relics is in the care of the National Trust for Scotland, which means that all grass is cut, flowers grow in orderly beds, and each separate item is clearly labelled. The Nunnery is in ruins, but it is quite easy to make sense out of them because of this care in presenting the site intelligibly to visitors. The nuns were really Augustinian canonesses (which meant, like their male counterparts, that they were expected to lead a far more intellectual life of study and discussion than the ordinary Benedictine nuns or monks did), and their house was founded by Reginald, son of Somerled, in about 1200. The first prioress was Reginald's sister Bethoc (Beatrice). The first colony of canonesses was most likely brought from a similar foundation in Ireland. There were never many of them; the last two prioresses before the Reformation were MacLeans, so its modest endowments from land in Mull passed to the MacLeans of Mull; when their property was forfeited in 1690 the Earls of Argyll acquired it.

What remains standing consists of two gables and a wall of the Refectory, the foundation walls of the service buildings and cloister (which is laid out as a garden), and the west wall and three round-arched bays of the church, in the romanesque style usual for the period, the best example in the West Highlands apart from the chapel of Dunstaffnage. There is also a repaired and roofed chapel of St Ronan's to the north, which houses a museum, mostly for carved grave-slabs: one of them is of Prioress Anna MacLean, dated 1543. The garden atmosphere of the site is enhanced by the provision of benches. Relax on one of these, enjoy the sunshine picking out the colours of wild-flowers growing on parts of the old red sandstone walls, and the ubiquitous gulls planing over them, the dazzling, shining waters of the Sound with the little ferry fussing on one of its innumerable crossings, and you may feel the island's peace, disturbed only by the saw-mill sounds of the rookery in a neighbouring clump of trees.

It is well to go early to Iona, to avoid the throngs that arrive by the ferry-load from around 11.30 onwards; it is very difficult to savour the essential serenity of the place if several hundreds of others are also trying, in their various ways, to feel it (and some are not trying at all, and some are trying in another sense). Most writers express something of this sentiment on visiting Iona. The much-travelled H. V. Morton, for example, writes that 'Iona is a solemn, haunted place . . . . .And when you stand on its hills and look west over the Atlantic where the outermost isles rise like ships at anchor, when you see the vivid Atlantic sunsets staining the granite hills and the white sands, you feel that this is a place apart: a little sanctuary for ever dedicated to God.'

The path from the Nunnery now makes for the Abbey, swinging left past the first of the high crosses of Iona. This is MacLean's Cross, probably commissioned by one of the clan in the late fifteenth century. It is covered with an intricate interlaced design, with a figure on its western side, facing the parish church, of Christ Crucified. Oddly enough for so revered a site, when the Reformation closed both abbey and nunnery, and neither church was kept in repair, Iona was without a parish church for nearly 200 years. Eventually in 1824 an Act of Parliament decreed that forty-two new churches should be built in the Highlands, and in 1828 Iona's rose, to a design by Thomas Telford (who also designed one at the head of Loch Uisg); inside and out it is plain and simple, dignified and restrained, a fitting accompaniment to the virtuoso of the Abbey and its surroundings.

Just across the road from the church is the St Columba Hotel, which with the Argyll Hotel down in the village on the foreshore constitutes Iona's accommodation for visitors: except that the inmates of the Abbey have opened their Guest-house in its historic function, and you can stay there in so beatific a setting. None of these remains open in the winter months.

Next to the St Columba Hotel is the burial ground, *Reilig Odhrain*, and St Oran's Chapel standing within it. *Reilig Odhrain* has a large number of carved grave-slabs commemorating many members of prominent West Highland families, but the best of them are in the Abbey Museum. Tradition says that it is also the burial-place for forty-eight kings of Scotland, Ireland, Norway, and even one of France. Dean Munro, in 1549, found three little mausoleum tombs, each inscribed 'Tumulus Regum Scotiae, Hyberniae, and Norwegiae' respectively. None of these remains, and no-one knows where these interments are, and even the official guide says 'it is likely that these supposed burials are fiction.'

St Oran's Chapel is definitely fact, because there it is, the earliest surviving building on the island. It is thought to have been built as a family mausoleum or mortuary chapel by Somerled or his son Reginald, which makes it late twelfth century, and that date certainly accords with the small, stone, rectangular shape and the characteristic dog-tooth ornamentation around the doorway. In ruins for centuries, it was restored and re-roofed in 1957.

At the gateway to the Abbey precincts there is a kiosk and a young man who tells you that admittance is free, and so is the hand-out information sheet, but that maintenance is costly and any donations are appreciated: a box for them is prominent.

Two Celtic crosses stand before the Abbey, St Martin's and St John's. St Martin's is original, carved and erected in the late eighth century, from stone brought from mid-Argyll; its carvings are similar to those on the Kildalton Cross in Islay. St John's Cross is a replica, as more than thirty years ago the original was blown over and smashed in a gale. It has been pieced together again in Edinburgh, was returned to Iona in 1989, and is housed in a glass case in the Abbey museum: the replica remains outside.

Close beside the doorway to the Abbey Church is a tiny little stone building called St Columba's Shrine. It was rebuilt from the foundations in 1962, and contains no relics of St Columba because there are none, but it stands on the site traditionally said to be the saint's burial-place. The Benedictine Abbey was founded, like the Nunnery, by Reginald, Somerled's son, in about 1200. Its lands were all in the Isles and Lorn, in the gift of the Lord of the Isles. It stands on the site of St Columba's original little wooden huts, the Abbey Church on the site of successive churches since the first. Its plan is cruciform, its style is twelfth-century romanesque, with round-headed arches. There was a major reconstruction in the fifteenth century, with Gothic pointed windows and a new tower, and the combination of styles is interesting.

The story of the silver cross on the communion table was told in the *Sunday Post* in March, 1989. A friend of Lord MacLeod of Fuinary, who founded the Iona Community, wanted to give something to the Abbey Church, so together they searched, but found nothing suitable until they went to the sale of the remaining work of a recently deceased silversmith. Among his creations was a magnificent silver cross, exactly what was needed, but the silversmith's widow explained that it was not for sale: her husband, she said, had wanted it to be given without any charge to Iona Abbey.

In the south transept there are marble effigies of the 8th Duke of Argyll and his duchess, because it was the Duke who gave in 1899 the sites in Iona, containing what were then ruins, to the Cathedral Trustees, to hold in perpetuity for the nation. Weather-erosion has made this difficult, but they have done it. The Trust restored the Abbey Church between 1902 and 1910; in 1938 Lord MacLeod, then Dr George Macleod, founded the Iona Community as a Church of Scotland brotherhood, to use Iona as a base, but to spread the Gospel throughout Scotland and elsewhere, rather as St Columba did in the first place. They began the work of restoring the other buildings, finishing them in 1965 with John Brown's slates from the Luing quarry. In 1979 the trustees of the 10th Duke of Argyll sold the rest of the island to the Fraser Foundation, which gave it to the nation in memory of Lord Fraser of Allander, and the Secretary of State for Scotland in turn gave it to the National Trust for Scotland.

The restoration work has been superbly done. The cloister has been reconstructed to appear as its thirteenth-century original, with double columns and pointed arches; in the centre is a large bronze creation of the Lithuanian sculptor Jacques Lipschitz, representing the Descent of the Spirit. All buildings are in full use by the Community except for the visitors' shop and the Guest-house rooms, and as you stroll in the cloister you may savour an appetising cooking-smell drifting down from the Refectory, over the shop. The Abbey Museum is in a building detached from the central range and thought therefore to have been on the Infirmary site. Unrestored chapels within the precinct lie as tumbled ruins, and so does the bishop's house; without the sacred bounds are traces of the ditch and rampart, or vallum, that enclosed the earliest of the monastic settlements.

If the time is now gone 11.30 am, hordes of tourists will be streaming along the road from the ferry, and you must take to the hills. Return towards the Nunnery, but take a track to the right past the Village Hall and go off among the pastures and the sheep, and the croft-houses, across the windy centre of the island, over the ridge and down to the beautiful west coast. At the Bay at the Back of the Ocean, on a fine day, you might be in the Caribbean: or you could be right here, for there is an essentially Hebridean flavour about it. The flavour is distilled from the bright green, sheep-cropped machair, the white shell-sand, the gulls and plovers that chase each other, the jagged little skerries rising above the surface of a sea of many colours, from pale inshore green to deep ocean indigo, bordering on violet out to the west. The essential ingredient is solitude, for there will not be crowds here, a mile's walk from the jetty.

The crofts and farms of Iona lie all in the centre and on the east coast; the rest, in the south and in the north-west, is all hill and moorland. Sites like St Columba's Bay, where is he said to have first landed, or Cairn of the Back to Ireland, or the Marble Quarry, are hard to find because there are no tracks. There is one leaving Bay at the Back of the Ocean southward, across the very primitive golf course on the machair, and up to the sandy hills, but it loses itself at Loch Staoineig in the middle of a peat-moss, and progress becomes uncertain and hazardous. It hardly matters, since if you want the island's holy, blessed peace, the hills and the western bays are the real sanctuary.

Back on the east coast there are several new houses and some sandy beaches, one of which is called Martyrs' Bay. There was a hiatus in the monastery's history caused by the Vikings, who raided it several times in the late eighth century, and in 806 slaughtered sixty-eight of the monks in this particular bay. 'The white sands and the pale green waters of the sea above them were on that day of terror stained deeply with human blood,' says Seton Gordon, as if he was there at the time. The survivors removed for safety to Kells in Ireland. A war memorial, of much later slaughter, stands there now, hard by a church converted into a private house but retaining its bell-seating.

There is so much to see in Iona, and most visitors who come for the day (or even a couple of hours if they are involved in a coach-tour, or one of the cruises that calls at other places) have no time to see more than a fraction of it. To take your time, to be there when the tourists are not, to savour the sense of 'peace and holy quiet', that is the ideal way to know and love Iona. Members of the Community and any of the Iona residents will tell you.

Boats leave the quayside in Iona to take visitors to Staffa. There is no shortage of means for going there, because in addition to other boats running from Fionnphort, there are cruises run from Mull and from Ulva in Mull by Turus Mara, which you can book from Oban, Fort William, or Tobermory Tourist Offices, and there are day cruises run by Caledonian MacBrayne to Staffa by way of Mull and Iona, from Oban. The attraction, of course, is extraordinary rock formations, and the caves.

Felix Mendelssohn came to Staffa in 1829 and wrote his overture, *Fingal's Cave*, three years later; he evidently had some ideas for it at the time, because as soon as returned to the mainland where he was staying, and opened the piano there, he had no sooner fingered a few notes when his Scottish host reminded him that it was the Sabbath Day, and music was not permitted. Sir Joseph Banks, President of the Royal Society, had already alerted public interest in the island in 1772, and thereafter a constant flow of visitors came to admire its wonders. Johnson and Boswell were prevented by heavy seas from landing, but Queen Victoria came in 1847, and countless numbers of the rest of us who make up most of the world's population, before and since.

What happened to create the tall fluted hexagonal columns, curved into graceful shapes, is not, as might be thought, the work of the pre-Christian Celtic gods, nor of the mighty Fionn Mac Coul (or Fingal), but of a complicated geological process. The basaltic columns were built up by the steady cooling of lava-flows as they came into contact with a colder bedrock, and were exposed to the effects of northern Scottish weather: everybody knows what that can be like. As they contracted when they cooled they assumed, by a fluke, their hexagonal shape. The curves were caused by the shape of the underlying rock over which the lava flowed. All this wonderfully technical information I owe to John Brooks, the writer of a Mull guide-book. Fingal's Cave is the biggest of several in the south of the island: 230 feet long, 60 feet high, 50 feet wide at the sea-entrance. Banks named it, because he thought his Gaelic guide, when he asked what it was called, said the Cave of Fionn. What he probably said, was *An Uamh Bhinn*, which means the Cave of Melody. Whatever mistake Banks made about naming it, he was clearly impressed, as have been all other visitors. 'Compared to this what are the cathedrals or the palaces built by men! Mere models or playthings, imitations as diminutive as his works will always be when compared to those of nature. Where is now the boast of the architect! Regularity, the only part in which he fancied himself to exceed his mistress, Nature, is here found in her possession, and here it has been for ages undescribed.' So thought Sir Joseph, but the Islanders, of course, knew it well, and knew its acoustics too which possibly presented Mendels-sohn with the harmonies of wave-sounds for his overture to *An Uamh Bhinn*.

Queen Victoria wrote in in her Journal, 'As we rounded the point, the wonderful basaltic formation came into sight. The appearance it presents is most extraordinary; and when we turned the corner to go into the renowned Fingal's Cave, the effect was splendid, like a great entrance to a vaulted hall: it

looked almost awful as we entered, and the barge heaved up and
down on the swell of the sea. The rocks, under water, were all
colours — pink, blue and green — which had a most beautiful
and varied effect. It was the first time the British standard with a
Queen of Great Britain, and her husband and children, had ever
entered Fingal's Cave, and the men gave three cheers, which
sounded very impressive there . . . .'

There are five caves altogether, with varying degrees of
accessibility; the island is uninhabited.

The northern districts of Mull constitute the major part of it;
to see them you need to return along the long peninsula called
the Ross of Mull, south of Loch Scridain on A849, and turn left
at the head of the loch on B8035. This narrow and erratic road
skirts the riven flanks of Ben More, 3,171 feet, the highest
mountain in Mull, then at Kilfinichen Bay uses *Gleann Seilisdeir*,
the valley between *Coirc Bheinn*, 1,837 feet, and *Beinn na Sreine*,
1,704 feet, to reach Loch na Keal. The Forestry Commission
have used it too, to fill up with conifer plantations.

You come down to the sea-shore again at the cliffs of Gribun,
where fallen rocks lie everywhere and landslides are a constant
danger. Seton Gordon tells the story of a postman using this
road along the foot of the cliffs, when he found his way blocked
by a landslide. He was looking for somewhere to turn round and
go back when another grumbling, ground-trembling, thunderous crash told him that another avalanche of rock had landed
behind him. He could go neither way until the road had been
cleared. A much more horrendous story is told of a couple who
arrived at one of the cottages on the shore for their wedding
night; a great storm broke at midnight, and the torrential rain
and raging wind disturbed a mighty boulder from the cliff,
weighing thousands of tons. It crashed straight on top of the
cottage, crushing it flat, and the young lovers were never seen
again.

Immediately ahead of you here, out in the loch, is the island of
Inchkenneth, where facing the shore you can see a couple of

houses and a ruined chapel and graveyard. Cainnech, one of St Columba's followers, had his cell here, and when the weather was too bad to allow the funeral cortège of a Scottish king to go to Iona, they would bury him at Inchkenneth instead. Boswell and Johnson came here in 1773 to visit Sir Allan MacLean of Duart, and found it 'a pretty little island, a mile long, and about half a mile broad, all good land.' Johnson was so pleased with the Sunday he passed there that he wrote some Latin verses entitled 'Insula Sancti Kennethi', and a couple of days later Sir Allan took them to see MacKinnon's Cave, which is south of Gribun. 'Tradition says,' writes Boswell, 'that a piper and twelve men once advanced into this cave, nobody can tell how far; and never returned. . .' Dr Johnson said it was the greatest natural curiosity he had ever seen. It is inaccessible except at low tide, and then, evidently, one needs great caution and a good torch.

Beyond Inchkenneth is the much larger island of Ulva, and round a point and farther on into Loch na Keil there is Eorsa. Seton Gordon says Loch na Keil should be spelt *Loch nan Ceall* and means Loch of the Churches. W. H. Murray says that *ceal* is an old Gaelic word for cliff, which certainly seems appropriate. MacAlpine's Dictionary gives for *ceal*: 'hue of the countenance: *is bochd an ceal a th'ort*, you have a miserable expression of countenance.' So would anyone, with a thousand-ton rock landing on them.

At Knock the little road suddenly dog-legs, where the stream from Loch Ba runs beneath it into the head of the loch, and here there are stone walls and banks of rhododendrons belonging to Gruline House. This point is called the 'neck of Mull' as it is only three miles to Salen on the Sound of Mull, and it is a wonder it is not called Tarbert. At Gruline House there is a mausoleum which has become a shrine for visiting Australian pilgrims, because in it is buried Lachlan MacQuarie (1761–1824), who after emigrating to Australia became the first Governor of New South Wales, and has been called the 'Father of Australia'. He came back home to Mull, lived at Gruline

House and built a model crofting village at Salen.

The road, now called B8073, continues along the north side of Loch na Keal in a frenzy of wriggling, up violently steep hairpins and down the other side into who knows what, since it is all single-track and you cannot see what is coming. Not that much will be coming except other tourists: Mull lost 85% of its population in the Clearances and has never got them back. You can see Eorsa and Ulva from the northern side; Ulva is private, and so is the smaller Gometra at its western end. Round the point past the road to the Ulva Ferry, in Laggan Bay, is Lagganulva where there is a sixty-foot waterfall. If Mull weather is up to its usual tricks there will be so much water falling from the sky that the thought of walking to see some more will be off-putting.

The stretch of water between the mainland and Ulva is Loch Tuath, and from the road (still behaving like a demented earwig) you can, if you stop the car, and it isn't raining, enjoy the view of the Treshnish Isles, Dutchman's Cap and all. This south-facing lochside is like Loch Buie, brilliant with lush vegetation. Tiny hamlets, sometimes with only a couple of houses, appear from time to time, their gardens gay with flowers, but apart from multitudes of sheep there are few distractions from the deep inviolate peace.

You leave the lochside to climb over the flanks of *Cruachan Odhar*, steeply northward, through the barren interior and down to Calgary Bay, and Calgary at its head; there is a caravan site, a beach of pure white sand, and Calgary House. Colonel J. F. MacLeod, commander of the Royal Canadian North-West Mounted Police, was once a visitor to Calgary House, and it was his memory of it that made him suggest Calgary as the name of a new city founded in Alberta in 1876. One of the curiosities of Mull landscapes is that they alternate between the green and luxuriant, as at Loch Buie, Loch Tuath, and Calgary, and the wild, stony and totally barren, as in almost anywhere in the interior. On leaving Calgary, hectically uphill round several acute hairpin bends, you head for the latter variety in abundance in crossing the peninsula of Mornish, until you come to Dervaig, at the head of the narrow Loch Cuan.

Dervaig is by far the largest village in Mull so far, with houses, shops and hotels, all set on a hillside on end. It has a lovely little church with a slim 'pencil' tower, like so many in Ireland, and it has a theatre: not the biggest in the world, with just forty-three seats, it is called the Mull Little Theatre and it produces five plays in a season. There is a new luxury hotel and restaurant next door, to cater for theatre-goers from the mainland. The fully professional company will be working flat-out, playing to packed audiences on most nights from June to September, with no room for understudies: there are only two of them in the company! Just out of town and on a minor road going south to Loch Tuath there is the Old Byre Heritage Centre, which has won two national awards for its portrayal of the turmoil and distress caused by the notorious nineteenth-century Clearances.

The hills of Quinish and Mishnish in northern Mull are completely wild, separated by Glen Gorm which is afforested, with Forest Walks tracked out by the Forestry Commission; there are some man-made hill-lochs in this wilderness, with fishing by licence. Suddenly, the road dips steeply into Tobermory.

Tobar Mhoire, St Mary's Well, has the best anchorage in the Inner Hebrides, a bay a mile wide and long, its entrance sealed by Calve Island. It had never been a fishing port, but in 1788 the British Fisheries Association tried to make it into one. It built all those attractive cottages along the quayside, now painted in different colours, and fishing did prosper for a while. Then the railway came to Oban in 1880 and Tobermory collapsed. It now relies heavily on the tourist trade, with nine major hotels and guest-houses, countless bed-and-breakfast houses, and plenty of self-catering cottages and flats; there are also boat-hire firms, pleasure-cruises, wildlife expeditions, the House of Treshnish Gardens, the Mull and Iona Folklore Museum, and a nine-hole golf course. It is the main shopping centre for Mull, and there is a traffic problem; when we drove through, hoping to stop and explore, a large coach was trying to inch its way along the main street, with cars parked all along one side. All parking places on the quayside were occupied and there appeared to be no others: it was raining, too. This was in early June, not the high season.

There is debate about the identity of the Spanish ship from the battered Armada that put into Tobermory Bay in 1588. It might have been the *Florencia*, but there is evidence that it returned to Spain; perhaps it was the *San Juan de Sicilia*, but as it is still under 30 feet of clay it is hard to tell. MacLean of Duart went to negotiate with the captain, who lent him 100 armed men for an attack on Mingary Castle in Ardnamurchan and for an expedition against MacLean of Coll. However, perhaps by example of clan feuding, it was blown up by Donald MacLean of Morvern, along with himself and a treasure-chest worth £300,000 said to be aboard. Charles I granted the wreck to the Marquis of Argyll: with permission from the present Duke, strenuous efforts have been made to locate and salvage the wreck, so far without success.

There are some fine walks through the forests and along the coast from Tobermory, one of them going northward to the picturesquely-named Bloody Bay, where there was a sea-battle in 1439 between the MacLeans in support of John MacDonald, 4th Lord of the Isles, and his son Angus, who was backed up by Allan MacRuaraidh, Chief of Clanranald. Angus won, Mac-Lean of Duart was captured, and the eldest son of MacLeod of Lewis killed. It was just another family difference of opinion.

The road south of Tobermory, A848, is single-track as usual but good; it is cut out of the hills like a terrace, as they plunge down to the Sound of Mull. Opposite lies the dark Morvern mountain-mass. At Aros Mains, the Aros river comes tumbling down from Loch Frisa in the hills to the little bay. On its northern promontory stand the ruins of 14th-century Aros Castle, built by the Lord of the Isles. Looking northward up the

Sound it was possible from Aros to see a warning beacon lit at Mingary, near Kilchoan in Ardnamurchan, and vice-versa. Until 1308 the site had been a MacDougall stronghold, but Bruce gave it to Angus Og MacDonald for his support. It was last in use officially in 1608, when James VI (I of England) sent Lord Ochiltree as his viceroy with orders to sort out the disorderly island chiefs. He invited them all to a dinner aboard his flagship, the 'Moon', and they all came. The Bishop of the Isles preached a sermon, Lord Ochiltree proposed the Loyal Toast – and then informed then that they were all under arrest. They were taken to Edinburgh, and only released when they promised to ratify the new Statutes of Iona of 1609, which brought long-overdue reforms to the government of the Isles. Why did the Clan Chiefs of the Highlands and Islands ever trust the Stuart Kings?

At Salen, the model village just three miles from Governor MacQuarie's Gruline House on Loch na Keal, the road becomes two-way for the only stretch on the island, so you can make rapid progress to Pennygowan on the Forsa river. Half a mile east of the river there is a ruined chapel where, it is said, an early MacLean of Duart practised black magic, with his wife in attendance, trying to summon the Devil by roasting cats. I regret that I have been unable to discover whether the recipe was successful, and have not tried it myself.

From Fishnish Bay, a few miles on from the scene of MacLean's satanic barbecue, a ferry service runs to Lochaline in Morvern, provided by Caledonian MacBrayne plenty of times each day. The Morvern coast, the entrance to Lochaline and its lighthouse are clearly visible provided one of those infernal mists is not shrouding the Sound. If you have not taken the ferry to Lochaline, the road will bring you very quickly now back to Craignure and the ferry to Oban. Mull, with or without fine weather, is a fascinating mixture of interest and scenery, and sooner or later, you will probably want to return.

10

Morvern and Ardnamurchan

Morvern is not the most visited part of the West Highlands, because it is very mountainous and barren, there is only one road, and there are few obvious tourist attractions. For those reasons it has a great deal of charm. There are two ways of reaching it from the vicinity of Oban: one is to go by ferry to Craignure, then from Fishnish to Lochaline, the other is to motor across the Ballachulish Bridge, then cross by the Corran Ferry, and either through Glen Tarbert to Strontian, or along the shore to Kingairloch and inland. There are no more direct ways of going to Morvern.

Morvern in Gaelic is *A'Mhorbhairn*, the Sea-gap, meaning the gap of the Sound of Mull. It is a roughly diamond-shaped peninsula connected to the rest of mainland Scotland only by the six-mile Glen Tarbert, the isthmus between Loch Linnhe and Loch Sunart. Three of the diamond's sides are twelve miles long, the fourth, along the Sound of Mull, is twenty miles. The hill and moorland within its capacious interior is not high – there is not much over 1,900 feet – but wild and trackless, and its population is minimal. To see it all you need to be an eagle. To see any of it at all, let us assume that you are taking the Corran Ferry. It is a small open-both-ends car ferry, like those that run between Kyle of Lochalsh and Kyleakin in Skye, but

199

Lochaline

Loch Sunart

smaller. The crossing of Loch Linnhe takes about five minutes if the weather is fair, but the narrowing of the loch here means that currents are strong, and a tide-race against a high wide can be tempestuous. Several of the smaller and less powerful boats used before the 1939–45 war sank.

Beyond Sallachan Point the road, a good two-way one, swerves right to run along the head of a small bay, whence you have a fine view down Loch Linnhe and along the endless steep cliff-edged hills from Ardgour to Kingairloch in Morvern, sweeping down to the steel-blue loch. The road is A861 and just past Inversanda Bay you lose it, because it goes up Glen Tarbert.

If you relinquish for a while the chance to see the 2,903-feet *Garbh Bheinn* on the northern side of Glen Tarbert (on its north-eastern face there are massive 1,000-foot cliffs), you can take a little single-track road, B8043, which crosses the Tarbert river and dodges into a glen behind the sea-cliffs for a few miles before emerging at the loch-side again at Kilmalieu, to creep precariously along the base of some extremely fearsome cliffs. This is the Morvern district called Kingairloch, where if you go into the hundreds of square miles of hills you need expect to find no paths, and no people. The road twists around the bay *Camus na Croise*, where the Glengalmadale river plunges into the sea by the steep eastern shoulder of *Beinn na Cille*, 2,136 feet, and then you are flanking an inlet from Loch Linnhe called Loch a'Choire, and the hamlet of Kingairloch. There are some Forestry Commission plantations in the glen behind Kingairloch, and these are the only ones in the whole of this untrammelled district. Sheep, as usual, greatly outnumber humans, as they have done since the Clearances when the imbalance was intentionally created.

Into this wilderness you now plunge, past a small freshwater loch called Loch Uisge. *Uisge* is just water, it is *Uisge-beatha* which is the water of life, like *aqua vitae*, and it is the rest of the world that has called it whisky. The water of Loch Uisge is no doubt pure and crystal clear, but unfortunately it is not whisky. After what seems to have been about a hundred miles of this frightful little road it arrives at the A884 and by way of relief you expect a dual carriageway at least: it is still single-track, with passing-places. All the A-roads in Mull (bar one) are in that category, and so are the majority north of the Great Glen. There are not so many tourists up here. At least the A884 is good, and fairly straight, and a daring driver may reach speeds of nearly 40 mph. This is only possible because hardly anyone else is on the road: it is not at all like Argyll. There is a phenomenon of the Argyll roads, and that is the Crawler. He is invariably a visitor, quite often drives a powerful car, like a Rover, Volvo or BMW, but will never exceed 40 mph. Argyll roads are mostly two-way, but they twist and turn, and there are very few stretches for passing from behind. Each Crawler is therefore followed by a long string of angry and frustrated drivers, especially if they are locals and want to go about their daily business at speeds of 55–60 mph which are reasonable on those roads. The Crawler, no doubt, does not know the road, is on holiday, has Granny in the back seat and wishes to admire the scenery, but his adherence to his 40 mph has caused a near-miss that I have witnessed, and probably some accidents that I have not. And not counting those with caravans in tow, who cannot help it, there are very many Crawlers.

There is a code for using single-track roads; there are plenty of passing places, and if you see a car approaching, you pull into one. Its driver will sometimes do the same, so you flash your headlights to indicate that he may proceed. If you see in your mirror a local driver pursuing you with every indication that he wants to go somewhere in a hurry, it is civil to pull into a passing place and let him. Most will be visibly grateful, and part of the code is to indicate that you are, too, when someone makes way for you, with a smile and a wave. Not all visitors understand this practice, but it does save a great deal of irritation, and it makes for safe driving on these long, and usually lonely roads.

The A884 descends the glen of *Allt Beitheach*, a wide stream in a wide valley with one or two forestry plantations on its sides, and enters *Gleann Geal*, the White Glen, named perhaps from the falls and rapids along the river, causing white water. Apart from the blocks of conifers, this is mainly boggy moorland, with a ration of one lonely house for every two miles. There is water everywhere as the *Gleann Geal* water joins that from *Gleann Dubh*: white and black mixing together in rare harmony. The combined streams unite with that from Loch Arienas and as the River Aline run down swiftly into Loch Aline.

Loch Alainn, the Lovely Loch, is long and narrow, heavily wooded on both sides, and with an even narrower entrance from the Sound of Mull. Near the loch-head the road passes through a village called Larachbeg. It stands on croft-land given to the islanders of St Kilda, when they were evacuated in 1930. St Kilda is the farthest and most isolated of all the Outer Hebrides, as much as fifty miles west of Lewis, a mere dot in the ocean. The islanders' life was desperately hard, their health deteriorated and the authorities felt they could not be responsible for them if they stayed. As it was, quite a number died when they came to the mainland, but the survivors flourished and the younger ones appreciated the change in their circumstances.

A little square fifteenth-century keep, close by the river's entrance to the loch, is Kinlochaline Castle, which was the seat of Clan MacInnes when they were subject to the Lords of the Isles. Their name is derived from *Mac Aonghas*, Angus, and they claim that they are descended from the Angus who was one of the sons of Erc, the first leaders of the Scots of Dalriada. Their fortunes merged with those of MacDonald of the Isles, and under them they were lords of both Morvern and Ardgour. However, there was an occasion in 1390 when for unstated reasons (in my source) MacInnes and his five sons were all murdered at Ardtornish Castle by the Lord of the Isles, and their lands given to the MacLeans. The present fifteenth-century keep will therefore have been built by Clan MacLean.

Beyond Kinlochaline Castle stands a vast Victorian pile, all towers and turrets in the local stone, called Ardtornish Castle, not to be confused with the real thing, which is a crumbled ruin on Ardtornish Point in the Sound of Mull. This grandiose mansion has celebrated gardens (south-facing, warm and sheltered) and is now divided into separate apartments for self-catering holidays; facilities are numerous, since there are 35,000 acres of hills, woodland, rivers and lochs at the doorstep, available all year round.

The wooded west side of Loch Aline is the fringe of an immense forestry plantation covering thousands of acres, which means that timber-felling is a major occupation hereabouts. So also is sandmining: in 1925 a bed of cretaceous sandstone, eighteen feet thick, was discovered by a geological survey, and by 1939 it had become Britain's only source of silica for optical glass. It is also used in the production of Caithness Glass. It is extracted by the ton and does nothing to further the loveliness of the Lovely Loch.

The village of Lochaline stands on the western side of the *Caolas na h-Airde*, Straits of the High Point, all on the side of a steep hill. There are jetties for the ferries and for the ships bearing away the timber and sand, there are moored yachts, and there is a sense of remoteness, not unconnected with the fact that the A884 goes no farther. You can see the outline of the old Ardtornish Castle, out on the point above the lighthouse, but it is practically impossible to go and inspect it unless you have plenty of time, or a boat. It was a major stronghold of the MacDonalds, and Scott used it as the setting for his epic poem *Lord of the Isles*.

> Nor lacked they steadier light to keep
> Their course upon the darkened deep;
> Ardtornish on her frowning steep
> Twixt cloud and ocean hung,
> Glanced with a thousand lights of glee;

And landward far, and far to sea,
Her festal radiance flung.

Festal radiance flung far inland would be quite hard, since the frowning steep tends to get in the way, but Scott's imagination has made a living place out of a tumbledown ruin, so he must be forgiven. The castle was built in the fourteenth-century by a Lord of the Isles, and on the passing of MacDonald power was taken by the MacLeans of Duart. There was no destructive siege, its ruin is the result of centuries of neglect; only the lower walls of the keep remain, fifteen feet high and ten feet thick.

A twelve-mile road, B849, serves the little communities on Morvern's shore on the Sound of Mull, leading west from Lochaline and ending at Drimnin. There is a strip of cultivable land along this shore, and it used to support quite large townships (perhaps with difficulty); but Morvern suffered as heavily from the Clearances as did Mull, and they were practically extinguished. The two hills *Sithean na Raplaich*, 1,806 feet, and *Beinn Bhuidhe*, 1,481 feet, rise above them, clothed in forestry conifers, and their northern flanks, foothills and coast on Loch Sunart are uninhabited. There are no roads beyond the B849 just mentioned, and the A884, so retreat along them is the only way a motorist may leave Morvern. Passing the spot where it is joined by the perilous B8043 from Kingairloch, the A884 passes beneath the glowering crags of *Beinn nam Beathrach*, 1,911 feet, climbs, then descends to the shores of lovely Loch Sunart (*Sueineart* in Gaelic, Sweyn's Fiord, pronounced Soonyert). Across the loch the great *Beinn Resipol*, 2,775 feet, raises its often snow-capped head; it dominates the whole district of Sunart, between the loch of that name and Loch Shiel. It is a district of few inhabitants and many magically enchanting treasures, of perfect little coves with white shell-sand, heathery tracks among hills, cliffs and corries, and an abundance of natural sounds, scents, plants and creatures.

The road along Glen Tarbert arrives at the head of the loch, and a little farther on, where the Strontian river enters it, lies the pleasant village of Strontian. *Sron an-t Sidhean,* Point of the Fairies, owes its importance to mining. The fairies may well have been miners, (like the Seven Dwarfs), but they were once of cardinal importance to the Highland folk. Originally they were the gods of the Celtic pagan religion, the spirits of earth, mountains, trees, rivers, lochs, who needed to be placated with offerings, charms and spells, which the Druidical priesthood understood. The early Christians were wise enough to assimilate, rather than abolish, the old beliefs, so that churches were built on shrine-sites, and angels were depicted as superior spirits who had overcome the older ones. Being immortal, however, the old gods were obliged to retreat into the caverns of the hills, whence they would issue to work for good or ill of the human inhabitants of the earth. They were called the *Daoine Sidhe,* the Shining Ones; from them, slowly and persistently over the centuries, came the Highlanders' fairy stories.

Lead-mining may not have been among their activities, but in the early eighteenth-century the local landowner, Sir Alexander Murray, a keen mineralogist, prospected and opened mines in the hills along the Strontian river. Various mining companies jumped in, the biggest was the York Building Company, and the townships that grew up along the glen were collectively known as New York, like the pier in Loch Awe. By the mid-eighteenth-century around 600 tons of lead were produced annually (in 1753 sixty tons of it were used to roof the new Inveraray Castle); but problems arose, and when Sir James Riddell bought the estate in 1769 most of the mines closed down. In 1764 a new substance called Strontianite was identified from among the extracted minerals, and in 1790 Thomas Hope isolated the element known as Strontium: but it was no more than a mineralogical curiosity because at that time there was no economic use for it. Some of the mines were reopened when the French wars demanded copious lead for shot, but the area's full prosperity never recovered: by 1871 none was left working.

Strontium has risen to vital importance in the Nuclear Age, but the mines have not been reopened for its extraction, and the only mining at Strontian has been for barytes, the sulphate of barium. This may not be good news for local employment, but at least the south-facing village has been allowed to regain its natural beauty, which has encouraged the tourist trade. There are self-catering summer chalets, a caravan park, two hotels, and the north bank of the craggy Strontian Glen has sensibly been made a Nature Reserve with a marked-out trail, for which the Forestry Commission supplies a guide.

Beinn Resipol, the local mountain, overlooks both Loch Sunart and Loch Shiel, including at the latter's narrowest point the little *Eilean Fhianain*, St Finan's Isle, which was the sacred burial ground for the entire district. The tracks of coffin-bearing groups therefore crossed the hills, and although the tracks themselves have disappeared, there are several cairns which were built to mark the way. There are two ways by which you can most easily climb Beinn Resipol; one is to take an old mine-track from Ariundle (part of 'New York') up the stream *Allt na Cailleach* to *Bealach nan Carn*, Pass of the Cairn: you can see the eastern end of the summit ridge from there, and while it might take time, you can get there in the end. The other way is to start from the village of Resipole on the lochside: about 100 yards east of the caravan and camping site a gate gives access to the southern bank of the lovely *Allt mhic Chiarain*, and if you follow the stream you can find your way almost to the summit. It is not a difficult mountain, so they say, except when it is covered in snow.

The south-facing northern shore of Loch Sunart is beautiful. It is set about with luxuriant woodland, tiny rocky bays, little islands and only occasional hamlets, all the way to Salen. Viking place-names abound along Sweyn's Fiord, but there is evidence of much earlier occupation. There are chambered cairns at *Camas nan Geall* and near Kilchoan, from the Middle Stone Age, and there are standing stones also at *Camas nan Geall* and near Branault, left by Bronze Age residents. There are also numerous Celtic Iron Age duns, or hill-forts. The Vikings still held the whole area even after Somerled's time, until the crucial treaty of 1266 when they ceded all their territory in the West Highlands and Islands to the Scottish king.

Salen, at the head of an inlet, is delightful: *An t-Sailean* means tidal saltings, but its safe anchorage made it prosper, and when the stone jetty was built during the nineteenth-century it became a favourite port of call for pleasure-steamers; more importantly for the neighbourhood it also hosted its principal cattle-fair, which brought in all the crofters and farmers from the hills. It was never advisable, however, to stray too far from the clamorous centre of this vibrant metropolis, for just above the village lies the small *Lochan na Dunaich*, the Loch of Misfortune, so called because it was inhabited by a murderous *each uisge*, the water-horse (and still is, for all I know). It looked just like a fine stallion, except for wisps of water-weed in its mane, but anyone unwise enough to mount it was carried instantly straight into the lochan and devoured. The splendid A861, along which you have motored from Strontian at a good 25 mph, because it is single-track and straight as a corkscrew, now leaves Loch Sunart at Salen and heads towards Acharacle and Loch Shiel. You are on the threshold of Ardnamurchan, and to penetrate its mysteries you have either to take to the hills, in which case you will certainly get lost, or take instead the Queen's Highway B8007, which makes all Highland roads so far seem like the M1 by comparison. It sticks to the heavily wooded lochside at the base of the almost sheer hillside, and so that you may stick to it, progress cannot be rapid.

Ardnamurchan extends a long way westward, so far, that at its tip it becomes the farthest westernmost point of the British mainland. By the time you have motored along the B8007 for an hour or so you will think it stretches half way to America. The Atlantic Ocean, moreover, is implicit in its name, because *Ard na Mor Chuain* means Height of the Great Seas: as you will see when you go to its western extremity, this is no exaggeration.

Even after the cession of Ardnamurchan and Sunart to the Scottish crown in 1266, they were still held, illegally, by a Norse tyrant with the engaging name of Muchdragon Mac ri Lochlann, but the Gaelic population was encouraged to resist by a younger son of Angus Mor MacDonald of Islay called *Iain Springach*, John the Bold. For his successful efforts against the tyrant he was rewarded by King John Balliol with the title Lord of Ardnamurchan. Clan MacIain of Ardnamurchan prospered mightily under the protection of the MacDonalds of the Isles, but when the Lordship was forfeited in 1493 grimmer times arrived, for reasons which will be explained in due course.

With great difficulty your road creeps over the shoulder of Ben Laga, 1,679 feet, and on a promontory projecting into the loch you can still see the remains of an Iron Age fort called *Dun Ghallain*. Somewhere beneath the fort lie the bones of a tragic pair of lovers: a high-born young Celtic chief fell for a beautiful but humble maiden of Salen. The chief's mother was furious at this morganatic attachment, and by the evil arts of magic had the girl transmogrified into a swan. The young chief went hunting, and as sure as fate shot the swan with a well-aimed arrow; as the swan died it resumed the form of his lady-love, also expiring. In frenzied despair he reversed his sword and fell on it. Exactly why they were buried in *Dun Ghallain* is not clear, but presumably it was the young chief's own stronghold. Perhaps it served him right for shooting a swan.

From Ben Laga the little road descends to Glenborrodale, where there is a little inlet, a couple of hotels, and Glenborrodale Castle, a Victorian extravaganza in rosy pink red sandstone, embowered in masses of polychrome rhododendrons. It is apparently now owned by Mr Peter de Savary, and is another, very grand, hotel. In point of fact, although built in the approved baronial style it just fails to be Victorian, since it was built in 1902, by a diamond merchant called C. D. Rudd. The islands in the loch just here, called Risga, Carna and Oronsay, with many tiny companions lying off the lonely northern shores of Morvern, are breeding-grounds for multitudes of sea-birds.

At Glenmore there is a good environmental centre which explains all the natural life of Ardnamurchan, but the road to it from Glenborrodale is haunted. If you see a funeral procession moving along it, with coach, hoofbeats and lights, it means that there will be a death in the area. Along this road it must happen pretty often.

Ardslignish is a high promontory above the little *Camas nan Geall*, Bay of the Cells, mentioned earlier because of the ancient monuments hereabouts. In addition to the cairn and the standing stone, there is an eighteenth-century chapel and burial ground of the Campbells of Ardslignish, and the sad outlines of numerous long-deserted cottages. The standing stone, a tall pillar of red sandstone with a cross and the figure of a dog carved on it, is called *Cladh Chiarain*. The dedication to St Ciaran may have been made by St Columba, who according to Adamnan came here in the course of a journey farther north. The field at the head of the bay is surrounded by steep 250-foot slopes, and over it towers the height of Ben Hiant, 1,731 feet, the Holy Mountain, perhaps because of the cell in the bay.

The road now leaves the lochside and winds inland to avoid Ben Hiant; by this time you will be convinced that its maker (probably one of the *Daoine Sithean*) was determined to discourage any foreign traveller upon it, but you should be reassured, for there is worse to come. Inland, you have to negotiate *Beinn nan Losgann*, 1,026 feet, and in the process there are numerous blind summits, on the far side of which the road always turns abruptly, but you never know which way: straight ahead is usually a sheer drop, a lochan, a stream, or a swamp. However, if you pause for breath and to take your clammy hands off the steering-wheel at a convenient passing place, you may gasp with admiration for the view. You are now looking north, to a misty grey-blue sea in which appear the mauve shapes of the islands Eigg, Muck and Rhum, and in the distance the unmistakable

outline of the Black Cuillin of Skye. They hang in space before
you, like some mirage that will vanish if you blink, or like some
enchanted vision that entices you to follow, always at the same
distance, until you fall exhausted.

If you have survived this detour, refrained from driving into
Loch Mudle or any of the other fore-mentioned hazards, and
still possess some shreds of your nervous system intact, you
return southward to the village of Kilchoan on Loch Sunart,
which has two new churches and one old one, an hotel, and half
a mile before the village, a track leading down to the shattered
remains at the water's edge of Mingary Castle. It was built in the
thirteenth-century in a supremely strong position: its hexagonal
curtain walls are faced on four sides by the sea, on the other two
by a ditch cut into the basaltic rock. The main gate was on the
seaward side, where the rock forms a natural causeway, and
stone steps mount to the walls. There was also a landward
entrance, with a bridge across the ditch.

When James IV ordered the forfeiture of the Lordship of the
Isles, he held two courts at Mingary Castle, in October 1493
and May 1495, to receive the island chiefs and accept their
allegiance. The only one to agree in full and give complete and
lasting submission was MacIain of Ardnamurchan. The others
despised him for it, and began a series of assaults on his castle
over several years, culminating in 1517, when Sir John MacDonald of Lochalsh stormed and took it. The MacIains never
regained their former power; it was for another attack on it that
MacLean of Duart borrowed the Spanish soldiers from Tobermory Bay in 1588 and besieged it for three days. He was
unsuccessful, but left his mark: the eastern side of the bay is still
called *Port nan Spainteach*. By the beginning of the seventeenth-
century, the Campbells had begun their insidious process of
gaining land wherever they could, at the expense of any weaker
clans, and were in virtual control of Ardnamurchan and Sunart.
The MacIains were now forced into being landless outlaws,
were officially proscribed in 1624, and thereafter disappeared as

a clan. The Campbells continued to hold the entire peninsula until 1723 when they sold it to Sir Alexander Murray, the lead-mining enthusiast.

The Campbells, as Highland folk, might not have acted in the same way as Sir Alexander's successors as landowners: they were all alien to the West Highlands and their inhabitants' way of life. The tragic consequence of the '45 rebellion was that Highlanders as a whole were seen as dangerous and pernicious vermin which ought to be exterminated, a thesis which had already led in 1692 to the Glencoe massacre. First the family of Sir James Riddell, then James Dalgleish, aided by his notorious factor Donald MacColl, evicted their tenants and brought in sheep, helping themselves to fat profits from the newly mechanized and expanding woollen industry; by their insouciant selfishness they destroyed a people and their way of life.

The road B8007 continues its potentially homicidal way across the last of the peninsula, now entirely treeless and almost soil-less too: rocky crags, screes and cliffs resisting the sweeping, searching wind. High up on the spiny ridge, where some grass and a few trees have been encouraged to brave the Atlantic blasts, the Sonachan Hotel stands, boasting proudly that it is the most westerly hotel on the British mainland, and specializing in local produce: this surely must consist principally of fish, since the land produces next to nothing except sheep. The last mile or two of the road to the lighthouse, over the bare, barren wastes, crawling crab-wise between mighty crags, wriggles like a frenetic eel before arriving at a narrow space where you can park and, at a pinch, turn round. From there you can walk the last few hundred yards up to the lighthouse. It has been a long way, seventeen miles even from Salen, but here you are on the edge of the Highland world. Below you the great, grey, dark and menacing Atlantic rollers bear down upon the shore and crash foaming with malice against the black rocks. Northward, there is Skye, blurred and uncertain in the haze; southward, Mull, and south-west the low dusky outline of Coll. The lighthouse itself at the Point of Ardnamurchan is 118 feet of grey granite which, set up on its 60-foot cliff, makes its light visible for eighteen miles.

Northern Ardnamurchan can be reached by side-roads even more horrific than B8007 ('licensed to kill'?) so it is probably better to stay at the Sonachan Hotel, or even at a caravan down at Sanna Bay, and explore it on foot. There are four bays, all separated by rocky points, and all with pure white shell-sand, reefs, sharp rocks, and patches of bright green sea in between. Similar tiny tracks lead from Kilchoan to the scattered settlements farther east, to Fascadale, Achateny, Kilmory, Branault, and Ockle. On the road to Branault there is a tall Bronze Age standing stone called *Cladh Chatain*; east of Kilmory is a great, well-preserved Iron Age fort called *Dun Mor*, and beyond Ockle is another called *Dun Rubha na h-Uamha*, Fort of the Rocky Promontory of the Cave. The cave in question was used in the seventeenth-century by certain of Clan Campbell to complete the extermination of the remaining MacIains: they lit a fire at the cave's entrance and suffocated them all. At Swordle (*Suardail*, Grassy Field) in 1853, three little townships were cleared of their tenants: sixteen of them had been forced to build new houses at their own expense by the landowner, and now they were thrown out, with no compensation, to make way for a sheep farm. Forty years later, we are told, the sheep farm failed, but still you may see far more sheep than people in Ardnamurchan.

Carnasserie Castle

Carved Grave-slabs at Kilmartin

Tarbert in Knapdale

South point Pier, Gigha

St Columbia's Chapel, Mull of Kintyre

Skipness Castle

Port Charlotte, Islay

Bowmore, Islay

Port Ellen, Islay

Finlaggan Castle, Islay

Kildalton Cross, Islay

Maclean's Cross, Iona

St Martin's Cross, Iona

Dunollie Castle

St Odhrain's Chapel, Iona

Post Office at Lochbuie, Mull

The White Sands of Morar

11

Moidart and Ardgour

A strange, watery country opens out north of the three-mile neck of land between Salen and Acharacle, between Lochs Sunart and Shiel. The roads change direction so often, there are so many bays, inlets, and lochs, that it is difficult to understand the shape of the landscape, the lie of the land. Acharacle is the southern border-outpost of the country called Moidart, one of the areas of the West Highlands known as the *Garbh Chriochan*, the Rough Bounds, where roads are rare and the countryside is rugged and hard.

Acharacle stands at the foot of Loch Shiel, where its fresh and beautiful waters flow through a channel and out to Loch Moidart. It owes its name to a point on the channel that used to be fordable, because it is *Ath Tharracail*, Torquil's Ford. Traditionally it acquired its name from a battle at the ford between the eponymous Torquil, a Viking chieftain who had occupied the area, and the doughty Somerled. The modern bridge, built in 1935 to replace an earlier nineteenth-century version, still in place a little farther downstream, stands more or less on the site of the ford. Acharacle is basically a crofting township, but as it enjoys so delectable a view up lovely Loch Shiel it attracts fishing visitors to its three hotels.

There are several side-roads out of Acharacle to the sur-

Corran Ferry

Rhum and Eigg

rounding little townships, which are well worth exploring and constitute another excellent reason for staying in Acharacle; one is a turning left at the northern end of the village, B8044, which goes along the peninsula to Ardtoe. A tiny lane turns off left from this to Arivegaig, and there is a rough track which could take you along the southern shores of the almost landlocked Kentra Bay, where at low tide all is mud and sand, seaweed tang and waterfowl, to Gorteneorn, and then there is a track through the forestry plantation, redolent of pine, below Torr Beithe to Gortenfern; a little track to the right here will take you down to the beautiful white sands of *Camus an Lighe*, the Beach of Flooding. Uncertain years ago an old township is supposed to have been inundated beneath the shifting sands; they are called the Singing Sands, because when you scuff them with your feet they emit a peculiar high-pitched whine. The track could lead you on to Ockle, Swordle and Kilmory in Ardnamurchan, if you chose to let it.

If you continue on the exceedingly narrow B8044 across the flats of Kentra Moss, through the township of Kentra on the eastern side of its tidal bay, you can go to Ardtoe, or to Newton of Ardtoe, and in both cases you will run out of road, because it ends on the beach of each of these lovely little bays on this remote and haunting peninsula. On the southern side of the Shiel Bridge another tiny lane follows the left bank of the Shiel water to Shielfoot, where there is an Iron Age fort. Or you could walk along the right bank to Doirlinn, from which you can see, at the end of a tidal sand-spit in the South Channel of Loch Moidart, a rocky island bearing the considerable ruins of Castle Tioram (*tioram* means dry: the island is, and so is its approach at low tide). High, pentangular curtain walls enclose a turreted keep, the main entrance on the seaward side facing the island of Riska. It was built in 1353 by Lady Aimi MacDonald, divorced wife of John, the first Lord of the Isles; from her youngest son, Ranald, stem the MacDonalds of Clanranald, whose seat and stronghold Tioram became. Whether Lady Aimi chose the site, or simply built on an existing fort, its strength of position made it impregnable: it was taken only once, and that was as part of a trap.

The Earl of Argyll, sent by James IV to chastise Clanranald, besieged the Chief in Tioram, his galleys anchored in the loch by its western walls for five weeks; Argyll then broke off the siege and sailed away towards Ardnamurchan Point. Clanranald took advantage and went off to raise more of his clansmen to help. Argyll heard of this, returned swiftly and occupied the castle: but not for long. Clanranald with added strength pounced, seized the castle, and slaughtered the majority of its new Campbell garrison.

The castle's ultimate downfall was self-inflicted. Allan Dearg MacDonald of Clanranald (Allan the Red) had been out for James VII at Killiecrankie at the age of sixteen, and had to take refuge in France while William III's troops garrisoned his castle, from 1689 to 1698. In 1715, still a fervent Jacobite, he was out again, but on the eve of his departure had a vision which portended his own death in battle. If that happened, he could visualise the glee with which the hated enemy, Argyll, would take possession of his castle. So he ordered that as soon as he and his men had gone, it should be burnt. As he turned after climbing the old hill-track to the lochan at the summit of the hills overlooking Loch Moidart, he rested on a boulder still known as Clanranald's Seat, and watched the pall of smoke rising from his home, as if it were his own funeral pyre. Sure enough, he was killed at Sheriffmuir.

The track that runs along the headland by the lochside, from Castle Tioram, is called the Silver Walk, because in the late nineteenth-century, on the shore near the castle someone found a cache of silver Elizabethan coins; it is a fact that some silver was stolen from the castle during the seventeenth-century, for which two servants of Clanranald were hanged. A third, a girl, was tied by her hair to a low flat skerry, just offshore from this track, which is still called *Sgeir Nighinn an t-Sheumais*, the

Skerry of James's daughter. She was left there to drown in the rising tide.

All of these tracks and walks are within easy reach of Acharacle, from which the A861 road, single-track, after crossing Shiel Bridge, swings eastward along the foot of the hills between Loch Shiel and Loch Moidart. At Blain and at High Mingarry, a ruined township above the present Mingarry, there were famous smithies, and at the latter the armourers of Clanranald hammered out the helmets, dirks and claymores for his fighting men: their anvil still exists.

Through Dalnabreck and Langal you can gaze to your right towards the lovely waters of Loch Shiel, which throughout its length has no roads along either shore beyond Forestry Commission tracks or sheepwalks, and if you want to visit St Finan's Isle, at the narrowest strait of the loch, you will have to do as the coffin-parties used to do, and walk. There is a track from Langal, and another from the main road farther on, which serves Dalilea on the lochside, and there is a jetty from which boats may be hired. The island was the ancestral burial place of the MacDonalds of Clanranald, and many others; their graves are in and around St Finan's Chapel. There was once a school here, too, run by the celebrated Jacobite poet Alasdair Mac Mhaighstir Alasdair MacDonald, whose enormously long Gaelic name recalls that he was the son of Master Alasdair MacDonald of Dalilea House (a predecessor of the present Victorian building) who was Episcopalian minister for St Finan's Isle and, by the way, the whole of Moidart and Ardnamurchan. As he lived in the seventeenth and eighteenth-centuries, when there were no roads at all and precious few horses, he had to serve his parishioners on foot. Furthermore, most of his parishioners were Catholics, so he concentrated on the Episcopalians of Kilchoan. As he lived at Dalilea, this meant that he had to make the round trip to Kilchoan and back, about sixty miles, every Sunday.

His younger son Alasdair was born in about 1700. He was a

virulent Jacobite, out in the '45, urging on the clansmen with his hectic odes. Most of his poetry was therefore political; one which was not, concerns a boat's crew in a typical West Coast gale. It is translated from the Gaelic:

> Our whole crew grew dull of hearing
> In the tempest's scowl,
> So sharp the quavering cries of demons
> and the wild beasts' howl.
> With the oaken planks the weltering waves were wrestling
> In their noisy splashing;

Eventually the storm abates, and the gallery survives:

> The tempest rose from off us into places
> Lofty in the upper air,
> And after all its noisy barking
> Ruffled round us fair.
> Then we gave thanks to the High King,
> Who rein'd the wind's rude breath,
> And saved our good Clan Ranald
> From a bad and brutal death.

A fresh translation might give a better impression of Alasdair's talent.

The main road now climbs up the hill to a pass, from which a glance back will give you a fine view of Loch Shiel and Ben Resipol on its far side. At the pass, *Bealach an Tri Chriochan*, Pass of the Three Boundaries there is a large memorial cairn to one Captain Robertson who once owned the Kinlochmoidart estate and died in 1868. If you look north, you will see mile upon mile of the Rough Bounds of Moidart, a rugged wilderness of hill and moor, dashing burns and eerie hill-lochans where the curlews cry. The road then drops down to the head of Loch Moidart, where there is an imposing mansion built in 1880 on the site of Kinlochmoidart, where the Jacobites' plans were hatched in August, 1745.

James VIII (III of England), son of James VII and known as the Old Pretender, had tried twice to claim his throne back from the ruling House of Hanover, whose succession had been decided by Act of Parliament. The first time, in 1715, he arrived only when his supporters had been beaten; the second time in 1719 he did not arrive at all, and in 1745 he was too old, so he sent his son, Prince Charles Edward Stuart, to raise the clans for him and try once again, taking advantage of King George II's preoccupation with a war against France.

There had been enthusiasm (but hopeless leadership) in 1715, for the Highlanders felt badly let down by the Act of Union. The House of Stuart represented their last hope of retaining their culture, language, lands, and traditional way of life, the steady erosion of which they had experienced for years. The hideous massacre in Glencoe had taught them that no-one, from the Highland Line southward, could be trusted to honour an agreement, and the Campbells, the old enemies, always in with the government of the day, never had anyway. Nevertheless, times were moving on, and Sir Robert Walpole, with his policy of detachment from European wrangles, had created a wave of prosperity: confidence had waxed in the House of Hanover and its Whig ascendancy. Very few of those who called themselves Jacobites and drank the toast to the King over the Water, whether English or Scots, would dare risk now losing all they had acquired during the Walpole years in an armed attempt to oust King George and replace him with a Stuart; and the Stuarts, for their part, obstinately refused to yield in their adherence to the Catholic faith. English politicians had tried to persuade James in 1714, the better to justify his claim to be king of the mainly Protestant English, Welsh and Scots, who viewed Catholicism as the Devil's work and the Pope as Antichrist. James had refused then, and thrown away his only chance of being a king in fact rather than theory. A hundred years before, Henri IV of France, faced with the situation in reverse, with a Catholic majority against him, unable to enter his capital and be crowned, had said '*Paris vaut bien une messe*', ['Paris is worth a mass.'] converted to the faith of the majority and was accepted by them. Henri IV, admittedly, was a far wiser man than any Stuart, and the wonder is that any of the Highland chiefs who wanted a Catholic, Scottish king on the throne to safeguard their interests, trusted the Stuart family for a second, so much had they suffered from them in the past.

Prince Charles, who spoke poor English and no Gaelic, was a young man with boundless self-confidence and high ambitions. King Louis XV promised him soldiers, guns and money, but the weather drove his ships back to France. Charles landed with just seven companions, with only the grudging assistance of King Louis, and without even the wholehearted approval of his father. He landed near Arisaig in *Loch nan Uamh* and stayed for a while at Borrodale House, then moved on by sea to Loch Moidart. For seven days he stayed with Donald MacDonald of Kinloch-moidart while he made his plans, and word was sent out to the Clan Chiefs to join him at Glenfinnan with all their fighting forces.

Donald MacDonald paid for his faithful service to the Prince. After the carnage of Culloden, the Jacobites, their families and their estates all had to pay. Royal troops came and burnt Kinlochmoidart, while Isobel, Donald's wife, took her children way up the lonely Glen Moidart to Glenforslan (which is accessible now by way of a good walking track); while sheltering there she was told that her husband had been captured and beheaded. She went mad with grief.

Quite near Kinlochmoidart House, between the road and the loch, stand the Seven Men of Moidart, beech trees planted by local people after the rebellion to commemorate the original companions of the Prince who had come from France and landed with him. One of them was struck by lightning in the 1950s, one was blown down in a gale, and its replacement destroyed by cattle, and the rest have been torn and wind-damaged. There is a 1745 Association, which petitioned the

Countryside Commission for Scotland and the Highland Region to replace them. Seven new beech trees, at a cost of £1,000, have been planted behind the originals, protected by fencing and shrubbery, and the Highland Region authority has even created a new lay-by so that visitors may see them.

The western entrance to Loch Moidart is almost blocked by the islands Shona and Shona Beag, which are joined by a tiny isthmus, and the channel separating them from the shore dries out at low tide. Their entire populations were packed off to Australia in about 1853, but there are some cottages on them again now, if only holiday homes. Shoney, from whom their name comes, was a Celtic sea-god; right up to the late nineteenth-century people still offered him meal and milk so that he would regulate the sea-weather.

The road that climbs steeply up to *Bealach Carach*, the Dizzy Pass, and runs northward across the stony Moidart peninsula, was only opened in 1966 and is a good, smooth, two-way road. By way of Glen Uig it offers access to the beautiful north coast of Moidart which once could only be reached on foot. There was an old coffin-track, which can still be seen to the east of the road, but that was all, and now the wild and marvellous landscape of the glen and the shores of Glenuig Bay on the Sound of Arisaig may be enjoyed by anyone. There is a little lane by the inn at Glenuig that skirts a bit of the coast to the west, as far as Samalaman House, opposite the island of the same name; in a house on the same site there used to be a Catholic seminary for the training of what they called 'heather priests'. From the hills above this there are fine views of the islands Muck, the smallest and nearest, Eigg, Rhum, and Canna. *Muc* means sow, and it has been termed Insula Porcorum by scholars. In 1773 Johnson and Boswell met its laird: 'It was somewhat droll to hear this Laird called by his title. Muck would have sounded ill; so he was called Isle of Muck, which went off with great readiness.' It is small, only two miles by three-quarters, but Boswell reports the laird's boast that he had 'seven score of souls upon it'. Eigg has one precipitous crag, *An Sgurr*, which rises sheer to 1,291 feet.

The island is notorious for another of those ghastly clan massacres which occurred in the feuding past, and is similar to the way the Campbells extirpated the last of the Ardnamurchan MacIains. The men of Eigg, MacDonalds of Clanranald, had maltreated messengers sent by the MacLeods of Skye; also a MacLeod chief having devoted his amorous attention on too many of the Eigg young ladies, they put him in a boat and set him adrift. A war party of MacLeods sailed from Skye in their galleys in the fierce cold of early spring, when Eigg was under snow to the shoreline: most of the Eigg men were away from the island at the time, so the majority of the islanders went and hid in a great cave on the eastern coast, bar two familities who hid in another one. The Skye men searched the houses and found no-one, and were just about to re-embark when they saw one man who had left the cave and climbed a hill to keep watch. They followed his foot-prints in the snow (which had since covered those of all the rest) to the cave, and discovered the hiding-place. They lit a great fire in the cave's entrance; they piled wet thatch from the roofs on it to make smoke, and waited outside. When the screams, moans, coughs and groans had silenced, they departed. Only the two families who had sheltered in another cave survived; it seems to have happened in 1577, and 395 of the Eigg population died. The MacDonalds had their revenge, but it was short-lived, as we shall see.

Rhum is much bigger and belongs to the Nature Conservancy Council, which means that the whole island is a nature reserve. Mr Chris Eatough, Chief Warden, has an office that overlooks Loch Scresort, the anchorage on the east coast of the island, with views of the Sleat peninsula on Skye and the mountains of Knoydart. He describes the creatures he can see just by looking out of his window: mallards in the burn by the post office, greylag geese on the grass by the camping site, curlews, sand-pipers and oyster-catchers in the sandy bay, herons and the omnipresent herring and black-backed gulls. There are golden eagles nesting in the island, seals on the rocks, red deer in the woods; otters too are often seen. 'I suppose,' he says, 'my view is too good to be true and could detract from the work in hand. But likewise, it provides me with inspiration.'

Ferries run to all these islands from Mallaig, three days a week, by the courtesy of Caledonian MacBrayne.

From Glenuig the good A861 takes you along the shore eastward, past *Eilean nan Gobhar*, where there is a vitrified fort, into Loch Ailort. Huge towering hills rear up all around the loch, giving a more dramatic, awe-inspiring feeling than the kinder, greener lochsides of the south-west. The mass of Rhos-Bheinn, 2,895 feet, with six peaks, overlooks the southern shore, and the hard hills of the Ardnish peninsula opposite offer little comfort. Loch Ailort, its name from the Norse *All fjord*, Eel fiord (or possibly Deep fiord) is five miles long. Across the bridge over the Ailort river the good road encounters a T-junction, where the A830 from Fort William starts on its wriggly way to Mallaig. At this point we shall turn right and follow it towards Fort William. It shares a shoulder of the hills above the Ailort river with the West Highland Railway, a masterpiece of engineering which takes passengers from Fort William to the ferry-port Mallaig. Road and railway part company at the head of Loch Eilt, which is a beautiful freshwater loch, three miles long; if transposed to, say, Surrey, it would be designated an Area of Oustanding Natural Beauty, and invaded every weekend in summer by hordes from the London suburbs. As it is, with a road on one side and a railway on the other, it is hardly noticed; the equally beautiful *Loch Beoraid*, two miles north in the middle of the hills, has neither road nor railway and is never heard of at all. At the eastern end of Loch Eilt road and railway converge again and pass by the head of Loch Shiel at the place called Glenfinnan.

Loch Shiel is fed by the Finnan river, from Glen Finnan, which is named from the sixth-century St Finan who built his cell on the little island in the loch. He came from Kilchoan, and when he died in 575 his island cell became a shrine for pilgrimages. Glenfinnan was always a crossroads: the water-route up Loch Shiel from Ardnamurchan and Sunart, the two road-routes from the Great Glen to the east and Moidart and Morar from the west, and by Glen Finnan all the numberless glens to the north; as the crow flies it is twenty-five miles between Glenfinnan and the next modern road, at the head of Loch Duich. In the eighteenth-century most of the glens in that tract of country supported families, and it was from these that Prince Charles wanted fighting men. From Kinlochmoidart the Prince was rowed up Loch Shiel to Glenaladale, and thence to Glenfinnan to raise his standard on 19 August, 1745, and wait for the clans to arrive in their tens of thousands.

They might have done: 'The military array of this Hieland country,' says Bailie Nicol Jarvie in Scott's *Rob Roy*, 'were a' the men-folk between aughteen and fifty-six brought out that could bear arms, couldna come weel short of fifty-seven thousand five hundred men.' Many of the chiefs, however, were wary of committing themselves and their people to another rising, because they knew more of the political climate than did the Prince. Those that came to his side on 19 August numbered less than 2,000, and although this swelled considerably, his force seldom exceeded 5,000 throughout his campaign. Cameron of Lochiel, who had met the Prince at Kinlochmoidart, and tried to persuade him to go straight back to France, was there first, followed by the MacDonalds of Clanranald. Others followed, some then and some later: MacDonalds of Keppoch, Glengarry and Glencoe, MacLeans of Mull and the Isles, the outlawed MacGregors of Balquidder, the Stewarts of Appin; many of the clansmen had been coerced into rising under threat of eviction or roof-burning, particularly those from Atholl, and many were inspired less by loyalty to the Stuart cause than by hatred of the Campbells, who were raised by the Government in a regular regiment and as a Militia against them. Perhaps instinctively, perhaps knowingly in some minds, the Highlanders rose and fought for Prince Charles, their 'Bonnie Prince Charlie', in a last-ditch defence of their ancient Celtic culture, a social organization and economy that was centuries out of date by current standards, the last tribal society in Europe. A Stuart king, they hoped, would protect them, would ensure that justice would be done to them. Many of the Clan Chiefs had already seen, from the failure of the earlier risings and the comparatively mild governmental retaliation, and from the negotiated legal prerogatives they had already been able to obtain, that all their careful, patient striving would be totally overthrown by such reckless irresponsibility as an armed rising. It could result, they thought and, as it turned out, rightly, in the destruction of what they were trying to preserve.

Such a society was probably doomed in the advance of modern civilisation, but at least, if the Chiefs' advice had been taken and the Prince had stayed in France, the changes might have come gradually and far less painfully. Prince Charles's rash folly in raising his standard at Glenfinnan, his repeated refusal to take advice from experienced campaigners like Lord George Murray leading inexorably to his failure, and his glaring culpability in fighting the battle at Culloden on ground he was told was indefensible and a gift to the enemy, led to so bitter a humiliation for the proud Highlanders, not merely those who had taken part, but as the more cautious Chiefs had feared, the Gaels as a whole, that his glorification as 'Bonnie Prince Charlie', romantic hero, seems inapt, hollow, and false.

There is in the green fields at the head of the loch a tall grey tower with a figure on top; it is not a statue of Prince Charles, but more fittingly the figure of a Highlander to represent all of those who died for such a hopeless cause. It was built in 1815 by Alexander MacDonald of Glenaladale, descendant of the man who accommodated the Prince and his companions on the night of 18 August, and who served as a major in the Clanranald regiment. He had taken 150 men from Glenaladale to join the regiment; within a century the glen was utterly empty.

There is also a Visitor Centre at Glenfinnan, because the site belongs to the National Trust for Scotland, and there is an exposition of the whole campaign from Glenfinnan to Derby and back to the Culloden debacle. There are commentaries in four languages and even a snack bar, and it is all open from March to June and September to October from 10 am to 5.30 pm each day, and in July and August, 9.30 am to 6.30 pm.

Loch Shiel lies diagonally north-east to south-west; due south from Glenfinnan is the country of Ardgour, which is again completely roadless except on its periphery, twelve miles direct to the Glen Tarbert road from Glenfinnan and another twelve south-eastward from Loch Shiel to Loch Linnhe. There are great hills of over 2,000 feet like *Sgurr Dhomhnuill*, 2,914 feet, and *Beinn Mheadhoin*, 2,579 feet; there are great glens like Glen Cona, Glen Scaddle and Glen Gour, and the smallest population of all these wild districts. From the fifteenth-century it had been held by the MacLeans of Ardgour, an offshoot of the MacLeans of Duart, but now, what is not owned by the Forestry Commission is divided among sporting owners who rent out the shooting at some profit. Their identities are not well known, but in common with the ownership of vast tracts of land in the Highlands, they tend not to be Highlanders, nor Scottish, nor even English; some are Arabs, some Japanese, some from every other moneyed race.

The northern bound of Ardgour is Loch Eil, a broad loch which connects with Loch Linnhe, with a railway on the north side and roads on both sides.

12

Fort William and Ben Nevis

An enormous and somewhat elastic area on both sides of the entrance to the Great Glen is known as Lochaber, because it means mouth of the loch. *Aber* is not Gaelic, it is British, or Pictish, and there was a highly important Pictish fortress on the site of Inverlochy Castle. It would be surprising if this meeting-place of routes throughout the West Highlands did not give rise first to a fortress, then a crossroads, and finally, a railway junction. The Pictish fortress, which apparently was built by the fairies in one night (they should be employed on motorway repairs) figures in an astonishing treaty, signed there in 790 between King Eoghan MacAodh of the Picts and emissaries from the Emperor Charlemagne of the Franks. The outcome was that more than 4,000 Pictish warriors went to serve in the great Charles's campaigns. We owe this information to Hector Boece, who wrote his *Historia Scotorum* in the sixteenth-century (his source is less certain); if Hector's spelling had not been so shaky, and he had copied Mons Graupius correctly, the Grampian Mountains would be called the Graupians. He also says that King Eoghan II in the ninth-century built another great citadel (or fortress) to which many foreigners came from all parts of the known world.

The existing building called Inverlochy Castle was built about

Fort William and Ben Nevis

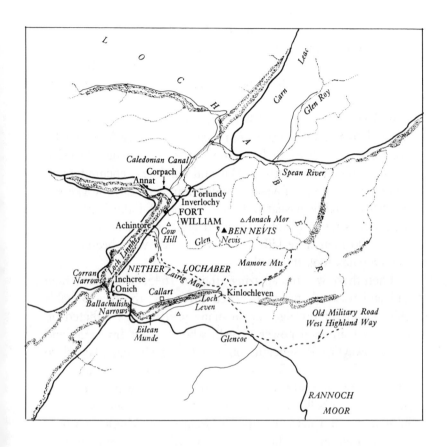

231

1275 by Black John Comyn, the Lord of Badenoch, who was on Edward I's side in the wars of independence; Bruce's triumph at Bannockburn in 1314 meant that the Comyns lost power, and the castle's condition began to deteriorate. It was not restored until 1509 when James IV appointed the Earl of Huntly as Sheriff of Inverness-shire and he used it as his centre for justice in Lochaber.

In 1431 the castle had been the scene of a furious battle. James I had captured and imprisoned Alexander MacDonald, 3rd Lord of the Isles, in Tantallon Castle, for rebellion in 1429; his army under the Earls of Mar and Caithness encountered a much smaller force of MacDonalds commanded by the Lord of the Isles's eighteen-year-old cousin Donald Balloch MacDonald, and after a terribly bloody struggle, in which it was said that 1,000 men were killed, the king's men were beaten. The MacDonalds took the castle.

Then there was the amazing affair of 1645. Montrose's men had laid waste Argyll and sacked Inveraray, the MacDonalds enjoying sweet revenge for so many past wrongs inflicted on them by Campbell power. Argyll, who had left Inveraray and sailed away to Roseneath, on the Gareloch, complained to Edinburgh, and militias were raised in the south, and the MacKenzies of Seaforth in the north. Argyll returned, rounded up his Campbell clansmen to join a few battalions of the militiamen, and marched up the Great Glen. Montrose would be forced up the glen: between the MacKenzies from Inverness, General Baillie's Lowland militia sealing off the southern passes, and the mighty Clan Campbell from Inverlochy, Montrose's ragged army of Irishmen, MacDonalds, Camerons and Stewarts, abetted by the notorious Sir Alasdair MacColla Ciotach MacDonald, would be crushed.

Montrose had other ideas. The January weather was appalling: blizzards swept the Highlands with thick drifting snow, but Montrose led his men southward from Loch Ness, up into the hills. They climbed 2,500 feet over *Carn Leac* and down to Glen

Roy and the Spean river, through raging snowstorms, lashing winds, avalanche and drift. They came over the shoulder of Ben Nevis, down upon Argyll's men as they lay encamped about Inverlochy.

They had been there a few days, sending out scouts to try to discover what Montrose was doing. They had come 'by the middle of the day,' says Neil Munro in *John Splendid*, 'to the plain on which lay the castle of Inverlochy – a staunch quadrangular edifice with round towers at the angles, and surrounded by a moat that smelled anything but freshly.' Argyll could not believe that the whole of Montrose's force had come down from the mountains: a skirmish would dispose of them. He took to his galley in Loch Linnhe, while 5,000 of his clansmen, with the Lowland militia, stood to arms before the old castle. At first light on the morning of 2 February, 1645, after a breakfast of oatmeal mixed with snow, Montrose's men charged. The Lowlanders broke and ran at once, but the Campbells, hemmed in by the collapse of their flanks, fought for the honour of their Chief, already compromised by his caution. They were pressed back to the lochside and died in the water, or the pursuit over the hillsides towards Loch Leven. 1,500 Campbells were killed, and the clan's power was lamed for a generation. The heather of MacDonald, at last, was raised over the myrtle of Campbell.

After the defeat, capture and execution of Charles I, and after, too, the execution of the finest strategist of the time, Graham of Montrose, Cromwell's military government deemed it necessary to keep the royalist clans of Cameron, MacDonald and Stewart in check; a fort was built at the head of Loch Linnhe, at the mouth (then) of the Nevis river. Work began in 1654, and soon a garrison of 250 of General Monck's men were established, beginning a long association of Inverlochy with the redcoats. A new fort was built in stone, to replace the first wooden one, in 1690 by General Hugh MacKay of Scourie, and named Fort William in honour of the new king. The wretched

233

litte huddle of thatched huts that grew up beside it was called Maryburgh, after the Queen, James VII's daughter. The fort was built substantially in the military style of the period which had been dictated by the great French engineer Vauban, with walls twenty feet high, stone turrets at each corner, ditch and ravelin; on the lochside was a sally-port, to landward an arched gateway with a drawbridge. The moat was filled with water from either the loch or the Nevis river. 1,000 men with their officers and the governor could be accommodated within.

The governor in 1691 was Colonel John Hill, who had shared in the direction of the original fort's construction in 1654 and succeeded as governor two years later. At the Restoration, however, he was obliged to hand the keys over to Cameron of Lochiel, and sail away down Loch Linnhe. The Camerons pulled down the *Gearasdan dubh nan Inbhir-Lochaidh*, the Black garrison of Inverlochy, as they called it, and burnt the timber. Thirty years later Hill was back as the governor of the new fort. The loyal clans had risen for the exiled James VII under Graham of Claverhouse, Viscount Dundee, fought Killiecrankie and ultimately lost their advantage because Dundee had been killed there. Once more the Highlands needed to be pacified, and more than anyone, the MacDonalds, Camerons and Stewarts brought to heel. Lowland administrators in William III's government, such as Sir John Dalrymple of Stair in Ayrshire, regarded the Highlanders with contempt as barbaric thieves and murderers. The first attempt to pacify them was by bribing them, but the clans still loyal to James refused to be bribed. William III, fighting in Flanders in defence of his own Netherlands, issued a royal pardon to all former rebels providing they took an oath of allegiance to him before 1 January, 1692. Those who did not would be punished 'with the utmost extremity of the law'.

The Jacobite clans sent urgent messages to James in France asking to be released from allegiance to him so that they might take the oath; James's dilatory reply was probably responsible for the tragedy that was to follow. Little but sorrow ever came of the Highlanders' loyalty to the House of Stuart.

As winter advanced and the Chiefs, still waiting for word from James, had not sworn the oath, Stair and the Campbell Chiefs prepared a plot. The proposed recipients of condign punishment, the scapegoats who would act as exemplars to all, were not to be the bigger clans like the Camerons of Lochaber or the MacDonalds of Glengarry or Keppoch, but the MacDonalds of Glencoe, who were not numerous but had a long-standing reputation for cattle-reiving, burning, slaughter and insurrection. Cattle-stealing was an economic necessity to many of the Highland clans, because by this time the population had outgrown what the glens could produce to support it. Their loyalty was to their Chief, and beyond this to Clan Donald; their chief enemies were the Campbells, who had robbed Clan Donald of the Lordship of the Isles and much more besides. Stair believed he would be performing a public service if 'this thieving tribe were rooted out and cut off.'

In the last week of December a messenger arrived from the exiled James: the Chiefs ought to do 'what may be most for their own safety'. For several it was much too short notice, in such severe winter weather: for one it was fatal. A blizzard swept the Highlands in that last week of December, 1691; old MacIain, Chief of the MacDonalds of Glencoe, rode at last to Fort William, hoping that he could take the oath before Governor Hill, whom he knew, rather than before a Campbell Sheriff in a Campbell town. Hill could not, but understood MacIain's pride. Many of his clan had been hanged in Inveraray, and he himself had been imprisoned there. 'Ardkinglas is a good man', said Hill, 'there is no shame in submitting before him.' Hill knew the movement of soldiers already taking place, with Stair, Argyll, and Breadalbane all planning the MacDonalds' extermination. He could not warn MacIain in so many words, but wrote a letter to Ardkinglas beseeching clemency for old MacIain should he fail to arrive on time. MacIain and his gillies set off on the long, arduous and frustrating journey to Inveraray.

Fort William was besieged by Prince Charles's Jacobite forces in the spring of 1746, but its garrison under Governor Campbell resisted for three weeks after deliberately burning the houses of Maryburgh, which had been built of timber and thatch in case this precaution ever became necessary. The siege was raised.

Poor James Stewart of Glen Duror, *Seumas a'Ghlinne*, was imprisoned in the fort from the time of his arrest to his trial and execution, in November, 1752. Everyone knew, then, before, and certainly after this tragic affair, that the day of the Jacobites was over. The Government's savage repression after the '45 had its effect, the lairds were beginning to realise that money could be forthcoming in floods if they cleared away the clansfolk for the sake of sheep, and the garrison had little to do. It endured until the mid-nineteenth century, and by that time its duty was directed at trying to control smuggling. In 1864 the fort was sold, and in 1889 sold again by compulsory purchase to the West Highland Railway Company, which demolished the entire fort save the officers' mess to make way for engine sheds. The inner arch of the main gateway, however, was removed and re-erected at the entrance to the military burial-ground at Craigs, where it can still be seen. Eventually the officers' block too was demolished in 1948.

The railway made Fort William, as it made Oban, but in the meantime it had changed its name twice: in 1793 it became Gordonsburgh, because the Duke of Gordon had bought it, and in 1834 it changed to Duncansburgh after another new owner, Sir Duncan Cameron of Fassiefern. It was in Sir Duncan's time that the present High Street was laid out, and the side-streets down to the lochside. Telford's engineering triumph, the Caledonian Canal, opened in 1822, and Fort William began at last to thrive as a commercial centre, principal sea-port of the new shipping-route. Stage-coach roads were improved to link Fort William with Inverness and Glasgow, to be supplanted in due course by the railway. The population rose, and in the

1890s the Nevis river was harnessed to one of the first Hydro-Electric power stations, so that by 1896 the town led all Britain in being lit by locally produced electricity.

In 1889 the railway line from Craigendoran was begun, in 1894 it was opened, and Fort William began to expand again: steamer services were extended and hotels built because the railway brought tourists to this accessible and convenient centre for touring the West Highlands. The motor-car continued and overtook the railway in recent years, so that even roads, latterly, have begun to improve. In addition to these sources of income, industry has arrived and the population enlarged still more. The British Aluminium factory at Inverlochy began production in 1929, the big paper-mill at Annat, near Corpach, was finished in 1963.

Fort William lacks the immediate appeal of Oban; the lochside is attractive, but the scenery is far less picturesque on the whole. Ben Nevis is obscured from view by Cow Hill, 942 feet (and by misty clouds most of the time from anywhere else); there are few exciting buildings, hardly anything remains of the old fort except the walls on the lochside, and Inverlochy Castle is very hard to find. It is surrounded by trees so cannot be seen from a distance, and is not well signposted. There is a footpath from the walls of the fort, which enclose a grassy picnic area, and a turning off the A82 road, nearly opposite the Aluminium works. It is easier, if misleading, to find the other Inverlochy Castle, a huge Victorian building which is now a luxury hotel catering for the more affluent kind of tourist: it is at Torlundy, on the A82.

There is, however, a distillery dispensing the good Ben Nevis malt whisky, and Long John (the founder, John MacDonald, was 6'4" tall), there is Ben Nevis itself, and there is the West Highland Museum in Cameron Square, opened in 1922 and housed in one of the oldest buildings in the town. The Museum contains far too much for a full description; one of the rooms has been entirely furnished as a reconstruction of Governor

Hill's study at the old fort: one may imagine him sitting at his table, receiving with alarm the huge figure of MacIain, his shaggy white hair and fiercely uptilted moustache glistening with snow. There are rooms full of weapons, including the gun that may have shot Colin Campbell of Glenure, and some military relics: the 79th Foot, Queen's Own Cameron Highlanders, were raised and based originally in Fort William. There is a display of local wildlife, photographs of the area in past years, a geological and archaeological survey describing the 'parallel roads' of Glen Roy, and Stone Age inhabitants, and much about the old Highland way of life, including a reconstructed room in a cottage. There is a Jacobite room, with mementoes of Prince Charles and his clandestine supporters in later years, particularly the famous 'Secret Portrait': a board with smears of paint on it like an artist's palette, meaningless until a polished metal cylinder is placed within the crescent of the smears, when they converge and reflect a portrait of the Prince. There is a good deal, too, not unnaturally, of the clan tartans, the way to don a *feileadh mor*, the big belted plaid, and the way the clan system was broken up. The West Highland Museum should be visited by anyone interested in the history and background of not only Fort William but of the whole of the West Highlands.

There is also a little Scottish Craft Exhibition and Ben Nevis Centre in the High Street, where you may find out more about the ancient indigenous crafts (the products of which, even the malt whisky, may be bought in the adjacent shop), and much information about Ben Nevis. Those still in the dark may go to the Cameron Centre, which is an Information and Interpretative Centre for tourists.

One of the principal reasons why many people stay in Fort William is to climb Ben Nevis, at 4,406 feet the highest mountain in Britain. Its name is from the Gaelic *Beinn neamh-bhathais*, Mountain with its head in the clouds. It is not a particularly attractive mountain scenically, and as its name implies, is often shrouded in grey clouds. It is climbed frequently because it is the highest. Even I have climbed it, and I am no mountaineer. There were nine of us, we were on a camping expedition to the Highlands in 1962, we had been camping at Invergarry and had moved to Fort William, and while four members of the party opted for a steamer trip down Loch Linnhe to Oban, the remaining five decided to climb Ben Nevis. 'There are two ways of doing it,' said Geoff Sanders, one of the five, 'One is like the North Wall of the Eiger, the other is like walking through Herne Bay Park.' Although Herne Bay Park has neither the scenic attractions nor the seemingly 45-degree elevation, he was broadly right. We drove along Glen Nevis, left our transport at an appropriate park and found the track. 'The track itself was not steep,' I wrote at the time, 'but neither was it smooth, and after the first 1,500 feet we were quite glad to rest, sit on a rock and have our lunch. Far below us was the quiet pastoral peacefulness of Glen Nevis: opposite, the top of the Forestry Commission plantations along the corresponding mountainside. Just above us was a plateau, a shoulder between a minor hill and Nevis himself, in which was a small, still tarn. It even looked cold.' We reached the bare rock, and the mist. 'If you are alone on that dead mountainside, with the mist swirling about you, moistening your clothes but not your lips, and that jagged, awkward path winding ahead into nothing, you feel the loneliest person in the world.' We found some frozen, crystalline snow up there, and quite a number of other climbers descending, some with children. We plodded on, the mist thinned, and suddenly, at the side of the track, was the side of the mountain that Herne Bay Park climbers avoid: 'a roaring black chasm, sheer-sided with dripping bare black rock, dropping horribly into the grey clouds.' We had reached the top, where there were several memorials, the ruins of the old observatory, some crows, and 'a terrible lot of toffee papers, bottle tops and empty beer tins.' We were in sunshine, above the clouds, but they were all we could see: we had to wait until a moment on the way down, when 'suddenly before us the clouds were lifting and we could see not only our way down but the tarn on the shoulder, and then the hill beyond it, and then, oh! Sunshine gleaming brilliantly in bands of shining gold on Loch Arkaig and Loch Linnhe: mountains stretching far away from us, splashed here and there with sunlit greens and yellows, purples and browns, then deeper purple and blue of the peaks beyond the peaks. Another slight lift of the mist and there was the far end of Loch Linnhe, the islands and the straight grey line of the open sea. The Highlands were all ours in that moment.'

Harriers run up and down Ben Nevis in a race, on the first Saturday in September every year. The winner in 1989 was Keith Anderson, of Ambleside, in a time of 1 hour, 27 minutes, 41 seconds. 'The thing about us,' he said afterwards, 'is that, first and foremost, we love these hills. They are living things to us, because we have seen different aspects to their character. Really, winning trophies and medals doesn't matter. There's more satisfaction in knowing that, if you fall down, your rival will pick you up.'

In 1887 the Fort William 'bellman', or town crier, pushed a 73 lb wheelbarrow up Ben Nevis; in 1911 Henry Alexander drove a Model T Ford up it, and in 1928 George Simpson, with a passenger, drove an Austin 7 up it; others have driven motor-cycles up it. H. V. Morton climbed it, some time before 1929, and having done so fell into conversation with the men in his hotel bar: 'Hitherto padlocked Highland tongues unlock them-selves. Men tell the story of the strange and wonderful things they have seen on "the Ben"; one how he saw the sun come up over Scotland; another how he saw the sun sink in splendour; a third how he saw all the Highland peaks nosing their way for a hundred miles through a white waste of motionless cloud.

'I edge in and pay my tribute. I tell them of Swiss mountains I have climbed and of the sights I have seen from the Libyan Hills in Egypt, and from the crests of the Aures Mountains in North Africa. Nothing I have seen from any mountains approached the glory of blue hills against blue hills – the monarchs of Scotland, mile after mile, with their heads in the sunlight of an autumn day.'

Arthur Gardner climbed it 'in the snowy spring of 1922'. They lost the track in the snow and found the going extremely tough, but managed to find the summit: 'The snow on the top must have been exceedingly deep, as we suddenly found ourselves walking over the roof of the little inn which serves summer visitors with refreshments, the only sign of the building being a chimney-pot pushing up through the snow.' Men and women, having made the effort to climb up the long, stony trail, experience the same kind of emotions when they stand on the summit, whether or not the view is open to them. 'In the deep snow, with all Scotland lying at our feet,' writes Arthur Gardner, 'and soft mists drifting over the landscape and occasionally enveloping us in their folds, we felt wonderfully remote from the busy world in which we spend most of our lives. It is good at times to go up into the hills, like the prophets of old, and there, alone with the clouds of heaven above us, and the noblest of terrestrial forms at our feet, to imbibe something of the spirit of infinity and worship before the throne of the Creator of them in humility and awe.'

There is a camping and caravan site in Glen Nevis, and a Youth Hostel, and plenty of hotels, guest-houses and bed-and-breakfast houses in Fort William, and whole villages of self-catering cottages on the hillsides outside it. A new attraction, to keep the tourists coming in the winter, too, has now appeared: the slopes of *Aonach Mor*, another 4,000-foot giant to the east of Ben Nevis, have become a ski resort. In June, 1989, it was reported that the Austrian engineering company Dopplemyer had installed pylons to support a gondola which would take skiers up to 2,300 feet, from which point seven tows would taken them to the top of the slopes. The Nevis Range Development Company is responsible for the project; its chairman, Ian Jones, is reported as saying: 'We hope to develop the mountain and preserve the environment in a way which has hitherto been neglected.' We hope they have.

Most of the Highland towns hold Highland Games during the summer months, partly for the local people and partly to attract the tourists; there is dancing, pipe-playing, with if possible a pipe band, a shinty match or two, and the games themselves, involving activities such as hammer-throwing, shot-putting, caber-tossing, and quite often a tug-of-war. Fort William's are usually held in late July or early August, when most of the tourists will be there and the weather will be at its worst. There is also an Agricultural Show, principally for local farmers.

Nether Lochaber is the triangle of territory stretching from Fort William at its apex, with Loch Linnhe its western rim, to Loch Leven in the south, with the mountains of Mamore sealing off the eastern side. There is a road into it, by way of Achintore up to Blar a'Chaorainn, and there are tracks which penetrate the wooded glens and ascend the rugged hills. One way of seeing it is to take the West Highland Way for this tract: a ninety-five-mile-long trail has been open for walkers since 1980. It starts from the northern Glasgow suburb Milngavie (pronounced Mulguy, if you can believe it), passes along old drove roads, footpaths, forest roads, old military roads and disused railway tracks en route, through some wonderfully unspoilt scenery, on the eastern side of Loch Lomond, across Rannoch Moor, to Glencoe and across the hills to Kinlochleven, and through this Nether Lochaber area to terminate at Fort William. It is reckoned that it takes a week to cover it all, and accommodation can be found in hotels, Youth Hostels, camping sites and bed-and-breakfast places: if you book in advance. The route is marked by the Countryside Commission for Scotland's symbol of a thistle within a hexagon, since it is that body which has devised it.

In Nether Lochaber the trail comes north-west from Kin-lochleven across the *Lairig Mor*, the Great Pass, then turns through the forests of Glen Nevis before winding down to Fort William; it is an ancient trackway across this wild and rugged area, trodden by many feet over the centuries. In the middle of it, west of Blar a'Chaorain, is Loch Lundavra, which is frequented by a *tarbh-uisge*, a water-bull, less fearsome than the *each-uisge* because it lures cows, rather than humans, into the loch. The military road over the *Lairig Mor* was built by General Caulfield, he who created the Rest-and-Be-Thankful road, but it was on the lines of the ancient trackway. The latter certainly existed in 1645, because a party of MacDonalds chased some Campbells along it after their victory at Inverlochy. They marked the spot where they stopped their pursuit by building a cairn, called *Carn Caimbeulach*, on the south side of the track about half a mile beyond Lundavra. It is traditional for passing MacDonalds to add a stone to this cairn, and for Campbells to take one off.

Along the northern shore of Loch Leven past *Caolas nan Con*, the Strait of the Dogs, there is a deserted mansion called Callart, on the site of an earlier house of the same name. During the seventeenth-century, in about 1640, every occupant of Callart except the laird's daughter Mary Cameron became infected with the plague, from a Spanish ship trading in Loch Leven. To prevent it from spreading, it was ordered that the house and everyone in it, living or dead, were to be burnt. Mary's lover, Diarmid Campbell of Inverawe, inclined to think this rather a pity, told Mary to let herself out of the house secretly at night, and swim, naked, across the loch to where he would meet her on the far shore. This she did, and clothed and mounted on swift horses, they hastened to Inverawe House, but Campbell of Inverawe refused to let them in until they had fulfilled a month's quarantine, in a bothy high up on the slopes of Beinn Cruachan. However, for the sake of family honour, he prudently had them married first. They survived their lonely honeymoon and were allowed to live at Inverawe. Happy endings seldom lighten the general gloom of Highland stories:

The West Highlands

in 1645 Diarmid Campbell was killed at Inverlochy, and poor Mary followed him to the grave later, of a broken heart.

The islands in Loch Leven here, in the wider reaches before the narrows, are mostly burial-places. One is *Eilean Munde*, where the Camerons of Callart (including, presumably, the plague-ridden ones), MacDonalds of Glencoe, and Stewarts of Ballachulish were interred, each clan having its own port of entry. The ghost of whoever has been most recently interred keeps watch over the rest; one rash youth, claiming superiority over all supernatural horrors, undertook to spend a night on the island. He regretted it. The Devil, clearly disapproving of such brash arrogance, left his claw-mark on the stone doorway of the ruined chapel, and you can still see it.

At Onich, beyond the modern bridge across the narrows and facing Loch Linnhe, in a field a few hundred yards west of the road, there stands a seven-foot tall monolith called *Cladh a'Charra*, the Stone of Stones. It was probably put there by local residents of about 2,000 BC, but its curiosity is that two holes have been made in it. Early religion often involved fertility rites, and this may have been the reason for them. A mile north of here at Inchree there is a marked Forestry walk of under two miles around the lovely Inchree Falls, from which you can enjoy fine views across the loch of the Kingairloch hills. The Corran Narrows, where the ferry runs, divide Loch Linnhe into its two parts, called *An Linnhe Saileach*, the Salt Pool, and *An Linnhe Dubh*, the Dark (or Black) Pool.

The new bridge across the Ballachulish narrows, replacing the ferry, and the newer, stronger Corran ferry, render communications in this district far quicker than they have ever been before. Imagine poor MacIain, faced with the task of journeying from Fort William to Inveraray in the space of a day if he was to save his clan from extirpation: even in winter, with a modern car on the modern roads he could have done it in a few hours.

244

13

Glencoe

'I glanced with a shiver down its terrible distance upon that nightmare of gulf and eminence, of gash, and peaks afloat upon swirling mists. It lay, a looming terror, forgotten of heaven and unfriendly to man (as one might readily imagine), haunted for ever with wailing airs and rumours, ghosts calling in the deeps of dusk and melancholy, legends of horror and remorse.' Neil Munro makes his protagonist, Elrigmore, say this of Glencoe in *John Splendid*.

H. V. Morton's view of it is similar: 'A man suddenly shot up into the moon might gaze at the cold, remote mountains with much the same chilly awe that he looks at the Pass of Glencoe. Here is a landscape without mercy.'

Messrs Bell, Bozman and Fairfax-Blakeborough, in *Hills and Mountains of Great Britain*, see a little farther: 'It takes time to absorb the subtle atmosphere of Glencoe, and the luxury traveller may see nothing whatever in the place but desolation. I have seen Glencoe in all its moods from a calm summer day to a wild night of winter storm, and it is always impressive and seems to me to justify the great pictures that have been made of it, for instance, by Horatio McCulloch.'

I too have seen Glencoe in a good many moods. In 1964 I took part in an extraordinary venture on the part of my friend

245

Peter Watkins to film the battle of Culloden and its aftermath, based on John Prebble's book. Peter was working for the BBC, so professional camera, sound, and make-up people accompanied us, but all the actors were amateurs: students, local folk, old friends, anyone in fact who had a face that Peter thought would fit in. After a fortnight's filming in the vicinity of Inverness, the whole outfit moved on to Glencoe village, and shot for another week in Glencoe and Glen Etive. Most of the time, rain lashed down relentlessly.

One day, Peter wanted to film an incident after the battle when the redcoats were searching for fugitive Jacobites, who had taken to the heather and the hills. A family was to be pursued up a mountainside. 'There's a marvellous corrie,' said Peter, 'up in MacDonald's Pass. I'm going to have the whole shooting-match up there today.' This was one of the glens leading into Glencoe, majestically beautiful, and forbiddingly steep: to take a whole film unit into it was not going to be a saunter along the beach. It was one of those days when rainstorms swooped down the glen, drenched everyone for ten minutes, then disappeared, to be replaced by a hot sun that made scrambling up the hillside an uncomfortable occupation. We got them all, actors, actresses in long skirts and totally inadequate footgear, young children, and Patrick, Peter's baby son, up that hillside, into the corrie. A mock-fight was arranged by our professional fight-arranger, Derek Ware. The children screamed, the men shouted; the baby was carefully laid on the ground beside a musket jabbed bayonet-first into the turf so that it looked as if the baby was impaled; an actor in a soldier's red coat was photographed holding the musket, in the act. An actress vigorously assaulted him from behind, while one of the little girls genuinely burst into tears, the whole gruesome scene overcoming her. The baby howled and was picked up by his real mother. 'Cut!'

Most of us were billeted in Glencoe village, but meals were a problem; Peter and his family were staying in the Kingshouse

Glencoe

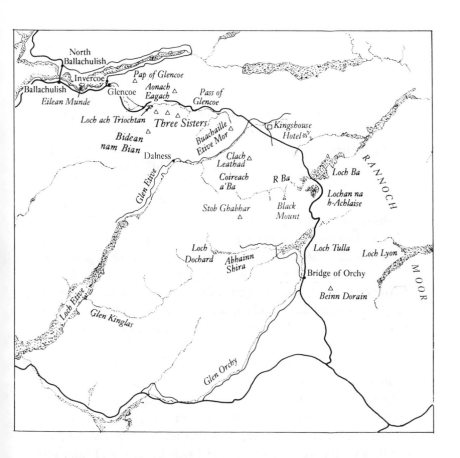

Hotel at the far end of the glen, so every night a number of us drove the whole twelve miles to join them at dinner, seeing the glen in all its mysterious moods, half gilded in the sun's last rays, half an impenetrable, morbid shadow; often teeming with water, lashing rain, thundering waterfalls, the river boiling, foaming, rich brown; every mountainside seemed to be streaked with water, gushing from every stone like a leaking bucket.

The head of the glen, marked by a great flat-topped rock on the old road, which is higher than the new at the point where the river Coe plunges over a high waterfall and gushes down through a narrow gorge, is called *Innean a'Cheathaich*, the Anvil of the Mist. On both sides of the glen the cliffs rise to 3,000 feet from the flats of *Loch ach triochtan*; on the south side the massive *Bidean nam Bian*, Peak of the Bens, with nine summits, walls it in; the Three Sisters are the ends of three spurs extending from Bidean, hanging over the glen in huge ugly bulges of black, sinister rock. The north side is the flank of *Aonach Eagach*, the Notched Ridge. The loch is at the base of *Aonach Dubh*, in whose upper face is the so-called Ossian's Cave. Ossian, son of Fingal or Fionn MacCumhail, was the legendary bard of these remote times, placed traditionally in the 3rd Century AD. He certainly did not live in the cave, whether or not he composed verse in it: it is extremely difficult to reach, and it is at an angle of about 45 degrees.

Legend has it that the Feinn, the standing army of Fingal, occupied the lower glen; they fought valiantly against the Norsemen, building four huge trenches on the slopes of the Pap of Glencoe (between Glencoe and Loch Leven), and built up earthworks as defences. They are said to have battled with the Norsemen at Laroch, a mile west of Glencoe village. There are eleven stone slabs near Laroch reputed to be the Vikings' graves. The victory won by Fingal and his warriors was dearly bought, for the slaughter was immense and they were never as strong again. But along *Bidean nam Bian* and *Aonach Eagach*, the Feinn are sleeping: the wind that howls about the tops is their breath, and one day they will arise at the call of Fingal's horn. No-one is sure what the name Glencoe means: some say it is the Glen of Dogs, recalling the hounds of Fionn; others say it is the glen of *comhan-taisg*, the plunder which the Feinn hid up in the hills.

Glencoe belonged to the Lordship of Lorn, so was MacDougall property until Bruce's time, then with the rest was given to Angus Og MacDonald of Islay who fought with Bruce at Bannockburn. The first MacDonald of Glencoe was Angus Og's bastard son Iain Og, also known as Iain Abràch. His father gave him Glencoe, and Iain gave his descendants, Chiefs of the MacDonalds of Glencoe, the title MacIain. Throughout their history, they supported Clan Donald and fought against the insidious advance of Clan Campbell; if Clan Donald supported the Stuart kings, so did MacIain. They were never numerous: the greatest number of warriors MacIain ever led was 150, so there can never have been any more than 500 men, women and children in all. They lived in little townships between Achtriachtan and Loch Leven.

MacIain's house at Carnoch stood on the flanks of the Pap of Glencoe, a stone-built, slate-roofed house, simple and austere, but luxurious compared with the thatched hovels of his people. He had no castle, and there was little in the glen to sustain fifty, let alone 500. So they ventured out from time to time on raids to other glens peopled by other clans, and earned for themselves the reputation that made them exemplary, to the Lowland mind of Dalrymple of Stair, of all that was savage, barbaric, and pernicious about the Highlanders, alien folk in alien dress speaking an alien tongue. What was more, they had spurned the new Reformation religion in favour of the old Episcopalian Church. Such people, according to those like Stair, were asking to be eliminated from the earth because they were a drag on progress to civilisation, an anachronism and a canker that must be cut out. So Stair enlisted the help of the great Clan Campbell, used the excuse of the oath to King William, and set about his duty.

Although he was late in submitting, MacIain's oath was accepted by the Sheriff, Campbell of Ardkinglas, who sent the certificate with his name and all the others who had sworn before him, and John Hill's letter begging MacIain to be accepted, to the Privy Council. Sadly, honest Ardkinglas, even then, was betrayed by men of his own clan, for there were many Campbells under the Master of Stair's malign influence: three of them went to the Clerks of the Council and said that MacIain's oath could not be accepted after the expiry of the set date: sheer malice was at work. Stair recommended that the whole clan should be wiped out: their total destruction, he said, would be regretted by none and would demonstrate the king's strength. King William was persuaded that genocide was a sad necessity, and orders were given that the troops at Inverlochy and Inverness should be used for the purpose. 'It is a great work of charity,' Stair wrote, 'to be exact in rooting out the damnable sept, the worst in all the Highlands.' Neither the king, nor Stair, had ever been to the Highlands.

John Hill in Fort William thought that his letter and Ardkinglas's recommendation had saved the MacDonalds, but Stair and the Campbells were already at work. The great hatred of the Lowlanders for them, recognised by Gaeldom in the phrase *Mi-run mor nan Gall*, was founded on fear of their strangeness, and it was compounded by Campbell hatred of those who were their ancient enemies.

Campbell of Glenlyon, a dissolute bankrupt, was to be the agency; he was given a commission, two companies of Argyll foot-soldiers, and orders to MacIain that they were to be billeted on the people of Glencoe. Dutifully, the MacDonalds received them into their poky cottages and prepared to give them the best that Highland hospitality could afford. The February weather was mild, the soldiers were called together and drilled each day, and gradually, although many of the Campbell troops had suffered at MacDonald hands in the past, and likewise the hosts from their guests, the rules of hospitality were inviolate, and friendship developed among the Highlanders.

The delay in the execution of Stair's order was due to John Hill's reluctance to be a party to such treachery, because he insisted that his own authority would be necessary. Eventually he compromised his integrity and gave an order for other troops to march to Glencoe 'and there put in due execution the orders you have received from the Commander-in-Chief.' The other soldiers, however, were not needed, for Glenlyon had his own orders, to begin the slaughter at five o'clock on the morning of 13 February. He gathered his troops, waited for the appointed hour, and then began the grisly work. Old MacIain was shot dead as he was trying hurriedly to dress himself, and all along the length of the glen from Invercoe to Achtriachtan there was shooting, as the soldiers performed their gruesome task. Some were bayonetted, some were burned in their cottages, but some were allowed to escape, for the orders stirred revulsion in the minds and stomachs of a number of the soldiers. Glenlyon failed to carry out his orders to the letter, for his men only killed thirty-eight in all, and there were nearly 400 of the clan in the glen. The rest escaped, but the weather had turned again and many died in the attempt to struggle over the mountain passes, thick with snow.

Highland history is full of massacre stories, committed by one clan against another. What revolted and disgusted Highland opinion was the treacherous abuse of hospitality involved in this of Glencoe, the murder by guests of their hosts, and this was one of the reasons why far fewer were killed than might have been, for Highland men in Glenlyon's force were too sickened to carry out their orders.

The massacre did not exterminate the MacDonalds of Glencoe: one of MacIain's sons survived, to be the new MacIain, and the people returned to their glen and built new homes. They were out in the 1715 rebellion, and in the '45. It was the Clearances that finished them off, not the Government.

Glencoe village, at the western end of the glen as it opens out to Loch Leven, is really Carnoch, where MacIain's house used to stand. Nothing is left of it, but a side-road from the old Bridge of Coe runs up-river to a hillock, on top of which is a tall Celtic cross with the inscription 'In memory of MacIain, Chief of Glencoe, who fell with his people in the massacre of Glencoe.' He was buried beside his forefathers in *Eilean Munde*. The modern village is oriented towards tourism, as now is the lower section of the glen; there is a Visitor Centre, which explains the story of the massacre, the Glencoe and North Lorn Folk Museum, in a crofter's cottage, and innumerable craft shops (one of which rejoices in the name 'Crafts and Things'); there is an Information Centre at Ballachulish, which explains the working of the Ballachulish slate quarries, and there are plenty of caravan and camping sites, and a Youth Hostel: apart from the historical interest, the glen is highly popular for climbing. Caution is always needed, and plenty of experience, because *Bidean nam Bian* is said to be second only to Ben Nevis for hazards to climbers, and there have been far too many fatal accidents. For those who prefer luxury in between exertions, there are five hotels and guest-houses in Glencoe, another four in Ballachulish, and several self-catering cottages and bed-and-breakfast houses.

One of the hotels, the Clachaig Inn, has recently been the centre of a howling blizzard of controversy, because its owners have put in planning application to build a dry ski-slope, nine chalets, a multi-gym and an adventure centre. Residents and visitors have concurred in heartfelt condemnation of the scheme, which would, they say, result in the spoliation of the glen. The perplexed and distressed owners of the inn say that it would not, since they had taken trouble to ensure that their development would be unobtrusive. The Highland Regional Council are likely to have the last word, but one might imagine old MacIain's shade chuckling at the vehemence of the opposition: after all, a dry ski-slope and nine chalets are not quite the same thing as being shot, along with most of your family and neighbours, are they?

Beyond the head of Glencoe, above the 'anvil' and the thunderous falls in the gorge, the valley broadens; on the south side the two 'herdsmen' stand, the mountains *Buachaille Etive Beag*, 3,029 feet, and *Buachaille Etive Mor*, 3,345 feet, and beyond the latter a side-road leads off through Glen Etive, to Dalness where Deirdre of the Sorrows played with her innocent young friends, the sons of Uisnach, and to the head of Loch Etive.

Opposite the Glen Etive turning is another, to the Kingshouse Hotel, which is still one of the loneliest, standing on the edge of the vast and bleak Rannoch Moor. It is certainly the oldest in Scotland, built in the eighteenth-century as a staging post between garrisons. Admittedly the eighteenth-century is just yesterday among English inns, but in the Highlands they usually built inns of wood and thatch, and burned them down from time to time. It is not uncommon to see a herd of roe deer grazing at the inn's threshold, so wild is the immediate neighbourhood. It has been extended recently for more accommodation, because apart from ordinary tourism and the rock-climbing experts in *Buachaille Etive Mor*, which reputedly has the best rock-climbing in Scotland, there is an additional reason now for staying there. Just across the road is a lane leading to the Winter Sports Centre on *Meall a'Bhuiridh*, 3,636 feet, (pronounced Mellavoory). From the old road to the Black Mount, a new road leads to the foot of the chairlift, which whisks you to a plateau at 2,250 feet, then a tow heaves you up another 1,350 feet, and you can, if you enjoy this kind of occupation, then slide all the way down again. In a good snowy year the ski season lasts until the end of June.

Rannoch Moor is a vast triangle of land, 1,000 feet above sea level, stretching between the Kingshouse Hotel and Loch Rannoch to the east, and Loch Tulla to the south, an area of fifty-six square miles. There is no road from east to west. It is the site of what once was a part of the ancient Wood of Caledon, a forest that used at one time to extend from Glencoe to Braemar, and from Glen Lyon to Glen Affric. It was the home of plenty of brown bears, wild boars, wolves and countless other creatures, but over the centuries it was destroyed by fire and felling; from the ninth to the twelfth centuries, by the Norsemen and by the Highlanders themselves, to kill the wolves and the brigands it harboured, then from the fifteenth to the eighteenth centuries for iron smelting and by army commanders to root out rebels. Small parts of it remain, a tiny area near Loch Tulla, and a larger one at the Black Wood of Rannoch.

There is plenty of water on the moor, rivers rise and flow from it, and there is a continuous line of water right across it: in theory at least it is possible to swim – or skate – from one side to the other. Not many people do, but there are hundreds of water-birds that might. In the lochans you will see divers, grebes, swans, numerous species of duck, and greenshanks. Anyone who tries walking across will soon find their shanks remarkably green, but as the ground is drained by the lochans it is reasonably dry in fine weather. In foul weather it is the most desolate place on earth, because it is so vast, grim, shelterless and trackless: a wilderness of peat-bog, water, heather, and countless dangers. The West Highland Way crosses it by keeping well to the western rim, following for the most part the old military road that goes down Glencoe. No-one would wish to be out on the moor at night, in bad weather. It is haunted, of course, but only at its far eastern end, on Loch Rannoch: a light in the form of a ball is sometimes seen skimming the surface of the water. It always rises at the same point, moves the same distance, and disappears at the same place. Occasionally, however, it has been seen to rise from the water and roll up the hill *Meall-dubh*; no-one has yet explained it.

The only road across the moor is the A82 through Glencoe, which runs very straight across the moor's undulations and threads a seemingly precarious way between the lochans, *Loch*

Ba to the left, *Lochan na h-Achlaise* and several others to the right; behind these last is the Black Mount, and the valley of the Ba river (across which the West Highland Way goes, by Ba Bridge). Westward, the Ba river rises in *Coireach a'Ba*, the biggest corrie in Scotland, under the frowning cliffs of *Clach Leathad*, 3,600 feet; southward from it is another great mass rearing high cliffs over the corrie, *Stob Ghabhar*, 3,565 feet. These are the eastern end of the range that stretches south-west down to Loch Etive.

Below the Black Mount the road dog-legs, runs down beside lovely tree-lined Loch Tulla, from which the Orchy river issues, is joined by the railway and the electricity cables, and goes down to Bridge of Orchy, where there is a railway station and a famous hotel, open from March to November for the exploration of the magnificent countryside around it; directly east is the smooth uninterrupted slope of *Beinn Dorain*, 3,524 feet, where Duncan Ban MacIntyre composed his verse about the red deer. If you cross the Bridge of Orchy on A8005, a single-track road, and go to Forest Lodge, you will pass what remains at Inveroran of the house where he was born. From Forest Lodge a track up *Abhainn Shira* takes you to Loch Dochard, and eventually after a long, fascinating and completely solitary walk, down Glen Kinglass to Loch Etive.

Half a mile south of Bridge of Orchy is a turning right to B8074 which runs all the way down Glen Orchy; it is fourteen miles long, is heavily wooded (mostly by the Forestry Commission) and always it follows the tumbling, turbulent Orchy as it hurtles over spectacular rapids and falls, like *Eas Urchaidh*, the Falls of Orchy. Fishing is by permit, which is another reason for staying at the Bridge of Orchy Hotel. There are few farmsteads and no villages, which was certainly not the case in Duncan Ban MacIntyre's time: the Clearances stripped the glen of people.

We are back now in the Campbell country of Argyll, and it is time to resume the journey north.

14

Morar, Knoydart, and Glen Shiel

The last chapter's diversion into Lochaber and Fort William began at the head of Loch Ailort, where the good A861 meets, at a T-junction, the A830. To penetrate into Arisaig and Morar you must take the left turning here, skirting the head of Loch Ailort. To your left and the west of the loch, the grey, rugged rocks belong to the Ardnish peninsula which divides the Sound of Arisaig between Loch Ailort and *Loch nan Uamh* (pronounced Loch nan Oor, Loch of the Caves). No-one lives in Ardnish: not many did in 1940, but those few were cleared out for the sake of security, when the army's 'hush-hush' training centre for what would become known as commandos was established at Inverailort Castle. They later moved to wider hunting-grounds in the Great Glen near Spean Bridge.

There is one track that can take you into Ardnish: it starts at Polnish, past the little Loch Dubh, crosses the railway line at its western end and heads off along the rocky peninsula's northern slopes. Unexpectedly in the middle you come to the lovely, remote *Loch Doire a'Ghearrain*, then you drop down to the ruins of a deserted township, Peanmeanach, above a little bay. It is five miles there, and no other way back, but what pleasures, what larks, Pip old Chap, as Joe Gargery might have said: the beauty of Highland walking is that in such places as this, which

256

is not a mountain that has to be climbed, nor a ski-slope, nor is it adjacent to craft-shops and places of refreshment, very few other folks bother to get out of their cars and put their boots on. As like as not, you will have it to yourself, to share with the wild sea-birds, the curlews and the herons.

The main road soon arrives at the head of *Loch nan Uamh*, where it dives under a viaduct of the railway. This is an extraordinary railway, opened in 1901, an engineering achievement to rival some of those in Switzerland; by viaducts, tunnels, cuttings and embankments, it wriggles its way from Fort William along this difficult coast to Mallaig.

The railway line is still discreetly near at hand, up in the trees above the road, when you see the Prince's Cairn on the road-and-lochside. It was placed here by the '45 Association to mark the spot where Prince Charles, on 20 September, 1746, at last was evacuated from the soil of Scotland, to be put aboard a French frigate *L'Heureux*, and taken away for ever from the country he had ruined. Curiously enough, his venture ended very near where it had begun, because just a short way farther on, at the gleaming sands below Borrodale House, he had landed from the French ship *du Teillay*. The house stands where the Borrodale burn plunges under the road on its way to the beach and the loch; Charles stayed in it as a guest of Angus MacDonald, a tenant of Clanranald, guarded by a hundred clansmen. It was here that he met the Clan Chiefs, and by force of personality and the charm possessed by some of the Stuarts, persuaded them that his lunatic adventure was feasible. Donald Cameron of Lochiel had gone to meet the Prince to put his case for abstaining: he left full of enthusiasm for him.

Four days after Culloden, Charles returned to Borrodale House, a fugitive. He was then put in a boat and rowed across the terrible Minch to Benbecula, and endured many adventures until he returned to the Morar coast. By that time Borrodale House had been burnt, in the aftermath of Culloden, and Angus MacDonald was living in a hut nearby. Charles lurked in a cave

South Morar

Loch Sheil from Glenfinnan

at the seaward end of a low ridge on the west side of the little bay, 40 feet deep with an opening so hard to find that no-one did. He was then smuggled through the cordon of troops to the mountains, where he hid until, in September, he was told of the approach of French ships, and brought down again to *Loch nan Uamh*. Although the house was burnt, its walls remained standing and it could be re-roofed and restored; it is therefore virtually unchanged in appearance, and the Prince's room can be identified as the one on the ground floor at the west front.

There is a path up the east bank of Glen Borrodale, from the bridge, leading right into the heart of South Morar, a moorland dotted with lochans, up as far as *Carn a Mhadaidh Ruaidh*, Cairn of the Red Fox, from which eminence it drops very steeply to Scamadale on the shores of Loch Morar. The view from the top, on a clear day, will be magnificent: of all Loch Morar, and the rugged sea-coast from *Loch nan Uamh* to the shining white Morar sands.

Arisaig, although it gives its name to the wide Sound to the south, stands at the head of its own little loch, which gives it a delightful setting and a very attractive, sheltered harbour. The loch is called *Loch nan Ceall*, Loch of the Holy Cells, and it is littered with tiny islands and skerries so that navigation is hazardous; nevertheless there are ferry services to the islands Eigg, Muck, Rhum and Canna in the summer months. Arisaig has a store and post office, six hotels and guest-houses, some self-catering chalets, and is on the edge not only of some of the finest beaches in the West Highlands, but of some of the best walking country too, up in the hills above Loch Morar.

The southern arm of *Loch nan Ceall* is formed by a long rocky peninsula called *Rubha Arisaig*. A lane winds its way from the village along its shores to an old steamer pier. The land here is not the most fertile in the world, and it is hardly surprising that in the end, its scanty soil proved unable to support its population, which largely emigrated. The hill at the western end of the peninsula is called *Cruach Doire na Doruinn*, Hill of Anguish, because the people would climb it to catch a last glimpse of the white-sailed ships carrying their loved ones away forever.

About half a mile north of Arisaig, close by the present Catholic Church of St Mary, are the ruins of a sixteenth-century chapel of Kilmory, dedicated to St Maolrubha (Maree), and in its churchyard are several carved grave-slabs, including one of a clerical figure; there is also a bronze plaque on the wall near the gate commemorating the Gaelic poet Alasdair Mhic Mhaigstir Alasdair MacDonald, who lived in *Rubha Arisaig* and is buried here in an unmarked grave. He was to have been taken to St Finan's Isle in Loch Shiel, like his father, but the weather was too stormy for the journey.

All this while, road and railway have kept each other company, but here they diverge and run to either side of a wide flat area of peat-moss called *Mointeach Mor*. It permits the railway, for the only stretch in the whole of its length, to run in anything like a straight line, but not for long. The road, A830, is anything but straight as it follows the vagaries of the shoreline. There are twelve or more coves and bays in the course of four miles from Arisaig to the Morar river estuary, and these are the famous white beaches of Morar. The sand is dazzling white silica, there are rocks and skerries off-shore, and for a coastline there is nothing to rival it, which is probably why there are so many caravan and camping sites along its foreshore; these are conveniently close to the sand and the sea, but tend to detract from the landscape's intrinsic beauty. There is also a nine-hole golf course south of Traigh House, on the machair between the beach and the Moss. If you can ignore the proliferation of caravans, you will enjoy the sight of the dark, indigo, rock-dotted sea contrasting with gleaming, silvery sands, backed by bright green machair and fringed with yellow irises. The sands themselves are yet uncluttered, unspoiled by beach-huts, ice-cream stalls and fun-fairs.

The Morar river is all of 200 yards long and consists mainly of falls, which have been harnessed by the Hydro-Electricity

Board, so are no longer the inspiring spectacle they once were. This tiny stretch of river is all that stops Loch Morar from being a sea-loch, and the extraordinary feature is, that as a fresh-water loch it is the deepest in Britain. There is another tiny neck of land between South Tarbet Bay on the loch's northern shore, and Tarbet on the southern shore of Loch Nevis; soundings in the middle of Loch Morar at this point have recorded 1,080 feet. This, naturally, is where the monster Morag lives.

There have been multifarious attempts to prove and to disprove the existence of a monster in Loch Ness, and there are roads on both sides of Loch Ness, and plenty of facilities to make investigation possible. Loch Morar on the other hand, bar a narrow lane that runs from Morar to Bracorina, just a mile or two along the northern shore, is quite roadless, so the monster has been left alone. Scientific findings, however, on Morag, were published in 1972, and she has been seen fairly often; she is described as being about thirty feet long, with a flat, snake-like head and dull brownish skin. She surfaces during long spells of warm, thundery weather, when the loch-water is still as glass. These were the conditions when in 1969 she surfaced beside the boat of two local fishermen, who had to beat her away with an oar.

Morag of course keeps well away from the shallower western end of the loch, near the river and estuary, and would never be visible to the water-sports enthusiasts who dash to and fro among the little islands off the northern shore. They operate mainly from *Bun an Loin*, a bay near Morar Lodge. The biggest of the islands is *Eilean Mor*, which until the '45 was the site of a Catholic seminary. After Culloden, Bishop Hugh MacDonald and old Lord Lovat took refuge there from the redcoats for a short while; discovered, they fled up the loch, but near the mouth of the Meoble river Lord Lovat was captured. He was eventually executed on Tower Hill in 1747; the bishop managed to shake off the pursuit and escaped to France, but the seminary was completely destroyed by the troops.

From Bracorina the lane diverges into tracks, one of which crosses the rugged, watery moorland, via stepping stones across *Lochan Stole*, to reach Stoul on Loch Nevis; the other continues as a path along the lochside to Brinacory, then Swordland, then either to Tarbet or the stone jetty on South Tarbet Bay. From here you can see the upper reaches of the loch; on one of those stuffy, storm-threatened, lowering days, when the midges torment you to madness and the water is clear to the bottom for many yards out, you may well catch a glimpse of the fearsome Morag. High hills and moorland surround the loch and no track goes near it, for east of it is wild Lochaber where no man lives or goes except on hunting expeditions after the red deer.

Morar is a village at the head of the tidal estuary of the Morar river; it was accorded a railway station, and that has brought it visitors, shops, a garage, a large hotel, two guest-houses and plenty of self-catering accommodation. A couple of miles farther along the main road, where it passes over the railway at Glasnacardoch, a track will take you up into the moorland to the beautiful little *Loch an Nostarie*, and from there, by way of the high *bealach* between *Carn a Gobhair* and *Carn mhic a'Ghille Chaim*, to another high and unvisited loch, *Loch Eiregoraidh*, where there are ruins of deserted cottages. Loch Nevis, the sea-loch to the north and east of the narrow ridge separating Loch Morar from it, is likewise roadless; the high hills to its north belong to the country of Knoydart, and at its head can be seen one of the sharpest peaks in Scotland, called by the Highlanders, thinking of sex as usual, *Sgurr na Ciche*, Hill of the Breast (3,412 feet).

Road, railway, and North Morar all terminate at Mallaig. Before the railway arrived in 1901 it was just a crofting township, no bigger than Mallaigvaig to its east. The harbour contributed to its prosperity, because fish landed there could be easily transported by rail, so Mallaig began to thrive. It has two hotels, the West Highland on the hill, and the Marine by the harbour; if you stay at the latter you will be well aware that the fish market starts early in the morning, and the catch is auctioned at the quayside. The local common herring, and black-backed gulls are well-informed of this fact, too.

Caledonian MacBrayne run ferries from Mallaig to the Small Isles, Rhum, Muck, Canna, and Eigg, four times a week, to Armadale in Skye every day, and to Kyle of Lochalsh three times a week. There is also a service to Castlebay in Barra on Sundays, which returns via Armadale. There are also smaller, passenger ferries to Inverie and to Camusrory at the head of Loch Nevis, in Knoydart: these are the only means of reaching Knoydart.

Mallaig is a busy, active little town, all set on the side of the hilly promontory west of its bay; the railway station, the ferry-piers, the fishing depot and boats, the screaming, flapping gulls, all combine to put the tourist in his place. He or she is welcome, but not essential. Mallaigvaig is still just a crofting township, as it was when Prince Charles was landed there early in the morning of 5 July, 1746, having been rowed over from Elgol in Skye during the night. Government troops were everywhere, a detachment quartered at Earnsaig at the mouth of Loch Nevis, not far away. Charles and his few companions slept in the open for three nights, then Charles and John MacKinnon rowed into Loch Nevis, only to encounter some troops rowing in the opposite direction. They pulled frantically, as if from Putney to Mortlake, landed at *Sron Raineach*, a steep and inhospitable shore not far from where they had started, climbed the steep *Aonach Mor* and dropped to sleep. They then decided to row across Loch Nevis to Scothouse in Inverie Bay to seek help from the Chief of Clanranald, then staying with MacDonald of Scothouse. Both of these had been keen supporters of Charles at first, but could offer no help now. Charles and MacKinnon returned to Mallaigvaig, thence to Borrodale House and the cave.

Knoydart too, like Moidart and Morar, is called *Garbh Chriochan*, the Rough Bounds, and in many ways it is far rougher; except for a very long and narrow track from the A87 by Loch Garry, far to the east, up Glen Garry and along the side of Loch Quoich to Kinlochhourn, on its north-eastern edge, it is completely inaccessible by road. It has, moreover, high mountains that line the two lochs Nevis and Hourn, and a minute population. The two lochs are both thirteen miles long, and their names mean, respectively, Heaven and Hell. Even on sunny days Loch Hourn is shadowed, since steep mountains rise on both sides to 3,000 feet and more, like *Ladhar Beinn*, 3,343 feet, the Forked Mountain (it is pronounced Larven), the most westerly Munro of the Scottish mainland. From the narrows at Barrisdale Bay, the inner loch is sharp-sided, straitened, and serpentine; on its Knoydart shore, for fully five months of the year, there is no sunshine.

Seton Gordon climbed to Loch Hourn from the *Gleann an Dubh Lochainn* which leads up from Inverie Bay, in what sounds like fairly average Knoydart weather: 'Heavy rain was falling as I climbed this track one September morning. The raindrops hissed upon the loch in the glen, refreshing the waters which were shrunken from many weeks of drought, and in the mist-filled corries the white waterfalls were awakening the music of the hills, silent for so long. At a height of rather more than 1,000 feet above the Atlantic the path reaches the watershed. Here, this sombre morning, I stood and looked down to the depths in which Loch Hourn lay. It resembled a lake of the infernal regions. Above it rose vast hills, grim, ghostly, and nebulous through banks of fog and soft-stealing rain-showers. Never in Scotland have I seen hills giving the impression of such vast size.'

So infernal a region must have its infernal occupants, and sure enough Loch Hourn harbours the dreadful Barrisdale Beast. 'Less than sixty years ago,' relates Alasdair Alpin MacGregor, 'there lived at Barrisdale, by the shores of Loch Hourn, a crofter who once encountered this monster. He assured his neighbours that this ungainly creature had gigantic wings, and was three-legged. He often saw it in flight across the hills of Knoydart, especially about Barrisdale itself; and he averred that on one occasion, when it was making for him with evil design, he rushed for the shelter of his cottage. As the crofter himself used to relate up until the time of his death, he just succeeded in slamming the door in the monster's face.' The Bull of Barrisdale, as it is also called, has been heard from one end of Loch Hourn to the other, because its roaring is louder and more fearsome than the belling of stags, and it travels rapidly: the roaring seems to come from one corrie, then from another far distant. One old man of Barrisdale, Ranald Mac-Master, quite often discovered its tracks, 'a paw and a claw', on the hills, and on the sandy beaches of Barrisdale Bay.

Loch Nevis is a different matter: the Knoydart mountains shelter it from the north, but the sun does appear over the much lower hills of Morar, so it is warmer and occasionally sunlit. It still receives 80–100 inches of rain a year. The chief centre of population is Inverie Bay, which is a wide and spacious bay, guarded by the mountain *Sgurr Coire Choinnichean*, and the headland *Rubha Raonuill*, and it therefore rejoices in the kind of luxuriant growth found at Loch Buie in Mull. Over a thousand people lived here until the Clearances, in Inverie, Sandaig, Doune, Airor, and Inverguseran; Knoydart then belonged to the MacDonells of Glengarry. After the '45 there was some emigration to Canada, but the land stayed in Glengarry's hands, even after Angus, the sixteenth Chief, sold all the rest and emigrated to Australia. He returned to Inverie and died in 1852, but by that time the population of 600 had thinned still further because of potato blight, and the failure of the herring to oblige by migrating in the usual numbers to Loch Nevis; both of these factors caused famine, so there was more emigration. Finally, Glengarry's widow evicted the remaining crofters to make way for sheep: 400 were turned out of Airor, Sundaig, Doune and Inverie, and driven aboard a transport ship, their cottages destroyed. She then sold Knoydart to a Lowland ironmaster.

266

Some people have returned to Knoydart; there is crofting, and there are sheep still, and the Forestry Commission employs several. There is also deer-stalking for those who can afford it. There are small roads for vans, tractors, and Forestry Landrovers, otherwise only the paths, starting with the one described and used by Seton Gordon, which goes from Inverie and follows the Inverie river up *Gleann an Dubh Lochain* to Barrisdale Bay. The second main track turns off this glen eastward, along *Gleann Meadail*, which climbs to a pass of 1,709 feet, then falls to Kinlochnevis, where at Camusrory there is a Mountain Rescue kit. There is another track from Inverie which goes north over *Mam Uidhe*, a hill of 445 feet, to *Gleann na Guiserein*, a wide valley from the base of *Ladhar Bheinn* to Inverguseran on the western coast.

There is accommodation available in Knoydart nowadays: there is the Pier House Guest-house at Inverie, which has four rooms; a cottage advertising bed-and-breakfast, and a bungalow for rent, also at Inverie. Otherwise you have to camp.

East of the Rough Bounds, the country of Lochaber stretches away to the Great Glen and beyond; between the only two major roads, A830 along Loch Eil and A87 through Glen Shiel, lie the parallel Lochs Arkaig, Quoich, and Garry. East of the Great Glen the main road from Fort William to Inverness, A82, runs alongside the railway to Spean Bridge where, after a straight of more than four miles, it does a violent turn and doubles up the hill. Lochaber extends northward here to the Corrieyairack Pass, used by Montrose and his men to spring his surprise on Argyll in 1645. It is the country of MacDonald of Keppoch, and it includes the two Glens Roy and Gloy, both comprising the Glen Roy Nature Reserve, and both famous for their so-called Parallel Roads. These look like trackways scoured out like terraces on the hillsides, precisely the same height each side of the glen, and one above the other at some distance. They are best seen in Glen Roy where they show up green and wide at the southern end, in three bands, at 857 feet, 1,068, and 1,149 respectively. They were not, of course, man-made: no man ever made roads so symmetrically perfect. At the end of the last Ice Age a great glacier, flowing north from the Ben Nevis massif, dammed the outlets from the glens. The springing mountain waters formed deep lakes; as the ice retreated, or as breaches were made in it, the lake-water receded, leaving behind the beaches they had made on the hillsides. More hundreds of years passed, then another breach, another subsidence, and another beach. The Parallel Roads are the beaches.

When you have charged up the winding hill from Spean Bridge you arrive at a high, windy plateau, and immediately on your left there is a large memorial consisting of the figures of three men. They represent the Commandos who were trained in the Great Glen for their daring exploits in the 1939–45 war. The figures were designed by Scott Sutherland, they were raised in 1952, and the site was chosen by the Rev. John Birkbeck, M. C., Padre to the Commandos, who was one of those asked to find somewhere appropriate for it. This report appeared in the Glasgow Sunday Post, 2 April, 1989: 'Last week, at 80, this stalwart and fearless man died in Aberdeen where he ministered for many years. I have many memories of him – his piercing eyes that saw straight through humbug and hypocrisy, his ceaseless travels, his pen that kept writing far into the night, his refusal to be defeated by illness, his gentleness with the old and the sick. And for me, the memorial on that windswept moor is his memorial too – a true soldier of faith who fought to the end for all he believed in.'

The three commandos are gazing towards the mist-shrouded Ben Nevis; the road directly beneath them turns from the A82 to the foot of Loch Lochy, and then towards Loch Arkaig in the hills; near Loch Arkaig is Achnacarry House, home of Cameron of Lochiel since 1660. That is, the site is, because the original castle was wrecked by Cumberland's happy Vandals in 1746 after Culloden, and the present house was built on the site in 1802 by the twenty-second Chief. It was burnt during the

1939–45 war, but restored in 1952, and is still the home of Cameron of Lochiel. 'It is', says W. H. Murray, 'the only fine building in Lochaber.' It is not open to the public. Loch Arkaig, above the house, is still relatively undefiled by the hand of man, except of those who put caravans in proximity to it.

The A82 road keeps to the east side of Loch Lochy, which is much set about with caravan sites and battalions of self-catering chalets, and crosses the Caledonian Canal at Laggan. Just here, in the mid-sixteenth-century, there was an example of the fierce clan feuding which broke out when the steadying influence of the MacDonald Lords of the Isles was removed. There was a terrible battle between the MacDonalds of Clanranald and the Frasers of Lovat, over the right to certain disputed lands. 800 men entered the fray: it was a hot July day, so they fought in their shifts, and the affair has been remembered as the Battle of the Shirts; at dusk that day all but fourteen of them were dead, including the Chief and eighty gentlemen of Clan Fraser.

As the road passes along the western side of Loch Oich, a monument comes into sight, called *Tobar nan Ceann*, the Well of the Heads. It was raised by the twenty-seventh Chief of Glengarry in 1812, a pyramid on a square column, and it recalls another horrific Highland story, inscribed on each of the four sides of the column in Gaelic, English, French, and Latin. In 1663 young MacDonald of Keppoch and his two brothers were murdered in their own castle, which stood on *Tom Beag*, a rounded hillock where the Roy river joins the Spean. The culprits were guests, and some were kinsmen; Ian Lom, Keppoch's bard, sought help from Sir James MacDonald of Sleat (of whom the Keppoch MacDonalds were a sept) and the murderers were rounded up. They were rounded off, too, and their seven heads, having been washed in the well by Loch Oich, were presented to the Chief of the MacDonells of Glengarry in his castle, nearby. The well no longer exists, because the road was widened, but the seven carved heads can be seen adorning the pyramid on the monument.

At Invergarry the road leaves the Great Glen and swings inland, above the MacDonells' old castle on *Creag Fhithich*, Rock of the Raven. It was built in 1602, after their major seat at Strome was blown up in a feud with the MacKenzies. The castle sheltered Prince Charles before and after Culloden and was wrecked and burnt by Cumberland's men. A mansion was built to replace it, and this is now the Glengarry Castle Hotel, a luxurious haven for those whose tastes run to deer-stalking, grouse-shooting, and salmon fishing. There is also the Invergarry Hotel, a little farther down the scale.

The Glen Garry road is good and fast, which is rather a pity because Loch Garry, girt with birches, rowans and oaks, is beautiful. Mid-way along the loch, a minor road leaves the A87 to the left, towards Tomdoun; it runs alongside a big hydro-electric scheme, Loch Quoich, and after a long, long time, reaches Kinlochhourn and the Barrisdale Forest. The A87 swings away from the loch up into the hills, which are here devoid of trees, bleak and windswept; as it dips and climbs high above Loch Loyne, if you look westward you may see an endless panorama of mountains and glens, knowing that it is all wilderness, where birds and animals may live undisturbed — that is, until some of the guests at the Invergarry Castle Hotel get at them.

The A87 meets the A887 from Glen Moriston, and at this T-junction you turn left for the long journey down Glen Shiel, first skirting the north side of Loch Cluanie. At the far end of the loch, where there is a dam, the Cluanie Inn offers the only human company in the entire glen. The road, I must own, is a good deal better than when I first motored along it, with two very good old friends, in 1957; it was then single-track with passing places, and since even then there was a fair amount of traffic both ways, progress deteriorated into a kind of Musical Chairs, in and out of the passing places. It took ages. Now, before you know it, you are in among the mountains again beyond Loch Cluanie, through a rugged glen between high hills, and to the north are the series of peaks called the Five Sisters of Kintail. They rise frowning over the Shiel River from Cluanie Forest down to Loch Duich, as they have ever since dim unrecorded times when they first took up their stations.

It happened that a man of those parts, living at the head of Loch Duich, had seven beautiful daughters, but as hardly anyone else had settled in Kintail in those days, they had no boy-friends and no hope of husbands, and the father, long since a widower, worried about their future. Then one night there was a great storm, and the girls went down to the lochside in the morning to see what the wind and waves had brought in. There was a ship, battered and smashed by the tempest, limping in to the beach. The girls, keeping an eye on it, wrapped their shawls over their heads to look like old women, and searched for driftwood on the beach. Presently two young men came ashore from the ship in a small boat, saw the girls, and wondered at such marvellous luck; they were good-looking young fellows, they were Irishmen, and so they very soon won the girls' confidence.

The young men were taken to the family home, where the father was pleased with them, for they seemed to be of good background and breeding; taking care not to let any of the other sailors know how lucky they were, they came for breakfast every morning until the ship was repaired and ready for sea again. By that time they had taken a great fancy for the two youngest girls, which upset the five elders who thought that the eldest two should be the first to have husbands. The sailors would have only the little ones, however, and asked the father for their hands in marriage. The father was delighted, but worried that the others were jealous; the sailors told him to be patient, because they had five brothers at home whom they would send as soon as possible to be husbands to the others.

They took the two girls and sailed away, and the five watched carefully each day for signs of a ship coming, bearing the five brothers. None came, so the father went to the Sage of Kintail, who had the Sight (he was the seventh son of a seventh son), and asked him when the brothers were coming. 'I see no brothers,' he said, 'they are their mother's only sons.' The father, greatly distressed, told the daughters this news, but they refused to believe him. They became impossible to live with, so the father went again to the Sage to ask his advice. 'Tell them,' said the Sage, 'that if they must waste their time waiting for these brothers, who will never come, and they want to remain beautiful, here is what they must do to catch some other young men who may come from a different direction. They must go to the head of the loch and stand there in a row, warm in summer, cold in winter, looking out all round so that wheresoever their suitors come from they will see them.'

So the Five Sisters of Kintail did so, and they have been there ever since, always beautiful, always admired, and still waiting.

At Shiel Bridge there is a turning signposted 'Scenic route to Glenelg' to the left. There are also camping and caravan sites, and a Youth Hostel, for there is wonderful walking and climbing country hereabouts. The Scenic Route climbs quickly, at 1:6 into the Ratagan Forest, to cross the Mam Ratagan Pass, and from here is a superb view back into the glen, with the Five Sisters immobile on the far side.

This was the site of the only battle of the little-known Second Jacobite Rebellion of 1719. James Stuart, the Old Pretender, described as James III of England and VIII of Scotland, had found an ally in King Philip V of Spain, who provided him with an army of 5,000 men, and arms for another 30,000; they sailed from Corunna, but were dispersed by England's ally, the weather, which produced a storm of singular severity. Only two Spanish frigates completed the voyage, bringing 300 of the white-coated soldiers to the shores of Loch Duich, below Eilean Donan Castle. Their Jacobite allies consisted only of Lochiel's Camerons, some Atholl men and MacKenzies, and the Mac-Gregors under Rob Roy himself. The Government troops occupied the narrow gorge of Glen Shiel, defended it with resolution and some mortars, and soon found that the High-landers had little liking for this kind of fighting. They drifted away, leaving the Spaniards to surrender. They left their name, as a memento, attached to the first of the Five Sisters, which was from then on called *Sgurr nan Spainteach*.

Over the top of the Mam Ratagan Pass, the road plunges down Glen More to Glenelg. Boswell and Johnson came this way, with a Highland gentlemen called Hay, who thought it only right that Johnson should be entertained on the way. He 'led the horse's head, talking to Dr Johnson as much as he could; and (having heard him, in the forenoon, express a pastoral pleasure on seeing the goats browsing) just when the Doctor was uttering his displeasure, the fellow cried, with a very Highland accent, "See such pretty goats!" Then he whistled, *whu!* and made them jump. Little did he conceive what Doctor Johnson was. Here now was a common ignorant Highland clown imagining that he could divert, as one does a child – *Dr Samuel Johnson*! The ludicrousness, absurdity, and extraordinary contrast between what the fellow fancied, and the reality, was truly comick.'

At that time there were barracks at Bernera, in the flat mouth of Glen More, 'but there was only a serjeant and a few men there.' They went to the inn at Glenelg. 'A maid shewed us up stairs into a room damp and dirty, with bare walls, a variety of bad smells, a coarse black greasy fir table, and forms of the same kind; and out of a wretched bed started a fellow from his sleep, like Edgar in *King Lear*, "Poor Tom's a cold."

'This inn was furnished with not a single article that we could either eat or drink . . .'

Today the Glenelg Inn, with nine bedrooms, has just about everything, is open from April to September, and even Dr Johnson would be well entertained there. Between Glen More and Loch Hourn, the Glenelg mountains are massive and forbidding; the highest is *Beinn Sgritheall*, 3,194 feet, one of the range that makes Loch Hourn so cheerless a sight. Despite the inhospitable nature of so much of this interior, however, there is evidence that plenty of human life managed to exist here in the Iron Age, because there are no less than two excellently preserved brochs, and another more delapidated on the shores of Loch Alsh.

Take the road south from Glenelg village along the Sound of Sleat and turn left at Eilanreach House up *Gleann Beag*; Dun Telve is a couple of miles up the glen road, and Dun Troddan a quarter of a mile beyond that. The best example of a broch is that of Mousa in Shetland, but these two are the second and third largest respectively. Dun Telve's walls stand to thirty-three feet, Dun Troddan's to twenty-five; both have passages, stairs, and rooms within the thickness of the walls, but Dun Troddan is only a half-section. No mortar was used, the stones are laid without gaps so that the outer surface is unbroken, the outer wall is concave (it slopes inward and then out again to become vertical), and the galleries within the walls spiral up to the top: altogether a superb piece of craftmanship by the Iron Age masons, who performed this feat at some time between the first century BC and the late first century AD. Their exact purpose is unknown; there is also a chambered cairn, and a fort called Dun Grugaig farther up the same glen, into which cattle could be driven and in which women and children could take shelter, for the inner courtyards of the brochs are far too small for that purpose. Probably they were watch-towers and temporary refuges.

The road down Glen More goes on to the ferry across the strait to Kylerhea; Skye is only 500 yards across the water, but the ferry runs only in the summer months. Johnson and Boswell crossed to Armadale, a much longer voyage, and according to a local story, they were lucky not to be chased by a monstrous sea-serpent which frequents the straits. A former minister of Glenelg, who died in 1875, had a yacht and often sailed it, but one day, in the company of his two daughters, another clergyman, and a boy called Donald MacCrimmon, his boat was nearly swamped by a huge monster which reared up out of the sea right next to them. It was 'as big and round as a herring barrel, and of great length. And it went wriggling up and down through the water, zig-zag, right and left like.' The serpent chased them to the mouth of Loch Hourn, then disappeared; they landed at Arnisdale and stayed there overnight. In the morning one of the daughters insisted on walking home, although it was thirteen miles. The others embarked in the yacht. At the mouth of Loch Hourn they again encountered the monster, but managed to evade it and reach home safely. A Skye man from Kylerhea saw it, too: 'Yess, yess, one tay I saw the fearful head of the peast go town the Kyle; and inteet it wass a week pefore hiss tail passed.' No wonder the ferry only runs in the summer, even now.

The most often-used ferry service runs from Kyle of Lochalsh to Kyleakin; from the Shiel Bridge at the head of Loch Duich you continue along the A87 on the northern shore of the loch. There is a narrow meeting-place of three lochs at the far end, where Loch Duich meets Loch Long and both spread out into Loch Alsh; situated exactly where activities could be spotted in all three, there stands Eilean Donan Castle.

There was a vitrified fort on the site when St Donan, who founded a monastery on Eigg in 616, was murdered along with fifty of his monks by pirates, probably Vikings. A castle was built in about 1230 by King Alexander II to combat the Norsemen who held Skye; when Alexander III had wrested the isles from them, he gave the castle to Colin Fitzgerald, son of the Earl of Desmond, for his services at the battle of Largs in 1263 when the Norsemen were beaten. The Earl of Ross granted Kintail to the MacKenzies in 1463, and this is the earliest proof of the Clan's tenure of the castle, but the MacRaes, who had migrated from wildest Wester Ross to Kintail and Glenelg in the fourteenth century and become firm allies of Clan Kenneth, were made hereditary constables of Eilean Donan in 1520.

In 1553 the MacRaes had to prove their worth when Donald Gorm MacDonald of Sleat launched an attack on the castle with

Eilean Donan Castle

400 men in galleys; the Constable, Duncan MacRae, shot him with an arrow, and the armada dispersed. The next excitement was the Jacobite rebellion of 1719, when the castle was its headquarters; three Royal Naval frigates sailed into Loch Alsh and bombarded the castle, reduced it to ruins, captured what was left of its Spanish garrison and all the stores, and the battle at Shiel Bridge finished off the rest. The castle remained in ruins, disintegrating slowly, until the MacRae family began its restoration by virtually rebuilding it in 1912; it was finished in 1932 and is now open to the public.

At Dornie there is a bridge over the entrance to Loch Long, and at Ardelve on the far side, there is a way of reaching, after many hard miles and a superabundance of determined and energetic walking and climbing, the Hidden Falls of Glomach, the most spectacular in all Great Britain. Their source is at 1,200 feet, from a loch above Glen Affric. The stream flows north for three miles, then plunges 500 feet down a chasm. W.

H. Murray, in *The West Highlands of Scotland*, describes exactly how you may see them.

'The public road goes five miles up Loch Long through farmland to end at the foot of Glen Elchaig, half a mile short of Killilan House. The second stage is rough going through thick alder woods. the road is gravelly, full of potholes, and marked "Private" at the start. But the owner of Killilan House grants motorists permission to drive five miles on to the *Allt a'Ghlomaich*. For the rest, boots are essential. You cross the river Elchaig by a footbridge built by the Rights of Way Society, and with 800 feet to climb follow a path up the left bank of the Glomach burn. The hillside above looks grassy, with some birch-scrub in the deep-cut ravine, but the path is boggy in the lower part, then rocky where it traverses the flank of the ravine. The burn below has several brown pools under small waterfalls – each a tempting bathing spot on hot days. A point is at last reached where the top of the Falls of Glomach at 1,100 feet may be glimpsed, and now the track divides.

'One branch keeps high on the easier, outer slopes to the top of the great chasm. This track does not give any good view of the fall. For that you must climb down a very steep zig-zag track on the west flank of the chasm to a platform, from which the upper and middle part of the fall can be well seen. The second branch is a lower track suitable only for mountaineers. It traverses into the upper chasm on precipitous, rocky, and grassy flanks. The route is often exposed and dangerous unless one is wearing climbing boots and the weather is dry. Do not use the route in wet weather. The narrow track ends on a horizontal rock-rib, from which one suddenly looks down into the cauldron under the great waterfall. The river comes over the brink in one gigantic spout of eighty feet, hits the top of a buttress, and there splits with deafening roar into two falls, which in heavy spate may coalesce. These plunge 220 feet in weighty curtains down the smooth-faced buttress to a misted rock-pool, then on again to a fifty-foot fall that cannot be seen. The cauldron formation is unique in Scotland in the combination of its hidden character with extreme narrowness and great depth.'

The Highlands keep their secrets and will not yield them to all the world.

The A87 from Ardelve follows the shores of Loch Alsh through some country which will be described in a later chapter, and arrives at the railway terminus and ferry-port of Kyle of Lochalsh. The ferry has been operating from Kyle to Kyleakin in Skye ever since the railway arrived, late in the last century. Some say, unkindly, so have the present ferry-boats. The boats are old, occasionally break down, and there are often long lines of cars and lorries waiting to cross, on both sides. A bridge is in the offing, a bridge that will replace the ferries, keep the flow of traffic rolling, and gladden the hearts of islanders who want to pay the same prices for everything they have to import as the mainlanders. Opposition comes, not unnaturally, from the ferry crews, from the conservation lobby, from those who think that an island ought to remain an island without a tangible link with the mainland, and from those who think that the volume of traffic in the tourist season might swell to unmanageable proportions, straining to the limit Skye's road system and means of accommodation.

The ferry fares are high, but one of the principal problems, that of the eternal question of money, inevitably arose: who would pay for the bridge? The Minister of State for Scotland visited Skye in early August, 1989, and was immediately stuck in the long queue of cars waiting to board the ferry and cross the Kyle; the engine of one of the old ferries had broken down, a smaller replacement could not cope, and at one point the line of cars stretched three miles back along the A87. The Minister announced that the Scottish Office would not oppose the scheme, but somebody else would have to pay for it. If built by a private company, the bridge would have to be paid for by those using it, at least at the going ferry-rate. Islanders objected, pointing out that other bridges, such as

278

those of the Tay, the Forth, and the Erskine across the Clyde, had tolls in pence, not pounds. The Highland Regional Council approved the scheme, but stressed that they would press for half-price concessions for local people (which they get on the ferries), and a Scottish Office spokesman said that the bridge would require a special Hybrid Bill to be drafted, and that construction could begin in 1992. After more debate and yet more delay, the first pillars of the Skye Bridge were put in place in September, 1993.

15

Isle of Skye

From the mainland, Skye appears to be entirely mountainous: the great brown hills rise massively, impenetrably, above its shores and sweep down into the sea. The little ferry heaves up its ramp with much clanking and chugs the short distance across to Kyleakin. To the left of the concrete slipway you can see a little ruined tower on a knoll: this is *Caisteal Maol*, built in the thirteenth-century by the daughter of the King of the Norsemen so that tolls could be extracted from all ship-captains using the strait. But she married a MacKinnon, so instead it became a MacKinnon fortress. It was probably originally three storeys high, and the walls are still nine feet thick.

There are two theories concerning the origin of Kyleakin's name: one is that it was named from Acunn, a follower of Fionn MacCumhail (Kylerhea, the strait between Skye and Glenelg, was named from Accun's brother Riadh); the Fingalian heroes fought the early Vikings in the third-century, or thereabouts. The other theory also concerns Vikings, and their King Haakon, who gave his name to Kyle Haakon.

Alexander III was doing his best to expel Norse influence and dominion from his kingdom. He had sent the Earl of Ross to harry the Norse garrison of Skye, which he had accomplished without undue concern for Human Rights, Women's Lib, or

280

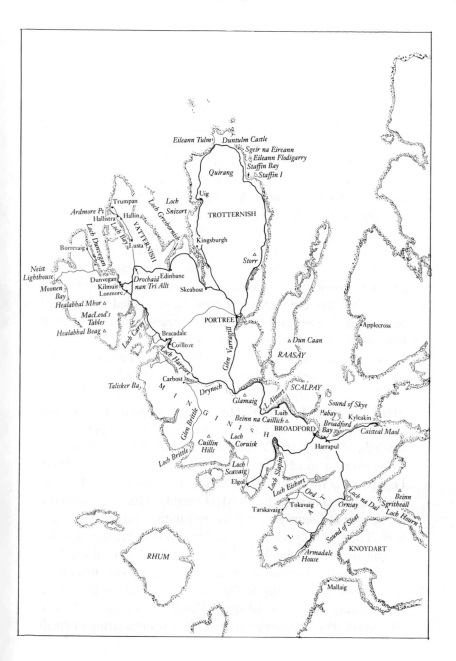

Prevention of Cruelty to Children, to say nothing of the tabloid press. King Haakon, taking umbrage, set forth with his longship fleet to teach Alexander a lesson. He sailed from Kirkwall in Orkney in July, 1263, and when he anchored in the Sound of Skye, between the island and the mainland, north of the Kyle, he was met by King Magnus of Man and sundry other local adherents. With his armada thus augmented he set sail for the Firth of Clyde, but the weather was at its Highland worst, and it was not until September that they entered the Firth. On 30 September a gale split the fleet apart, even tearing up the anchors of the king's huge ship. Store-ships were driven ashore at Largs on the Ayrshire coast and their crews assailed by Scottish archers. In the morning Haakon brought his ship and some of his men ashore, to find that all Alexander's army was drawn up on the ridge. There was a brief and indecisive encounter, then the Norsemen returned to their ships and sailed away. That was the battle of Largs. Haakon died in Kirkwall during that winter, and his successor negotiated a withdrawal from his Scottish territories three years later.

Skye is sixty miles long, but nowhere are you more than five miles from the sea, because it is deeply indented by sea-lochs which form six large peninsulas. The Gaels called it *Eilean a Sgiathanach*, the Winged Isle; the Vikings called it *Skuyö*, Cloud Island: either way, the name sounds like Skye. Its population, the bulk of whom are farmers and crofters, live on the coastal strips because much of the interior, like the rest of the West Highlands, is rocky and infertile. There is a good deal of forest, some of which belongs to the MacDonalds of Sleat, some to the MacLeods of Dunvegan, and the rest to the Forestry Commission. There is only one town, and that is Portree, the capital.

The road from the Kyleakin ferry, A850, runs along high ground on the shore of the Sound of Skye, passing Broadford Aerodrome, and dipping to the lower reaches about Broadford Bay, looking out to the island of Pabay. Broadford (in Gaelic *An-t'ath-leathan*, meaning broad ford) is really a string of small connected townships, starting with Harrapul; it is a good centre for Skye, because at Harrapul there is the Hebridean Hotel and the Isle of Skye Field Centre, where there are rooms to let, and at Broadford, the Broadford Hotel, a guest-house, and fifteen bed-and-breakfast houses. It is also attractive, backed to the west by the slopes of *Beinn na Caillich*, 2,403 feet, beyond it the Red Hills, and before it the wide bay, a haven for all manner of wild waterfowl whether the tide is in or out. Beyond little green Pabay you can see the mountains of Applecross on the mainland.

To visit the most southerly of the peninsulas, Sleat, you can take the A851 road from near Harrapul; it runs first through heathery moorland, devoid of habitation or even sheep, down to *Loch na Dal*, an inlet from the Sound of Sleat. From here and from Duisdalemore are superb views of *Beinn Sgritheall* in Glenelg, and of the wild hills of Knoydart, across the glittering Sound, and on either side of arctic Loch Hourn: high, dark, grim hills that seem to defy penetration.

From Ornsay Island, where at the head of the tiny bay there is a pier and an inn, the road runs inland for a while, emerging on the shore again at Knock Bay, where you can see the ivy-grown remains of Camus Castle. When Norway ceded the Isles to Scotland in 1266, Skye was granted to Angus MacDonald, then styled King of the Isles, who gave it in turn to Leod, the son of the Norse King Olav the Black of Man, and Clan MacLeod, his descendants, held both the island and this castle until the late fourteenth-century, when Clan Donald took Sleat back from them and re-occupied Camus Castle. At some unspecified time it is said to have been attacked by the MacLeods and defended successfully by a lady, *Mairi a'Caisteal*. She is unlikely to have been able, had she been there, to have defied the assault on it made in 1690 by Royal Naval warships, sent by William III to bring in the recalcitrant Sir Donald MacDonald. The ships bombarded Camus and MacDonald's house at Armadale, and then a landing-party burned them; unfortunately for the sailors, they were then ambushed by the irate MacDonalds and hanged from makeshift gibbets, fashioned from their own oars.

Armadale House remained in ruins until 1815 when the second Lord MacDonald built a new residential castle on the site. This also is now ruined, but has been carefully adapted as a 'Sculptured Ruin', which means that it has been sufficiently propped up not to fall down on the heads of passing visitors to the Clan Donald Centre, established in one of the former outhouses. It is surrounded by beautiful gardens, with many exotic and splendid trees, and terraces with benches from which to admire the view across the Sound of Sleat of the Knoydart hills. The Centre takes the form of an exhibition, with written panels, of the rise and fall of the Clan Donald Lordship of the Isles.

Much has been said already about the importance of this Lordship, confirmed by Bruce out of the quasi-autonomous Kingship of the Isles, created for the grandson of Somerled. What it achieved, for the space of nearly 200 years, was a period of comparative peace in the turbulent history of clan rivalry, in which the Lord exerted such power that he could intervene in quarrels and impose discipline from above. The Lordship evolved as an entirely Gaelic society with a thriving and colourful literature, art and culture, with its own tribal way of life and its own land-based economy. It was the political aspirations of the fifteenth-century Lords which stretched the patience of the Stewart Kings of Scotland to breaking-point and led them eventually to enrol the ambitious Campbells as their lieutenants. The Lordship was abolished in 1493, the Campbells were ascendant. It was from this time on, however, that the lawlessness of the Highlanders broke out in long-standing, festering feuds. The result of this anarchy was that the whole Gaelic society came under pressure from royal authority, from Lowland *mi-run mor nan Gall*, from the uncompromising, ruthless Covenanters. Adherence to the House of Stuart (the French spelling), resulting in the Glencoe massacre, the Jacobite risings and the final catastrophe of Culloden, could be viewed as more a desperate defence of the Gaelic world against hostile enemies anxious for its destruction, than for any real sympathy for the wretched Stuarts. In the end, the allegiance brought destruction more swiftly and sweepingly than if they had toed the official line. The condign punishments that followed Culloden, including the proscription, began the extinction, the Clearances completed it. Very few natural Gaelic speakers remain on the mainland, and only in Barra and the Uists is it spoken at home by the majority. The place-names remain, and the tiny remnant of the people, but as a living language Gaelic is almost defunct. To the bards of Clan Donald it all began with the collapse of the Lordship of the Isles. One of them, Giolla Colum mac an Ollaimh, wrote in the sixteenth-century book of the Dean of Lismore:

> It is no joy without Clan Donald,
> it is no strength to be without them;
> the best race in the round world:
> to them belongs every godly man.

The old stable-block near the entrance to Armadale Castle has been skilfully converted into a shop, a restaurant, a house, and two flats to rent. Down in Armadale Bay there is a steamer-pier where the ferry from Mallaig docks; there is also the Armadale Hotel with an annexe in the shape of an ancient stone cottage, roofed with corrugated iron, functioning as a public bar. A scattering of other cottages, and a Youth Hostel flying St Andrew's cross complete the scene, with some boats moored in the bay, and the inescapable, immaculately dressed gulls gliding easily over the bright, gleaming water.

Stone cottages are of uncertain date: in Johnson's time 'the houses in general are made of turf, covered with grass', as Boswell reports, so perhaps these are more recent than 1773. There is a small turning left from the A853 where it encounters the A851 (you have to return the same way along the coast of

Sleat since little further progress can be made), which climbs up to the totally uninhabited interior, and descends precipitately to its rugged northern shore with such immediacy that derangement of driver and destruction of vehicle appear to be the intention. If you pass this test of skill, which could try the nerve of any Grand Prix hero, then the reward (on a fine day) is the grandest view in the island. The whole range of the dark, jagged Cuillin greets you across Loch Eishort, and away in the sea westward, the mountains of Rhum. The Cuillin are not often seen, for they appear only rarely from their habitual cloud cover (the reason for the Norse name for the island); so when they are visible the sheer drama of their stark, dark, saw-tooth outline is the more intense.

At Tarskavaig on this coast there is a large crofting community and plenty of sheep which normally inhabit the middle of the road, with little intention of yielding to entreaties to move. There are new cottages among the old, and more yet at Tokavaig where the shore is of red sandstone. Here, on a blunt bluff with a good defensible position, is a tumbled old castle, whose broken walls are almost indistinguishable from the rock. It is Dunscaith Castle, and once it was the power-base of the MacDonalds of Sleat. It was previously Norse, and its name derives from one Queen Sgathach who is said to have instituted there a kind of ladies' military academy, to a hundred of whom at a time she taught the arts of war. One version says that her castle had 'seven great doors and seven great windows between every two doors of them, and thrice fifty couches between every two windows of them, and thrice fifty handsome marriageable girls in scarlet cloaks and in beautiful and blue attire attending and waiting upon Sgathach.' Viewing the ruins, one's imagination is somewhat cramped for space to envisage such a building: Buckingham Palace just would not fit on the rock. There are plenty of legends about Sgathach, including some of the hero Cuchulainn, Knight of the Red Branch of Ulster, and one in which Sgathach and her Amazon maids watched a Viking galley being shipwrecked on the shore below them; they rounded up the survivors, and tied each one by his long hair to a tree, leaving them swinging there until they died.

An arched bridge links the promontory of the castle with the mainland. It should not be crossed, as it is unsafe.

At Ord there is a small hotel, looking down on the little islets of the bay, and the majestic mountain-mass opposite; here you turn sharply right and follow the valley of the Ord river back to the A851.

Another road from Broadford, A881, skirts the flanks of *Beinn na Caillich* and makes for Loch Slapin, where the Red Hills and the Black Cuillin face each other across the loch; the Red Hills are round-topped and formed of crumbly pink granite, and the Cuillin, although also igneous, are spiky and dark, their colour varying according to the light from pale grey to dark brown and plum black. The western side of Loch Slapin is formed by another peninsula called Strathaird, dividing the loch from Loch Scavaig on the western side. The road goes to Elgol, and nearby is yet another Prince Charles's Cave, for here the Prince was guided by the elderly Chief of the MacKinnons, the clan which had held Strathaird since the fourteenth-century. From here in July, 1746, Charles made his way back to the Morar coast, where he hid in the cave near Borrodale House.

A little lane from Elgol crosses to the east coast of Strathaird, facing Sleat, where under the cliffs below the crofts of Glasnak-ille is Spar Cave, which Scott, in *The Lord of the Isles*, calls

> . . . mermaid's alabaster grot,
> Who bathes her limbs in sunless well,
> Deep in Straithaird's enchanted cell.

It used to have semi-opaque stalactites, but most of them have been vandalised by greedy tourists of other years.

Loch Scavaig is on the southern shores of the Cuillin, where the waters of Loch Coruisk descend from them to the sea. Dark blue, glittering with a million silver lights, shines Loch Coruisk in fine weather, beneath the grey heights; no pleasure to see lake or peaks when the dark clouds gather, as Scott says:

> Nor tree, nor shrub, nor plant, nor flower,
> Nor aught of vegetative power,
> The weary eye may ken.
> For all is rocks at random thrown,
> Black waves, bare crags, and banks of stone.

There are other approaches to the Cuillin, easier than this, but few more spectacular.

Go north from Broadford, on the A850 past the road to the Youth Hostel and through the forest on the lower slopes of *Beinn na Caillich*; it skirts the sea-coast so that you have good views of the island Scalpay, then follows the inward thrust of Loch Ainort through Luib, where there is a thatched cottage museum, furnished and set out with the articles and style of the early twentieth-century. It is on the loch-side, just below the road, and noticeable because thatches in this end of the twentieth-century are rare. From Loch Ainort the road winds up and over the shoulder of great, grey, glum Glamaig and past its frightful sheer face, and down to Sconser at Loch Sligachan, where there is a nine-hole golf course and a ferry to Raasay.

The island of Raasay's southern end, and its pointed peak, Dun Caan, can be seen across the narrows; the ferry is small, and has recently had its weight-load reduced from a maximum twenty-four tons to eighteen, because there has been no time to strip its paint. It is painted twice a year, and if it cannot be blasted off it just accumulates, and of course so does the weight. When blasted, it can shed as much as two tons of excess thickness. Johnson and Boswell visited Raasay, which Boswell says is fifteen miles long. 'This island,' he says, 'has abundance of black cattle, sheep, and goats; a good many horses, which are used for ploughing, carrying out dung, and other works of husbandry. I believe the people never ride. There are indeed no roads through the island, unless a few detached beaten tracks deserve that name. Most of the houses are upon the shore; so that all the people have little boats, and catch fish.' Boswell was told that 'in 1745, a hundred fighting men were reviewed here . . . They returned home all but fourteen.' It is hard to imagine such populous activity on the island now.

At the head of Loch Sligachan the river of the same name enters the sea, and shortly above its entry is the famous Sligachan Hotel, where H. V. Morton stayed. He describes his sensations after rising on his first morning there, in *In Search of Scotland*: 'The inn is built at an angle which, when you stand on the steps, cuts off the view to the right. You remain there, mesmerised by Glamaig, in whose shadow you stand. He is in the shape of Vesuvius. He looks as though he might at any moment give a terrible explosion and belch flame. You take a step towards him. You clear the boundary wall, and instantly out of the corner of your eye become aware of something tremendous to your right. You turn . . . the sight of the "Black" Cuillins hits you like a blow in the face!'

The Cuillin, which are not named from the Celtic hero Cuchullin but from the Old Norse *Kjöllen*, keel-shaped, form a seven-mile horseshoe, in which there are twenty-four sharp peaks. They are formed from two kinds of rock, a coarsely crystalline gabbro which is tough, and a smooth basalt, slippery when wet. Both were components of lava flows, but the basalt cooled quickly, the gabbro slowly, from which it acquired its crystalline texture. The gabbro, at first beneath the other's surface, was then gradually exposed by water erosion, was more resistant than the basalt, and remained in the form of the twenty-four jagged peaks. 'The traverse of the main ridge,' says W. H. Murray, 'gives 10,000 feet of ascent and the best day's mountaineering in Britain.' More than half of the peaks are invisible from the outside, you need to climb up to see them.

Another road meets the A850 at the Sligachan Hotel, called A863. If you follow it along the course of the Drynoch river to the head-waters of Loch Harport, and then turn left on B8009 and from that even sharper left, you can climb over some rocky, sheep-infested moorland, from which you can have superb views of the Cuillin, and find your way to Glen Brittle. The Cuillin never look benign, even on bright sunny days they are awesome and impressive, their serrated outline, snow-capped to late spring, shining like sharks' teeth. Glen Brittle is fertile, in direct contrast to the stony wilderness immediately to its east, and the Brittle river emerges at a sandy bay at the head of Loch Brittle. There is a Youth Hostel, and the grassy plain near the water's edge is usually dotted with the blues and oranges and greens of climbers' tents, for this has taken over from the Sligachan Hotel as a favourite starting-point and base for exploration of the mountains, at least seven of which are Munros. The sand on Loch Brittle's shores is black and fine, a ground-down basalt which does not come from the Cuillin. Under the shadow of the looming *Sgurr Alasdair* and his grim brothers, the climbers cook their suppers, ease off their boots, sniff the fresh breeze from the loch and swap mountain stories. The gulls plane over them, watching for scraps, and impervious to the tales: they have heard them all before.

The peninsula projecting westward from the Cuillin is called Minginish; there are a few other minor roads serving its crofting communities, and one which reaches Talisker Bay on its west coast; the famous Talisker Distillery is at Carbost on Loch Harport, making one of the finest malt whiskies in the Highlands and Islands, although each has its advocates and detractors. In Portree I tried to buy some, but at that time there appeared to have been a Talisker drought; I enquired of a butcher who, like the grocers, had a licence ('They sell liquor, so I couldn't see why I shouldn't'), and he sold me instead a bottle of *Poit Dhubh*, distilled in Eilean Iarmain in Skye. Its name, Black Pot, is a synonym for illicit whisky, which no doubt used to taste even better.

From Drynoch, at the head of Loch Harport, the A863 road runs into the bare, brown, heathery hills and returns to the

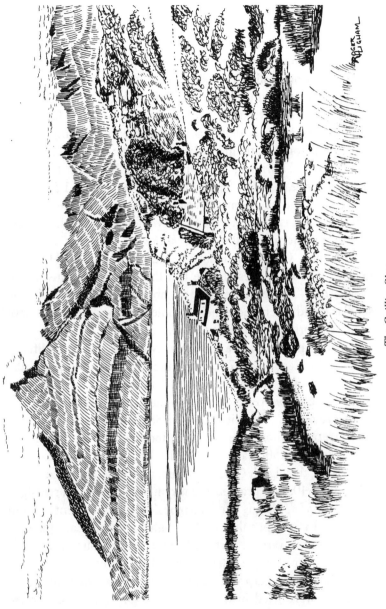

The Cuillin, Skye

waterside only at the mouth of the loch, opposite the lighthouse on Ardtreck Point. It follows the re-entrant inlet to Coillore, where the B885 crosses the island to Portree, then on the far side of the inlet is the crofting township of Bracadale, where there is a broch called *Dun Beag*, the Little Fort: this one is so small it is very hard to find! Not far from here, at another inlet called Loch Caroy, there are splendid views of MacLeod's Tables. It is not true that MacLeod was either a joiner or the inventor of some mathematical compendium; the Tables, in the peninsula of Duirinish, are flat-topped hills. They are called *Healabhal Bheag*, 1,601 feet, and *Healabhal Mhor*, 1,538 feet: notice how the small one (*Bheag*) is greater than the big one (*Mhor*). This is the Skyemen's way of confusing the artless visitor. Furthermore, the word *healabhal* does not occur in MacAlpine's Gaelic dictionary because there is no H in the Gaelic alphabet — despite the fact that it occurs in just about every word. These matters are so abstruse that only a Gaelic scholar could disentangle their complexities, and he would have to be well primed with *Poit Dhubh*.

On the far side of the Tables at Moonen Bay, the cliffs of Waterstein Head, at 967 feet, are the highest in Skye, and the Neist lighthouse at the head of the bay is Skye's most westerly point. It can be reached by a minor road which starts at Lonmore on the A863, it is called B884 and it passes a turning to Borreraig, where the MacCrimmon school of piping was conducted for 250 years. It was Alasdair Crotach MacLeod of Dunvegan, the eighth Chief, who first patronised the MacCrimmons in 1540, and granted them rent-free land at Borreraig.

Piobaireachd, playing the bag-pipes, is a very ancient form of music and is not peculiar to the Highlands; there are pipes in Ireland, and in various parts of Europe too, in country districts. In France, for example, they are called *la cornemuse*. The fact is, that although the harp was a more important bardic instrument, the pipes were used in the Highland regiments of the British Army, with drums, as a band, after the '45, and they have therefore become associated with the Highlands to a greater extent. Each clan, however, has its own Salute, Lament, and March, and the pipe-music is still played, and composed, by civil as well as military or police pipers. The sounds that the pipes produce are not to everyone's taste, but they do have a capacity to evoke strong emotions. Backed by the drums they lift the weariest of feet on a long march; they stir the blood of those about to engage in battle; at dances their rhythm is impossible to resist; their laments bring forth tears from the sternest of souls.

Dunvegan has a hotel-packed village (six including guest-houses) but its castle stands aloof from it, on a point near the head of Loch Dunvegan. At the castle's car-park there is a very splendid café and shop, you pay at the gates, and there is a long rhododendron-lined drive to what used to be the rear of the castle. 'Having dismounted,' says Boswell when he and Johnson were guests, 'we ascended a flight of steps, which was made by the late MacLeod, for the accommodation of persons coming to him by land, there formerly being, for security, no other access to the castle but from the sea; so that visitors who came by the land were under the necessity of getting into a boat, and sailed round to the only place where it could be approached.' The present bridge and porch date from some forty years after Johnson and Boswell's visit.

The first of the combined fortifications and dwelling-space on the rock of Dunvegan dates from the thirteenth-century, when *Liotr*, or Leod, son of Olav of Man, was given the land and built a massive curtain wall enclosing the rock, with the sea-gate the only access. Buildings inside will have been of wood, and thatched; no trace at all remains of any earlier structures on the site, probably going back to the Iron Age, as indicated by the name *dun*. The fourteenth-century keep was added by Malcolm MacLeod, third Chief. There are parts, like the dungeon and basement, which are just the same as when it was built. The so-called Fairy Tower was built in about 1500, with four floors, connected by a circular mural staircase; this was added by

Alasdair Crotach, the piping enthusiast. *Cruitach* means hunch-backed, a deformity that was visited upon poor Alasdair when he was clouted between the shoulders with a battle-axe. A central house to replace the austere keep as living-quarters was built in the early seventeenth-century, and the whole affair was remo-delled in 1790 by the twenty-third Chief, Norman the General, and again in the 1840s by the twenty-fifth Chief.

In addition to the portraits and other family treasures, there are some rare and singular wonders in Dunvegan. Most of them are in the Drawing-room, which is in the keep. There is the Dunvegan Cup, to start with; this is a drinking cup given to Sir Rory Mor MacLeod in 1596 by the O'Neills of Ulster for his support of their rebellion against the English, and although it is encased in exquisite silver filigree, with an inscribed date 1493, the wooden cup itself is reckoned to be much older, since the O'Neills claim that it belonged to their ancestor Niall Glun-dubh, High King of Ireland in the early tenth-century. Rory Mor's Horn is the other relic brought into the family by that worthy, the fifteenth Chief. It is a cow's horn, decorated with silver at the mouth, and is the Clan's traditional drinking-vessel. The Chief's heir, when he comes of age, must fill it with claret and drink it off 'without setting down or falling down'; it holds a bottle and a half, so takes a little practice. The present Chief, the twenty-ninth, did it on 14 August, 1956, in 1 minute, 57 seconds. It now has a false bottom, but all the same, practising must have been fun.

Quite the weirdest treasure in Dunvegan, in a glass case in the Drawing-room, is *Am Bratach Sith*, the Fairy Flag. It is a tattered fragment of yellow silk, and there are dozens of theories concerning its origin and how it came to be in the MacLeods' hands. One is that a crusading MacLeod was given it in Palestine: but it is thought to be at least 400 years older than the First Crusade. There are three or four versions of the fairy story, one of which I shall repeat. A dashing young Chief of Clan MacLeod once married a fairy, who was permitted to live with him for twenty years before returning to Fairyland. When the day came for them to part for ever, she took him to *Drochaid nan tri Allt*, Bridge of the Three Burns, which is three miles to the east of Dunvegan. She gave him the banner, and assured him that if the Clan was in deep danger, the banner should be waved, and all would be well. It has worked at various times: twice when the Clan was hard-pressed in battle, the flag was waved and victory was secured. In 1939 a fire threatened to destroy the entire castle, until the flag was carried out to safety. Then the blaze died down.

It might be the flag that King Harald Hardrada of Norway, that fearsome warrior, purloined when he plundered the pilgrim routes in the Middle East. He claimed that with it he could never be defeated in battle. At Stamford Bridge, in 1066, it was not disembarked from his galley, and he was killed amidst the frightful slaughter of his followers. The Norsemen might well have brought it away to Skye. On the other hand, it might have been given to the MacLeods by the fairies.

Quite adjacent to the elegantly-furnished Drawing-room is the thirteen-foot deep dungeon, the last four feet of which were cut out of the solid rock. It was an *oubliette*: the prisoners were thrown in, and forgotten, so they tended to die there. One horrific story illustrates its usefulness. John MacLeod, ninth Chief, died in 1557 leaving only a daughter, Mary, and an illegitimate son, Iain Dubh. While John's brothers and other kinsmen were away at the funeral, Iain Dubh seized Dunvegan. When the mourners returned he seized them too, killed both brothers and their sons, and threw the rest into the dungeon. There they languished, and were still doing so when Campbell of Argyll came along, anxious as Mary's guardian to investigate affairs at Dunvegan. Iain Dubh invited him and ten other Campbell chiefs to Dunvegan to discuss the matter; he pretended to agree to their terms, entertained them, and offered a final farewell banquet to assure them of his goodwill. They were all vastly diverted by the sumptuous victuals served them, until the end, when they found that the goblets set before them contained blood, and they had no sooner understood its full significance than they were dirked from behind, where they sat.

The Fairy Bridge, as *Drochaid nan tri Allt* is called, is where the B886 leaves the A850 east of Dunvegan. The modern road has its own bridge, but the old one, where the sorrowing MacLeod had to take leave of his fairy wife and received from her *Am Bratach Sith*, is still there, where three burns meet and run down to Loch Bay. The noble B886 expires at Lusta, on the bay, and continues as a narrow minor road. The bay widens to join Loch Dunvegan, strewn with islands and skerries, the sea is dark blue and the high cliffs are sharp against the sky. The road roughens into a track as it traces the high cliff-tops of the Waternish, or Vatternish peninsula. There are no trees, there are occasional crofting settlements like Hallin and Halistra, and there is a sign to Trumpan. If you take the left fork at this sign, you will find that the road loops back to it; after heading for Ardmore Point the lane swings right to a ruined chapel in a graveyard.

Not much is left of Trumpan Church, which is hardly surprising considering the nature of the following story. It is connected with the massacre of the MacDonalds of Eigg by a gang of MacLeods in 1577, recounted in Chapter 11. In May, 1578, the galleys of Clanranald landed on the shores of Vatternish at the time of morning service, when the church at Trumpan was full of its MacLeod congregation. The MacDonalds barred the door from the outside and set fire to the building; their pipers marched around, playing loudly to drown the screams of those choking and suffering inside, until the whole place was consumed and the cries ceased. Only one worshipper, a woman, managed to escape by squeezing through a tiny window in the corner, but suffered mortal injuries in the process.

By this time others in the neighbourhood had seen the smoke and heard the pipes, and before the Clanranald men could

Trumpan Church, Skye

return to their galleys and sail away, they were surrounded by a strong band of furiously indignant MacLeods. The fight was fierce, and escape for Clanranald difficult because the tide had ebbed, leaving their galleys stranded on the beach; nevertheless MacDonald valour seemed to be accounting for many Mac-Leods, until the Fairy Flag from Dunvegan was fetched and unfurled. Then the ranks of the MacLeods seemed mysteriously to be filled with fresh and vigorous warriors, and in the end only one galley was launched, manned by a handful of survivors from the battle. Stones from a dyke were piled up over the bodies of the Clanranald slain so that the action was named the Battle of the Spoiled Dyke.

In the churchyard at Trumpan is a Trial Stone, a small standing stone with a little hole in it. The practice was to establish guilt or innocence by blindfolding the accused and placing him or her before the stone; if he could put his finger straight into the hole, he was innocent, but if he fumbled and scratched about before locating it, he was guilty.

On a good day, a wonderful, bright, fresh day when the sky is so clear you can count an eagle's feathers, and the sea is so blue you would think it had rained dye, you can stand in Trumpan churchyard and look westward and see the outlines of the Uists and Lewis and Harris on the horizon. You can only do this on about four days in the year, so you have to be lucky, but if it happens, then you will sense the magic in the air, and you will wish to be nowhere else on earth.

No roads go to Vatternish Point, and precious few to anywhere else, so you have to return to the Fairy Bridge and continue along the A850 to Edinbane, where there is a good inn, the Lodge Hotel. There is also the Marshall Leisure and Recreation Centre, open on weekdays for all kinds of indoor games. From Edinbane on Loch Greshornish the road, good and wide, runs round to Loch Snizort Beag, and at Skeabost, where there is a privately-owned nine-hole golf course, you can cut through to the A856 in Trotternish peninsula. It is twenty miles long and eight miles wide, the biggest and most north-easterly peninsula of Skye. It is for the most part quite treeless, and inland, wild and mountainous. The people and their crofts are all on the coastal belts.

Always the sea is at hand, quite near at Kingsburgh, where a more modern house has replaced that of MacDonald of Kingsburgh, the husband of Flora MacDonaid. The little town of Uig, in Uig Bay, sheltered between high cliffs, has a pier for the ferries to Tarbert in Harris and Lochmaddy in North Uist. The road climbs in break-neck dog-legs up the northern side, to become A855 and single-track, but still it leads you northward towards the tip of the peninsula.

There are two reasons for pausing at Kilmuir: the Skye Museum, and Flora MacDonald's monument. The museum is based on a huddle of old, stone, thatched cottages, which are preserved and presented as they were when in use. They are long and low, and their thatches are weighed down with a fringe of stones depending on ropes. They are simple, rough and small: one is a forge, another has a spinning-wheel and a loom, a third is full of photographs of people in their occupations of the fairly recent past. The central cottage, with a peat fire smoking in the grate, is furnished just as if the occupants had gone out for a moment and would be straight back. The lady in charge has the Gaelic, and speaks it with anyone else who can. Few, these days, she says, have the Gaelic.

'Do the children here speak it at home?'

'Yes, but there are many incomers, who have no Gaelic, so they do not speak it among them.'

'Do you think radio and television have had an adverse effect on it?'

'Yes, and television the most. They sit in front of it so much. We are trying to keep it alive, but the life is so different now. I used to walk to school, and notice things on the way, like the ploughing and sowing, and the carts and horses used for everything, and the flowers and birds, but now they all go by bus, and take no notice of anything, and the work is all done by machines.'

An important relic is kept in this cottage, the pewter communion chalice from Trumpan Church, which appears to have escaped incineration.

Not far from the museum but higher up the slopes overlooking the sea-cliffs, there is a small burial-ground dominated by a huge and rather unlovely Celtic cross: the monument to Flora MacDonald, erected by one of her descendants. At Kingsburgh, Johnson and Boswell met Flora, and her husband Allan Mac-Donald. 'She is a little woman,' writes Boswell, 'of a genteel appearance, and uncommonly mild and well-bred.'

After Culloden, Prince Charles had been spirited away to South Uist in the Outer Hebrides, where Flora happened to have been visiting relatives. Some of Cumberland's troops were closing in, with the co-operation of the Royal Navy, so it was imperative to evacuate him. Flora, who was then twenty-three, was arrested on suspicion, but with great spirit and invention managed to procure from the officer commanding the Royal troops a pass back to her home in Skye for herself and 'Betty Bourke', her maid; five Uist men rowed, in an open boat, Flora and the disguised Prince across the perilous Minch in a night of terrifying storms, and through the Naval patrols, all the thirty-three miles to Skye. They dared not land at Vatternish because the MacLeods were against the Jacobites, so they rowed on across Loch Snizort to Monkstadt (or Mugstot) House, the home of Sir Alexander MacDonald, who was from home, actually at Fort Augustus with the Duke of Cumberland himself. His wife, Lady Margaret, was sympathetic, and ensured that Flora and the Prince, who was disguised as Betty Bourke, were smuggled through the cordon to Kingsburgh. He underwent numerous travels and perils throughout the island until he was at last brought away. Flora, as we have seen, was arrested, lodged for a while at Dunstaffnage, then taken to London for trial and imprisonment. On her release she married Allan MacDonald of Kingsburgh; they lived for eight years at Flodi-garry on the north-eastern coast of Trotternish. They had seven children, and Flora died in 1790 at the age of sixty-eight.

Along the coast, towards the extreme north of the island, the cliffs rise above the sea in majestic suddenness, and great hills soar up above the land; here on a rocky height above the cold sea-coast are the shattered fragments of Duntulm Castle, once a great MacDonald stronghold. The Norsemen had a fort on the site, and maybe the Iron Age Celts too: it was later held by the semi-Norse MacLeods, until purloined from them by MacDonald of Sleat. He moved his principal seat to Duntulm from Dunscaith in 1539, but when the Jacobite rising of 1715 failed, the land and castle were forfeited: Sleat remained, but Trotternish was taken, and with it Duntulm, which fell into ruin. Some of its masonry went into the building of the MacDonald house at Monkstadt. Duntulm today is a wreck, like Dunscaith, hardly recognisable as a once-mighty fortress: only its site proclaims its doughty impregnability, dominating the seascape and the little sharp-pointed *Eilean Tulm* beneath, commanding clear views westward to the Outer Hebrides, northward to the approaches from Norway, and eastward to the mainland at Gairloch in Wester Ross.

To the rear of the castle is a round grassy hillock called *Cnoc na h-Eiric*, the Hill of Pleas, where questions of land boundaries and other grievances would be heard by the Chief and his court, with the right reserved to appeal to the supreme MacDonald court at Finlaggan.

Strange outlandish shapes darken against the sky now, to your right hand as you round the headland of Trotternish and head eastward. They are the needle crags of the Quirang, rising like some mighty citadel, defending the secrets of the interior. Its name Quirang, *Cuith Raing*, means Pillared Stronghold, and it has among its tooth-like walls a smooth grassy plain called the Table, where cattle could be driven for safe keeping. Better to see it and enter it, a minor road could be used, which crosses the peninsula south of it, from Staffin Bay back to Uig Bay. In its shadow on the east coast is Flodigarry, the house where Allan and Flora MacDonald lived; it stands beside the present hotel above high, sheer cliffs, and looks over them to the islands *Sgeir na Eireann*, Eilean Flodigarry, and Staffin Island, which hems in Staffin Bay.

This coast has the most dramatic cliffs in the island. Brown basaltic columns rise sheer out of the water, making a vertical pattern for two miles: but they lie on a grey Jurassic sediment which crosses the columns horizontally. No wonder it reminded the Skye folk of a tartan pattern, so no wonder it is called the Kilt Rock.

The coastal strip, below the hills, is fertile, so there are frequent crofting settlements all the way, looking out to the mountains of Wester Ross, then the islands of Rona and Raasay. Opposite the northern tip of Raasay is another geological phenomenon; a mountain called the Storr rises to 2,358 feet at its southern end, with sheer cliffs dropping 600 feet to a green corrie fringed with pinnacles of rock, of light grey basalt. The

Portree, Skye

biggest, visible from the road and from quite a distance away, is the Old Man of Storr, a monolith 160 feet high, balanced on a craggy plinth. It can be reached by climbing 900 feet from the roadside, but cannot be climbed save by experts. Two of them, Don Whillans and James Barber, did so in 1955. Another of these pinnacles on the rim of the corrie is 100 feet high and is pierced by three great arches, like those at Carsaig in Mull.

As the road passes to the west of two freshwater lochs, *Leathan* and *Fada* (Broad, and Long), and Raasay comes more clearly into view beyond them, there is in the cliffs at the water's edge another Prince Charles's Cave, accessible only by boat, where the Prince was lodged for a brief time during his wanderings about the island.

Portree is soon reached, on its bay; it is the only town in the island, its capital, and its name, *Port Righ*, Port of the King, signifies its pre-eminence; so does its situation, which is superb. Colour-washed houses stand harmoniously by the quayside, reflected brilliantly in the limpid water, with others terraced up the steep hillside behind them. The main streets are on the clifftop, with shops, banks, post office, hotels (nine, and six guest-houses) and the meeting of four roads. It has a caravan and camping site, too, and in 1962 had a bakery, where the bread was baked behind the shop, and the smell of it as you came in from the road outside was not out of this world, but out of the modern world of sliced wrapped sterilised loaves from the supermarket: a heady, delicious, nostalgic smell of the past.

Glen Varragill takes you back to the Sligachan Hotel, the Glamaig, and the Black Cuillin. There is magic in the hills, lochs, rivers, and wide-open seascapes of Skye, magic in the queer rock-pinnacles of Trotternish, magic in the dark, awesome Cuillin, magic in the people with their memories of a life so different from the modern stereotype. Will it still be the same if a bridge connects it with the mainland? Perhaps, but one fears that it may not.

16

Wester Ross: Applecross and Gairloch

The peninsula between Loch Alsh and Loch Carron is not only full of beauty but also accessible, which is rather unusual for the West Highlands. The main A87 road runs along its southern coast to Kyle of Lochalsh, and from it the A890 cuts across to Loch Carron; the railway wriggles along its northern coast; with several stations, also round to Kyle. The hills are low and negotiable, the scenery spectacular.

On the south coast are the villages of Reraig and Balmacara. Balmacara means Village of the Rock, but its name has been given to the whole western part of this peninsula. The National Trust for Scotland owns 5,616 acres of it, and they have created the Lochalsh Woodland Garden, where there are walks laid out, open to everyone all the year round, every day, from 9 am to sunset. There is also an Information Desk which opens in the summer months only. Balmacara House is leased to the Scottish Education Authority and is used as a school for crofting.

Plockton, on the north coast, has a bay on outer Loch Carron and a harbour which at one time, before the railway was built, was used as a port by schooners trading from the Baltic, and by Lewis fishermen from Stornaway. The railway brought holiday

Wester Ross: Applecross and Gairloch

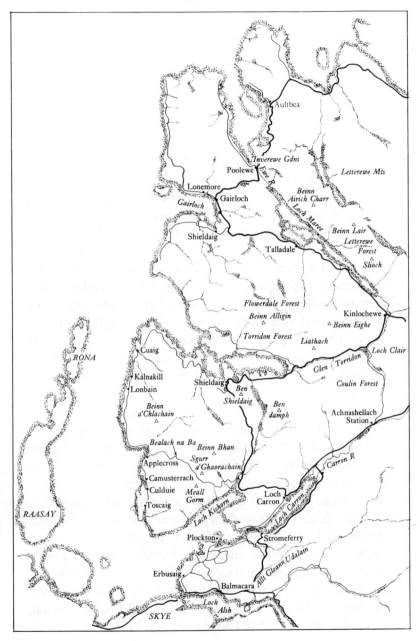

305

visitors, and there are two hotels and plenty of other accommodation. There is also an airstrip, built in 1966 by the Royal
Engineers, principally for an air ambulance service. It is a lovely
coastline, fringed with skerries and little islands, and at Erbusaig
there is even a bank of coral sand, where at low tide you may
find little branches of pale pink coral, if it has not all been carted
off already.

The road across the peninsula is A890, climbing into the hills
with *Allt Gleann Udalain*, winding through a green valley, then
down to Loch Carron at Stromeferry, which has the most
wonderfully informative sign in Scotland: 'Stromeferry — no
ferry.' This has been so since 1966, when a new road was built
alongside the railway, on the southern shore of the loch. Strome
Castle stood on the far side of the narrows — past tense because
nothing much remains of it. It was a stronghold of the
MacDonalds of Glengarry (who spell their name MacDonnell, a
better phonetic spelling from *MacDomhnaill*), who owned the
land, and acted as a frontier post in their struggles with the
MacKenzies. In the end, the MacKenzies managed to expedite
the castle's ascent to the four winds with a charge of gunpowder,
just three years before Messrs Catesby, Fawkes & Co. failed to
do the same thing to the House of Lords and King James VI and I.

Loch Carron's south side is heavily forest-clad, and shares
with the north side steep but not high mountains, and hardly any
cultivable land. Both road and railway are single-track and go on
to Inverness. At the head of the loch is the station of Strathcarron; Carron means winding or meandering (*car* in Gaelic is also
used to mean a swindler or twister) and the Carron river does
just that, along a mile-wide strath which made it eminently
suitable for the building of roads and railways.

Between Strathcarron and Glen Torridon there is a wide
stretch of hill and moorland called Coulin Forest, where the red
deer roam. A track leaves Achnashellach Station in Strathcarron, finds the Coulin river, Loch Coulin and Loch Clair, and
reaches the A896 in Glen Torridon. W. H. Murray says, 'on no

account should this walk be omitted from any exploration of the region.' It is seven or eight miles altogether.

Across the wide strath the road turns left along the other side of the loch to Lochcarron village, which is sometimes called Jeantown, and is a pretty place with a good harbour. It used to have a population of over 2,000 and a fishing fleet, but in the mid-nineteenth-century the herring-shoals stayed away from the sea-lochs, and the supply of salmon and sea-trout dried up too: so did the population. It has an hotel, and a petrol-station, with a ginger-haired lad working in his holidays (it was April): 'What can you tell us about the road to Applecross? Is it open?'

He looked dubious. 'Yes, but you must be careful. It is not like any other road.'

It is still A896, which although single-track is not bad; it rises to 450 feet, with a fine view north-east to the forest of Ben Damph, and all around the hills in August are several shades of purple with the heather. It descends abruptly to Loch Kishorn, which is south-facing and therefore lush with grass and hay-fields by the lochside, the brown heath rising on the hills behind. As the road swings round north, past the head of Loch Kishorn, to cross through Glenshieldaig to Loch Torridon, a minor road leads off left. At its entrance a sign will indicate the condition of the pass to Applecross; in our case, in April, it said: 'Pass open, but under snow — dangerous for caravans, lorries, and learners.' Or anyone else, for that matter, as we discovered.

First the little road, hardly wide enough for a normal-sized vehicle, follows the contour of great brown frowning *Beinn Bhan*, 2,938 feet, above the western shore of Loch Kishorn, and then it starts winding into the entrance of a deep glen between *Beinn Bhan* and *Sgurr a'Ghaorachain*, 2,539 feet; it makes for the other side, and starts to wind slowly along the western flanks of *Sgurr a'Ghaorachain* into a still deeper, darker glen between it and another height; *Meall Gorm*, 2,328 feet. The hills are bare, steep, barren and menacing; at the head of the glen the tiny road, having already climbed steeply, now ascends a precipitous cliff by means of a series of hairpin bends sharper and steeper than anything I have experienced. I have crossed the Pyrenees by most of their passes, but this one had me sweating and hoping that we should not meet anything coming the other way, since there seemed to be remarkably few passing places for so horrendous an ascent up such a narrow path. The engine of our 950 c.c. Fiesta, which had coped with passes of 6,000–8,000 feet in the Pyrenees with equanimity, began to complain, even in second gear. We crawled nervously up to the snow-bound top: the snow hung in slabs above the road, but was clear from it.

This was *Bealach na Ba*, the Pass of the Cattle; it climbs 2,053 feet in the course of six miles, the last part one in four. Sheer drops flank the road in this last part, hundreds of feet into the corrie between the two mountains. The driver has no time to look, fortunately. The view from the top is sensational: all of Skye lies below you, the snow-girt Cuillin lying like a man-trap, sharp and fierce, across the pale Sound.

The descent to Applecross is mild and gradual by comparison. The old name for this large and remote peninsula was *Comaraich*, the Sanctuary, a place of refuge made holy ground by the arrival in 673 of St Maolrubha, who built huts and a church on a grassy knoll near the mouth of the Crossan river. The Pictish word *aber* for river-mouth became *apor*, which combining with Crossan gave *Aporcrossan*, and that corrupted to Applecross. It remained a recognised sanctuary for all fugitives until the Reformation.

The village of Applecross is serene, untroubled, tranquil; there is a post office, an inn, and a long street of terraced houses whose gardens are on the foreshore just across the road: here their washing hangs out, garden sheds nestle against the beach-wall, and the children play. Oyster-catchers squabble on the water's edge, gulls and terns glide above, their plangent cries mingling with the soft sound of lapping water and the squeals of the laughing children; in the street their mothers pass the time of day in Gaelic. Behind the houses the tree-clad hills rise steeply, and across the little bay the high *Beinn a'Chlachain* shelters them from the worst of the northerly gales. An elderly gentleman walks towards us in the direction of the inn (it is that time of the day), and we ask him where we can find St Maolrubha's grave. He answers in the soft, hissing tones of the Gaelic speaker. 'Och, it iss chust round the head of the loch, you can see the church from here. Tid you know that St Maolrubha's iss the second oltest to St Columpa's? Yess, yess, inteet. Good tay to you!'

We retrieved our long-suffering car from the little car-park near the caravan site. How you get a caravan to Applecross by way of *Bealach na Ba* without losing your temper, wits, nerve and caravan, is beyond me. The little road traces the foreshore round to the head of the loch and the mouth of the Crossan river, just as the courteous gentleman had told us, and by the side of a large house there is the churchyard path, gate, church, and burial-ground.

Quite near the gate, within the walls of the burial-ground, there stands a huge red sandstone slab with the faint figure of a cross upon it; according to Seton Gordon this stone is 'to the memory of Ruadhri Mor Mac Caoigean who was slain by the Norsemen. He is believed to have been a chief of great strength and valour. The renowned Red Priest of Applecross is also buried here.' He does not say in what way the Red Priest was renowned, or who he was, but he was not St Maolrubha, whose grave lies in a corner of the churchyard by the ivy-grown ruins of a little chapel, which is certainly not St Maolrubha's original, since it is no earlier than thirteenth-century; two rounded stones, lying east to west instead of the more usual north to south, mark the saint's grave.

Maol, the head-cropping or tonsure, and *Rubha*, a variant of *Ruadh*, red, give the impression that his name derives from his red-haired appearance. He was a descendant of the royal house in Ireland of King Niall of the Nine Hostages. Born in County

Derry in 642 he sailed to Scotland in 671; he founded six churches along the west coast before settling at Applecross, and when he had established his monastic cell, with his brethren, he ruled as abbot for fifty years. He and his monks carried the Gospel across Ross and Cromarty into Sutherland. He died, aged eighty at Skail in Sutherland, and his body was brought back to Applecross, to lie in this quiet churchyard.

In the little parish church, which is plain and simple in the usual Church of Scotland manner, with the humblest of altars and lecterns but a high, white-painted pulpit, there are fragments of a Celtic cross that was found in the churchyard, said to date from the eighth century.

There is more chance in Applecross of experiencing that almost tangible peace, that benign sanctity of the early Christian places, than in Iona. But then, to reach Iona on the ferry from Fionnphort is not difficult; to come to Applecross you must cross the *Bealach na Ba.*

The dreaded *Bealach* is no longer the only way, in fact, of reaching the Sanctuary. The little roads run both ways along the coast from Applecross, south to Camusterrach, Culduie and Toscaig, but no farther. Northwards, and fairly recently, you can wend your slow way around the entire peninsula and regain the A896 at Shieldaig. In Seton Gordon's day it was 'not broader than a stalking path, so that no horse and cart can use it and no motor-car venture along it.' Although single-track, it is a good road; from Lonbain to Cuaig you can look westward and see all the mountains of Skye, and Raasay and Rona with a lighthouse on its most northerly point. Each of these little townships, Lonbain, Kalnakil, and Cuaig, have their few white croft-houses, but also numbers of broken-roofed, deserted houses too. Crofting will be terribly hard here, for it is rocky, treeless, infertile, inhospitable and uncharitable, a wilderness lacking even blades of grass for the sheep to eat.

This road takes you the very long, twisting, turning, up-and-down way around the northern tip of the peninsula into outer

Loch Torridon and along the shores of Loch Shieldaig, an inlet from it. After what seems like a hundred miles, it joins the A896 and very soon you are in Shieldaig, below the sheer, tree-grown cliff-face of Ben Shieldaig, 1,692 feet. Shieldaig, which gets its name from the Norse *Sild-vik*, Herring-bay, like Lochcarron was once famous for its fishing, as its name implies. Its houses front the quiet bay, looking out to Shieldaig Island, a coniferous bird-sanctuary. It has an inn on the waterfront, and like the majority of those in West Highland villages, even as remote as this, it can provide sustenance for passers-by. When I asked the young lady in this one if she could feed 'two hungry travellers', she thought I had said two hundred, and almost passed out.

As you progress from Shieldaig eastward along the southern shore of Loch Torridon, and look across the loch to the Torridon mountains, you are contemplating one of the oldest landscapes in Britain. The chain of mountains whose rock you see, was thrown up from the sea 300 million years ago; it was then reduced to sea-level by erosion, and when Scotland rose into shape, the root rocks of the old chain rose with it. Its sandstone sediment was deposited earlier than the Cambrian rock, which is the first in which fossils occur, and it is this which now caps the Torridon mountains with quartzite. The quartzite caps are 600 million years old, the sandstone beneath them older still, and the platform of gneiss on which the whole range stands, 1,500 million years old, which makes it the oldest rock known. It forms its own summits and cliffs in places, for example on the Letterewe range on the north side of Loch Maree.

The Torridon Forest was given to the National Trust for Scotland in 1967, an estate of 16,100 acres stretching over *Beinn Eighe*, 3,309 feet, including *Liathach*, which has seven tops, the highest of which is 3,456 feet, to *Beinn Alligin*, 3,232 feet. The whole area is a nature reserve, and at Torridon, where the A896 meets the minor road to Diabaig along the north of Loch

Torridon, there is a Countryside Centre and Deer Museum
with an audio-visual display on the region's wildlife; the Centre
is open from May to October, from Monday to Saturday 10 am
to 6 pm, Sundays 2 pm to 6 pm. The Deer Museum is not
staffed and is open all the year round. There is also a Youth
Hostel at Torridon because the climbing in these mountains is
greatly esteemed. Glen Torridon, along which the A896 now
takes you, is gaunt, bare, barren, and boulder-strewn. We have
seen red deer in it, walking across the road, but what they find to
eat there is not apparent. Nevertheless there are reputedly many
wild creatures in the Nature Reserve: there are certainly very
few tame ones.

The road meets A832 at Kinlochewe, which ought to be
called Kinlochmaree, but the loch's name, which used to be
Ewe, was changed to avoid confusion with the sea-loch of the
same name into which its waters flow. The village's name was
not. Kinlochewe is a good centre for exploring the region, with a
respectable hotel, plenty of self-catering accommodation and a
caravan site, and it is accessible from the A832 from Inverness.

The road follows the southern shore of Loch Maree, and it is
an excellent road, two-way for a change. Across the loch looms
old Slioch, 3,217 feet, named from *Sleagh*, a spear, which is the
highest point, above its crown of peaks, of the whole range on
the northern side of the loch. It is of sandstone, on a plinth of
gneiss, rising to the summits of *Beinn Lair*, 2,817 feet, and *Beinn
Airigh Charr*, 2,595 feet, which have huge cliffs on their
northern sides. The whole range is called the Letterewe Forest.

South of the loch, bordering on the Nature Reserve, is the
Flowerdale Forest. These forests are not nowadays entirely
timbered, where not replanted with conifers by the Forestry
Commission. They used to be, but over the centuries they have
been destroyed by fire and felling like the great forest of
Caledon. A few acres of old Scotch pines remain in the Nature
Reserve, which was bought by the Nature Conservancy Council.
In the area as a whole there are plenty of red deer; also there are

ptarmigan, rare elsewhere, golden eagles, wild cat, and the pine-marten, a long dark brown creature with a yellow throat.

Loch Maree is twelve miles long: its south-eastern end is dominated by the frowning Slioch, its north-western is wider and is set about with islands. In Talladale Bay, the Old Mill Hotel caters for fishing enthusiasts, since there are big sea-trout in the loch. Close by the Letterewe side of the loch is Isle Maree, which is thickly wooded with oak, ash, pine, birch, holly, willow and hazel. In the ancient Druidical days the island was a religious centre, and the oak was their symbol. St Maolrubha, on his missionary travels, planted the holly, and founded a cell there. The ruins of a chapel can still be seen in the undergrowth, and a dried-up and filled-in well. The latter was a favourite centre for pilgrimage, as it was thought that it had a curative value for mental disorders. It was also a wishing well, and if you wanted to make a wish you also had to push a coin into an old tree standing by. It was still alive when Queen Victoria visited the spot in 1877, but even by then far too much metal had been slotted edgeways into it, and it has since died.

From Talladale Bay the road leaves the lochside and enters Slattadale Forest, which used to be lovelier than it is now, because the Hydro-Electric Board has felled trees and built pylons instead, for a power station. The road arrives at a series of coastal bays called collectively Gairloch. *Gearr* in Gaelic means short, and Loch Gairloch penetrates only four miles inland. The first bay is called Charlestown, where there is a pier, a track up to Flowerdale House, the splendid Old Inn by a cool, clear burn, and a new bridge where the burn meets the bay. In January, 1982, heavy rainfall caused the partial destruction of the old bridge, built in 1800; it has now been restored as a footbridge, just in front of the inn. Flowerdale House was built in 1738 as the third residence on the site, of the Gairloch MacKenzies; the first was called *Tighe Dige*, House of the Moat.

The promontory that projects from the shore here, hemming in the little bay and giving it shelter as a harbour, is now the site of a nine-hole golf course, but was once the strategic position for a fort, *An Dun*; it shows traces of having been vitrified, having been built and used over a long period from the early Iron Age onwards. It seems that the MacBeaths, arriving from Assynt, refortified it in the thirteenth-century and defended themselves against the MacLeods in a struggle for possession of the land. In the end the MacLeods were rewarded for service to the Crown by a grant of legal title to Gairloch, so armed with this they drove the MacBeaths out.

The MacKenzies were also in contention for Gairloch, and after a particularly vile murder committed by the MacLeods, the King permitted the MacKenzies to destroy the MacLeods by 'Fire and Sword'. In 1494 they were granted Gairloch by charter, but they had their work cut out because they did not finally oust the MacLeods from the Gairloch dun until the mid-sixteenth-century.

Beyond the golf course and the dun is the main part of the township, with post office, banks and hotels. Altogether there are seven hotels and seven guest-houses in and around Gairloch, and their visitors may choose from fishing, sailing, canoeing, cruising, and the award-winning Gairloch Heritage Museum with its own restaurant attached, for their diversions. On the northern side of the loch, beyond Lonemore, there is a Youth Hostel, and there are caravan sites.

Minor roads serve the villages along the southern and northern sides of the loch, but the main road leaves the loch and turns sharp right, climbing over the rocky wastes to *Loch Tollaidh*, which is a high freshwater loch adorned by a couple of tiny islands. Another gruesome Highland story (better than Noddy for getting the children to sleep) is connected with it.

In 1480 the Laird of Gairloch was Allan MacLeod, who married a daughter of MacKenzie of Kintail, and had three sons with her. She died, and Allan married as a second wife a MacLeod of Lewis; of course, the inheritance would pass to the sons of the first marriage, and the brothers of the second,

MacLeod wife, resented the passing of the land to anyone with MacKenzie connections. The family was staying in a house on one of the little man-made islands in *Loch Tollaidh*; Allan MacLeod went fishing in the Ewe river, caught nothing, and lay down to sleep. The two MacLeod brothers arrived, full of vengeance, killed Allan, cut his head off and threw it in the river. Then they took his boat and went to the house on the island, where they told their sister what they had done to her husband, and took two of her step-sons, the third being fortunately absent. They led them away to a place called *Craig Bhadan an Aisc*, Rock of the Place of Burial, killed them, and took their blood-stained tunics with them to *Tighe Dige*, where they spent the night.

The distressed step-mother went to the house of an old family retainer, who that night went to *Tigh Dige*, found the tunics and stole them away. The stepmother then took the tunics to the boys' grandfather, MacKenzie of Kintail, who was understandably incensed. He sent his son, Hector Roy MacKenzie, to King James IV in Edinburgh, and elicited from him the 'Commission of Fire and Sword'. The two MacLeods were caught and killed by a MacRae, ally of the MacKenzies, in a bay near Gairloch called *Camus a'Bhata*. The MacKenzies took Gairloch. Considering the position of the step-mother, her actions show great strength of moral courage.

The Ewe river is nearly as short as that of Morar, so that a similarly slight tract of land separates Loch Maree from the sea at Loch Ewe. Just before the road follows the river down to the sea there is a beautiful view down Loch Maree, surely one of the most spectacular and delightful of the inland lochs.

Poolewe is a small crofting settlement where the river meets the loch, but it has two hotels and plenty of self-catering cottages, fishing again providing the most magnetic attraction for visitors. On the other hand, they might be horticultural enthusiasts, because a short way up the coast, where another small promontory called *Am Ploc Ard* juts into Loch Ewe, are the famous Inverewe Gardens, owned by the National Trust for Scotland, which ought to be visited and admired by gardeners and non-gardeners (like ourselves) alike.

'During the summer months', writes Mrs Mairi Sawyer in the foreword to the guide-book, 'hundreds of visitors wander through the gardens of Inverewe. Almost everyone expresses surprise at finding them here at all, and is amazed to see what trees, plants and shrubs flourish. Having motored, cycled or walked through many miles of peat-hags, bogs and wild rocks, they realise what this estate must have been like when my father, Osgood MacKenzie, bought it in 1862.'

Then, *Am Ploc Ard* was just heathery moorland with one willow tree growing on it among a mass of red Torridon sandstone. Osgood MacKenzie, whose forefathers were the post-MacLeod Lairds of Gairloch, planted a thick belt of Scotch firs and Corsican pines to act as a windbreak, and the mild air from the Gulf Stream has done the rest. Soil was brought in and shrubs and flowers and trees planted, to an extent that would not have been thought possible in so exposed a shore in the wild and windy North-West of Scotland. MacKenzie built a house there, too, but it was burnt down in 1914, to be replaced by another in 1936. Mrs Sawyer gave the whole estate to the National Trust for Scotland in 1952, a year before her death, and the Trust has run it, cared for it, and opened it for visitors ever since. There is a reception centre, a shop, and a restaurant; gardeners will know the best times to visit Inverewe, according to their preferences, but these times are given by the guide-book: rhododendrons are best from mid-April to mid-May, the rock-garden from May to June. July and August are good for herbaceous plants and annuals, and even the autumn is good for the fruits, the turning leaves, and the late-flowering hydrangeas and watsonias. The gardens are open, nevertheless, all year round, every day, from 9.30 am to sunset, but the Visitor Centre, shop and restaurant function only during the summer months, starting in late March and closing in late October.

316

There is even a camping and caravan site adjacent. One of the curious facts about Inverewe is that all of these exotic, sub-tropical plants are growing and flourishing at a latitude north of Moscow's.

17

Loch Broom and Ullapool

Inverewe is in the nethermost corner of Loch Ewe, where the Ewe river empties the waters of Loch Maree into the sea. The loch is eight miles long and three miles wide, and is almost entirely enclosed by the two peninsulas ending in *Rubha Reigh* to the south-west and Greenstone Point to the north-east; in the centre is a small pastoral island called Isle of Ewe. Since it is so nearly land-locked and therefore sheltered it is a good anchorage, and has consequently been used by the Royal Navy for quite some time. During the war of 1914–18, for example, there were many occasions when the loch was covered with the lean grey shapes of the ships of the Tenth Cruiser Squadron; many of these were converted merchantmen, others the older type of cruiser with tall masts, and three or four funnels apiece. They were exceedingly primitive compared with today's floating computers, their appetite for coal inexhaustible; anchored in the loch, they were taking a break from their ceaseless vigil against the dreaded submarines, the U-boats which had torpedoed so many merchant ships bringing food, fuel, and raw materials to Britain — and drowned many West Highlandmen, since so many had enrolled in one form of sea-going service or another. Very few ships will be seen in Loch Ewe now, but the Royal Navy still keeps some installations along its shores.

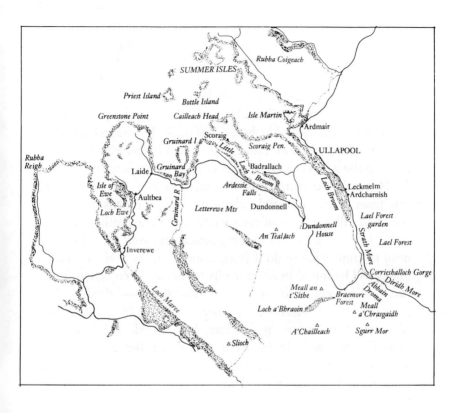

On the north-eastern shores of the loch are plenteous crofting townships, the chief of which is Aultbea, where there is a general store and post office, with a petrol pump, and two hotels. The chief attraction once more is the fishing, but this is a splendid district for climbing and walking — if you know what you are doing, for here there are no marked-out forest trails. Between Loch Maree and Loch Broom, an area of about 15 miles by 13, there is a hill-and-moorland wilderness punctuated by streams, lochans and lochs, and no roads. It is walled in to the south by the Letterewe range, dominated by Slioch; the same effect in the north is given by the mass of *An Teallach*, the Forge, 3,484 feet. If you go into this wilderness, or into any of the other vast areas of the Highlands where there are no roads or tracks, you need with you a list of essential requirements, without which you will be in danger of losing yourself and your life, and you need to know what to do if you get into trouble. Some of these things will be found in an appendix to this work, compiled from two publications, *Safety in Outdoor Education*, published by the Department of Education and Science through H.M.S.O., and *Notes for Hill-walkers* by William McConnell, published by himself and available in 1990. Disregard for all of these necessities can lead to tragedy, as has happened only too often, when those who presume to know better discover their folly too late.

The little waterside road through Aultbea along the north-eastern peninsula connects the white-painted, single-storey croft-houses and terminates at Mellon Charles, where there is still a Royal Naval base down by the water, recently refurbished. The A832 road from Aultbea crosses the neck of the peninsula; from the middle of it you suddenly come over a crest and there is a wonderful view northward of the island-strewn mouth of Loch Broom, with Gruinard Island in the foreground and the Summer Isles in the distance.

At Laide, on the shore of Gruinard Bay, where there is a caravan site more exposed than most to the vagaries of the northerly winds, the main road swings to the right to follow the coast, and a minor road departs left to serve the settlements on the northern side of the Greenstone Point peninsula. It is worth exploring, because it is a delightful stretch of coast, with quiet sandy coves and that peculiarly Highland sense of undisturbed peace — that is, when the aforesaid northerly winds are not reminding you that they come straight from the Arctic Circle. There are caves in the cliffs at Sand and Mellon Udrigle which were once used as places of worship, and nearby there is *Loch na Beiste*. This calm, picturesque inland freshwater loch got its name because there is a monster in it, or at least, there used to be. It appeared quite often, sometimes to the elders of the Kirk on Sunday mornings. They persuaded the landowner to drain the loch, but it proved impossible as there was a deep hole in the centre where the monster lurked. So they emptied fourteen barrels of lime into the hole, all the while trembling with apprehension in case the monster took umbrage and came leaping out at them. But it worked: the monster was never seen again. All the same, when you pass by the loch, which is on the right of the road when you have driven all the way down to Mellon Udrigle, reversed around the farmyard chickens, geese and lambs, and come back again, it would be as well to take care, for a monster with lime-dust in its eyes would not be charitably disposed towards strangers.

Out in the bay and constantly visible from the swerving road, as it follows the contours of the shoreline, is green and hilly Gruinard Island. For the last 45 years it has been inhabited by no-one, because it was infected. During the 1939–45 war, the War Office's Microbiological Research Establishment fastened on to the unfortunate island for an experiment in germ warfare. The disease anthrax was disseminated by aerosol, to see if it would infect cattle and sheep. The answer was yes, for sheep. Fortunately, this gruesome discovery was never put into practice, and the only beneficial result was the development of an effective vaccine against anthrax for humans and animals. The infection, however, remained in the island, and it was declared that decontamination would be far too expensive. The money, nevertheless, has at last been spent: half a million pounds of it. A newspaper article in early April, 1990, gives the joyful tidings that the last Ministry of Defence warning sign has been taken away, that Mr Michael Neubert of the Ministry has declared it safe, and he himself has led ashore the first visitors. The Ministry originally purchased it compulsorily, in 1947, for £500, and this is the sum it has agreed to receive from the nephew of the owner then, on 1st May. Its estimated worth now is more than £5 million.

Gruinard comes comes from the Norse *Grunna Fjord*, the Shallow Fiord; after passing over the Gruinard river and past Gruinard House, the road leaves the pink-sanded bay and heads inland towards Little Loch Broom. There are two Lochs Broom. Both of them, I am sorry to say, were given their names because of the high rainfall in the area, up to seventy-two inches a year at Dundonnell and 100 inches at Strathnasheallag: *Loch a'Bhraoin* means Loch of the Showers. They were created by the parallel rivers Dundonnell and Droma. Both issue as sea-lochs into the broad bay of the islands between Greenstone Point and *Rubha Coigeach*. The road keeps to the side of Little Loch Broom, under the shadow of the massive *An Teallach*. It is called the Forge because the misty cloud which always hangs about its eleven peaks looks like chimney smoke. Its principal ridge is eleven miles long, and it is all red Torridon sandstone, quite new compared with the gneiss, but still 800 million years old.

The peninsula between the two Lochs Broom, terminating in Cailleach Head, is named after one of its townships, Scoraig. The nearest road to Scoraig ends five miles farther east at Badrallach, and until October 1989, the children had to go into Ullapool by boat for school, and stay there for a week at a time. So the Scoraig people, eighty strong, decided that they needed their own school; the local landowner gave them a plot of land, the Free Church gave them a fire-ruined church, and the project began to take shape. So far there are only twelve pupils, and the headmaster is only in his early thirties, but the salient point is that the pupils themselves helped to build their school, certainly the smallest secondary school in Britain. They were all taught how to drive dumper trucks, mix cement, control the sixteen-foot boats that brought their building-materials and fittings, and one of the boys even wired the whole school for electricity, which has to be generated on the spot, like every other house in Scoraig.

At the head of Little Loch Broom, past the spectacular Ardessie Falls, is the splendid Dundonnell Hotel. As the name implies, the region was at one time Clan Donald land, until 1603 when MacDonell of Glengarry surrendered to MacKenzie of Kintail all his lands in Ross. Dundonnell House is a mile up the road, surrounded by plantations of deciduous trees, elm, beech, oak, sycamore, chestnut, lime; there are also the inescapable conifers of the Forestry Commission hereabouts, but Dundonnell House is privately owned. This is the area from which to begin climbing the ridge of *An Teallach*, and the deep trough beyond it called *Strath na Sealga*, or Strathnasheallag, but again, not without proper guidance and carrying the proper equipment.

From Dundonnell House in Strath Beag where the Dundonnell river flows into the loch, the A832 road goes inland, climbing beside the river, which crashes down several falls beside the towering cliff-face of *Carn a'Bhiorain*. Then you are in the Dundonnell Forest, and if you think this is like driving along the A35 in the New Forest you could not be more wrong; there is scarcely a tree in this forest, no cover of any kind within sight, just a straight road over brown moorland, marked out with red poles at intervals so that you can find the road when it is snow-covered. It is known as Destitution Road, appropriately for its poverty of vegetation, but built to give work during the dreadful days of the potato famine in 1851, when the only other alternatives to destitution were emigration or death. Ahead are

323

the mountains, first the fairly minor *Meall an t-Sithe*, Hill of the Fairies, then three Munros, *A'Chailleach*, *Meall a'Chrasgaith*, and *Sgurr Mor*. From the little inland freshwater *Loch a'Bhraoin*, the pluvious original for the name of the two sea-lochs, the Abhainn Cuileig rushes to join the Droma, and the road follows it into Braemore Forest, where there are at least some trees. Just here is another wonder of the West Highlands, and as there is a car-park by the road-side and a gate, path and bridge, there is no obstacle to viewing the Corrieshalloch (*Coire sealach*) Gorge.

The River Droma flows through the pass of Diridh More between the mountains *Beinn Dearg*, 3,547 feet, and *Sgurr Mor*, 3,637 feet. At the passing of the last Ice Age the torrent from the melting ice-caps surged down between these heights and cut a mile-long gorge, 200 feet deep, through solid rock. The National Trust for Scotland owns it, which is why there are wooden steps down to its verge, and fences on either side of the path, and a bridge across it. There is a notice on the bridge warning that no more than six people should be on it at one time, and my wife swears that she could feel it swaying in the wind, but it is perfectly safe; just upstream the little *Abhainn Droma* falls over a precipice and gushes deep down under you; on the black, wet, slippery sides of this sunless chasm trees grow, dwarf rowan, hazel, birch and alder. Across the bridge the path leads you downstream to a little belvedere (only two on it at a time) from which you can look upstream to the bridge and the waterfall beyond it. Sufferers from vertigo should not look down, but it is an awesome and thrilling sight.

The road itself crosses the gorge some half-mile farther upstream, and meets the A835; if you turn left you can then run down the eastern side of the gorge in Strath More. To your right are the looming heights of the huge *Beinn Dearg*, the Red Mountain (most of them are of red Torridon sandstone), and for exploration of it there are tracks through Lael Forest on its slopes, where the Forestry Commission have marked out walks. Even in their plantations here, there are indigenous trees among the ubiquitous conifers: ash, birch, oak, alder, rowan and Scotch pine, so that Strath More, and later on Loch Broomside, are more attractive to the eye than much of the landscape of the north-west. There is a Forest Garden at Lael, too, in which the Commission have cultivated 150 different species of trees and shrubs.

The road runs downhill all the way, through only two villages, Ardcharnich and Leckmelm, along the whole twelve miles to Ullapool, which lies in a bay of Loch Broom as it opens out towards the sea. Its name is Norse, from Ulli's steading (whoever Ulli may have been), and it was no more metropolitan than any other lochside village until 1788, when the British Fisheries Society saw fit to create a new fishing port, as they did in the same year at Tobermory. All the neat and harmonious houses along the quayside, painted white rather than multi-coloured as at Tobermory, date from this time, as does the regular layout of streets up the hill from the waterside. It is still an important fishing port, and fleets of lorries meet the boats as they come in, to cart off the catch to Aberdeen for canning and kippering. The Caledonian MacBrayne ferry to Stornaway in Lewis sails twice every day from Ullapool except Sundays; but the real prosperity of this contrived town these days is the tourist trade. As in Oban, Tobermory, and Fort William, tourism is big business. Ullapool can expect only forty-eight-inches of rain a year, because it is relatively free of the cloud-gathering mountains, and it offers a variety of activities, such as sea-angling, pony-trekking, sailing, and canoeing (at Ardmair, a mile down the lochside), and cruises to the islands. There are camping and caravan sites, and a Youth Hostel, for there is a wealth of walking and climbing in the wild hinterland; there is the Lochbroom Museum in the town with a history of the fishing and the Clearances, with displays of wildlife and geology too; there are twelve hotels and six guest-houses, not to mention several million self-catering cottages and bed-and-breakfast houses. If you want to know anything else, ask at the Information Centre, because there is one of those too.

It is the situation of Ullapool, like that of Oban, that is its chief attraction. The little town and most of its hotels sit on the waterfront looking at the still loch and the brown mountains of the Scoraig peninsula beyond. A few small ships swing at anchor: a boat ferries crewmen to and from the pier, the sea-birds glide overhead, mewing and crying, surveying the waters and swooping low for fish or scraps from the anchored ships. There is little other movement, just the Highland peace that seems to start from the mountains and spreads out over the lochs, compelling mere humans to obey its rules and control their disruptive instincts. The pale sea-mews, forever circling around and above all human activities, are like the spirits of departed Highlanders, viewing with distaste the pathetic efforts of modern man to inject some life back into the dehumanised landscape.

18

Sutherland

The country north-east of Ullapool is a rock-and-water peninsula called Coigach, which in Gaelic means Place of the Fifths, from an ancient Celtic custom of dividing land into five parts. Since one cannot grow much from either solid stone or standing pools of water, one fifth of not much would appear to be still less: starvation when the potatoes failed becomes immediately understandable. A fairly new and very good road leaves Ullapool and visits first Ardmair, in a corner of Loch Broom called Loch Kanaird, where, sheltered by Isle Martin, there flourish the fore-mentioned facilities for sundry aquatic pursuits, and camping and caravan sites for those pursuing them. Isle Martin has a hill of 397 feet and is named from one St Martin who built a chapel on its western side. It used to be inhabited: according to W. H. Murray it had a population of thirty in the early parts of this century, but they all left at the end of the 1939–45 war.

The road advances up Strath Kanaird beside Ben Mor Coigach, 2,438 feet, beyond which there is a chain of lochans stretching almost to the peninsula's coast at *Rubha Mor*. There is only one road, a very minor one, which leaves A835 at Drumrunie, enters Coigach by the northern side of Loch Lurgainn, the first of the chain, and serves all the villages and

settlements on the western side including the biggest, Achiltibuie, facing the offshore Summer Isles. Badentarbat Bay
separates Achiltibuie from the nearest and largest of the isles,
Tanera Mor, one ·and a half miles away. Its 800 acres used to
support a large community back in the great herring-fishing
days, but the last inhabitant left in 1946. Naturally, as there are
no longer humans there, the wildlife has proliferated, and it is
said that forty-three species of birds breed there. Sheep are
pastured on Tanera Mor, as they are on Tanera Beag, but
Horse Island, despite its name, is occupied by wild goats. There
are twelve islands altogether, and if you want a cruise among
them you can book one at the Post Office at Achiltibuie. Fishing
is also on offer, and there is a mysterious establishment called
The Hydroponicum, which claims it is the garden of the future,
offering a new lease of life not only to plants but to gardeners
too! There is also a Youth Hostel conveniently opposite Horse
Island, for the accommodation of other sorts of wild young goat.

In the very watery area between Ben Mor Coigach and *Cul
Mor*, 2,787 feet, among the foothills of *Stac Pollaidh*, 2,009 feet,
is Inverpolly Forest, a Nature Conservancy Reserve. *Stac
Pollaidh*, Stack of the Bog, is of red sandstone, but it has lost its
old quartzite cap: the weather has eroded it into thin needle-like
pinnacles, 'a great comb of rocks', as Arthur Gardner says.
These two mountains, with *Cul Beag*, 2,523 feet, to the south-
east, form a ring round a five-mile area of lochs and lochans, the
biggest of which is *Loch Sionascaig*; it is a fisherman's paraside,
but it is bare of trees and very bleak.

The A835 road passes between *Cul Mor* and the Cromalt
Hills, on the edge of a vast and trackless desert stretching
eastward for hundreds of square miles. On a steep cliff of the
nearest Cromalt is the Knockan Centre for climbers, where
rock-climbing and mountaineering skills are taught; strings of
them, appropriately equipped, may be seen ascending into the
misty clouds that hang over the hill, like lost souls in Dante's
Purgatorio, condemned for centuries to circle the mountain in

Sutherland

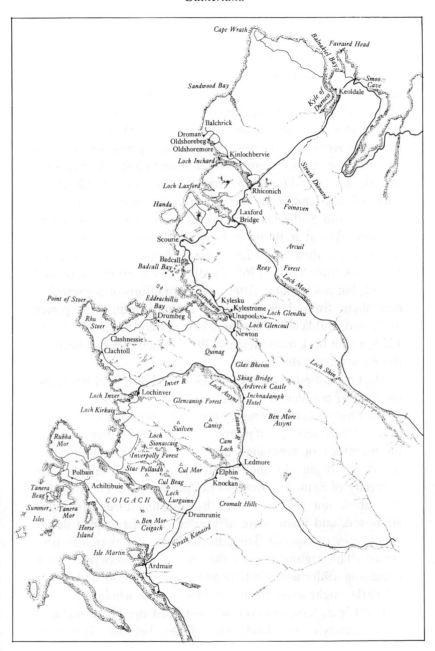

expiation of some dreadful sin (probably forgetting to bring a compass). Another string of lochs collectively known as the Cam Loch extend north-westward to the sea at Loch Kirkaig, providing the boundary between Coigach and Assynt. Humans in these parts are seldom seen, and even sheep are not so numerous. It is only where limestone protrudes into the granite masses that oases of fertility, such as at Knockan and Elphin, become possible. To the west (left hand side going north) it is all Archean gneiss, to the other side, Moine Schist, which pushed over the gneiss and turned the strata upside down, resulting in a chaos of rocks and hectic excitement in the minds of geologists.

Assynt and Sutherland are Viking names for what was their territory. Assynt is probably from the Norse *Ass*, rocky, and Sutherland is their South Land; they occupied the Orkneys and Shetlands from 875 to 1469. In 1034 they overran Sutherland as well, but not for long. After the valiant efforts of Somerled to oust them from their conquests farther south, their power weakened, and William the Lion, king of Scotland from 1165 to 1214, took it back from them in 1196. By then they had burnt all the forests along the coasts.

Most of Sutherland and Caithness is still devoid of trees, and the existing population is equally wanting in means of employment. There is currently raging fury in the pens of conservationists, that huge acreages of primitive bogland in the district, home for hundreds of breeding birds of all species including the rarest, are being ploughed for the planting of conifers. The Secretary of State for Scotland has put the point cogently that only areas not generally used by breeding birds are being afforested, and many more of greater value have been designated Sites of Special Scientific Interest, and therefore preserved. The argument goes that any interference with such remaining wildernesses in Scotland is a desecration, and National Parks ought to be created to preserve the whole.

The Clearances, however, which ruined the Highlands as a living society's homeland, still rankle, because they were effected so often by alien, English landlords. The worst, and most hated, for example, was George Granville Leveson-Gower, Marquis of Stafford. He married Elizabeth, Countess of Sutherland, who already owned most of it, and became Duke of Sutherland. Mainly through inheritance, he became the richest man in Britain, and spent thousands of pounds trying to improve his Highland estates. His method was to clear out the people from their homes and farms, and give them employment elsewhere, or else oblige them to emigrate. His factor, Patrick Sellar, became a byword for inhumanity, because it was he who personally effected the evictions. Such action invariably breeds exaggeration, founded on deep hostility, because age-old tenures, loyalties, and localities, were being disrupted.

Iain Crichton-Smith, in his novel *Consider the Lilies*, has Patrick Sellar come to visit an old lady, living in her family's cottage, and tell her that the Duke wants the cottage and he has sent him to put her out of it. ' "He's going to pull the house down." He said this as if it were the most ordinary thing in the world. Pulling her house down, when after all it was her house. She had never lived in any other house in all her seventy years. On the death of her parents — she hadn't married until they were both dead — her husband had come to live in this house. She had been born in the house, had spent her girlhood there, and had spent all the years of her marriage — such as they were — in it.'

Thousands of uncomprehending, Gaelic-speaking High-landers were evicted from their homes for no reason that they could understand, except that sheep were wanted and they were not, so they had to go. The question of employment has been of paramount significance ever since, and the emigrations did not stop with the Clearances, any more than they started with them. 'The noblest prospect which a Scotsman ever sees,' said Dr Johnson to Boswell, 'is the high road that leads him to England.'

Afforestation of some of Sutherland and Caithness, says the Secretary of State, will bring some employment to the region.

'About 60,000 hectares are now planted, supporting about 330 jobs. More are in prospect as the timber matures, and overall the total should reach about 1,000. Without further planting, at least two-thirds of the existing jobs will be lost and opportunities for downstream wood-processing will not materialise.'

There is also a governmental Enterprise Allowance Scheme which encourages small businesses to be established; in 1989 £20 million was devoted to this cause, and many Scots have taken advantage of it. Mr Jack Starke, the scheme's manager for the Highlands and Islands, has let it be known that almost any idea would be considered. The booming tourist industry has been the source of many of them.

The frontier of Assynt and of Sutherland is marked by the high hills on our left, of Suilven, 2,399 feet, and Canisp, 2,779 feet, and straight ahead of Ben More Assynt, 3,273 feet. At Ledmore, where a Forestry Commission fir-plantation clothes the otherwise naked landscape, the A835 meets the A837 at a T-junction, and turning left you follow the Loanan river, with Canisp to your left and Ben More Assynt right. The Cambrian limestone that provided the fertile strip at Knockan and Elphin has also been the cause of caves in the flanks of Ben More Assynt. The Nature Conservancy Council has a reserve there, which does not preclude the interest of potholers. The Traligill burn empties into Loch Assynt near the Inchnadamph Hotel, and a mile and a half uphill past the hotel, at the 600-foot contour, the Traligill drops underground, reappearing 350 yards lower down. The potholers, who do appear to live dangerously, find that here in wet weather they are dicing with death, because the caves tend to flood very suddenly.

Inchnadamph, Meadow of the Stags, benefits from the limestone because there is green pasture, and some of the croft-houses are built of white marble, which is the limestone in crystalline form. The Inchnadamph Hotel, open from March to October, is a fine centre for fishing, because the rivers and lochs are full of salmon, grilse, and brown trout, and the lucky fishermen might come across a rarity, a trout called a gillaroo (from *gille ruadh*, red lad), which originated in Ireland. It has adapted part of its stomach as a gizzard to crush the shells of molluscs. The hotel, standing in splendid isolation, also boasts a petrol pump, but never go there on a Thursday morning, because the petrol is delivered on Thursday afternoon, and they have usually run out.

Loch Assynt is six miles long, and its eastward part is completely bare of trees, the only features being the ruins of Calda House on the shore, and Ardvreck Castle on a promontory. Ardvreck (*Ard Bhreac*, the Speckled Point) was built in 1597 as a stronghold of MacLeod of Assynt. Before the Viking invasions, Assynt was ruled by the Thane of Sutherland; in the twelfth century he granted land to one MacNicol of Ullapool for his services against the Norsemen, and 200 years later the last MacNicol, a daughter, married a MacLeod of Lewis, to whom King David II granted Assynt by a charter dated 1346.

The family of MacLeod held the land for 326 years, losing it eventually by the greed of Neil MacLeod, the eleventh Chief, in the mid-seventeenth century. The story concerns the return of Montrose to Scotland. James Graham, Marquis of Montrose, had taken refuge in Holland when his campaign in 1646 came to an end with himself hiding in the mountains. When Charles I was executed in January, 1649, and with news of the violent barbarities of the Covenanters, he determined to return and champion young Charles II. In March, 1650, he sailed to the Orkneys, but from the beginning everything went wrong, part of his force having been diverted by gales and his transport ships wrecked; moreover, in the meantime Charles was trying to bargain with the Government. MacKenzie of Seaforth, whose clan had promised to join Montrose, delayed to await the result of Charles's negotiations, and Montrose and his hastily raised Orcadians were beaten at Carbisdale in Sutherland. Montrose escaped into Assynt, and sought refuge at Ardvreck Castle. There was a price on his head of £25,000, and despite his clan's inclination to rise on Montrose's behalf, their chief was tempted. He threw Montrose into his dungeon and alerted General Leslie at Tain. Montrose was led to Edinburgh and hanged on 21 May, 1650. The government paid MacLeod £20,000 in Scots coin (worth less than English) and the remainder in old, sour oatmeal. Seaforth realised that his delay had cost Montrose his life, and with remorseful rage devastated Assynt, taking off 9,000 head of cattle, horses and sheep. When Charles II was restored ten years later, he denounced MacLeod for a traitor, and Seaforth promptly seized Assynt. The castle stands on its crag, gaunt, grey, neglected and weather-wracked, a sad monument to a selfish man.

At Skiag Bridge, past the castle, the A894 leaves the lochside, skirting the eastern side of the mountain Quinag, 2,654 feet, and heads north, but the A837 remains faithful to the loch. Once when we drove past the castle, the eastern end of the loch's habitual bleakness was relieved by the apparition of a rainbow, beginning and ending in the loch-waters; the western end is enlivened by a multitude of islands which grow all the trees of the district: there are none at all on the banks. Houses are about as common as fish-and-chip shops on the moon, until at the head of the loch you pick up the Inver river and follow it down to Lochinver, a port at the head of a two-mile inlet from the sea called Loch Inver.

Lochinver is the nearest approach to a town since leaving Ullapool, having plenty of houses, many of which are new, three hotels and three guest-houses, a bank, a store-cum-post office which also runs the petrol station opposite, a police station, an Information Centre, and the equally informative Assynt Centre. Like Ullapool it owes its original existence to fishing, and at the quayside farther down the loch, dozens of fishing boats cluster together when the fleet is in. These days, Lochinver is a bigger fishing port than Ullapool, which is why there are new houses in the town. They have spilled over to the northern side of the river as it enters the loch, but the older buildings face west as the road

Lochinver

runs by the lochside towards the fishery.

Fishing is the chief attraction of Lochinver for tourists, sea-angling in hired boats, and salmon and trout-fishing from the rivers and lochs. Adjacent to the town is Glencanisp Forest, a playground for both fishermen and walkers accessible by tracks either side of Suilven. Because of its high, mile-and-a-half serrated summit ridge, the Vikings called it *Sul-fjall,* Pillar Mountain, but its modern name is a combination of the Norse element *Sul* with the Gaelic *Bheinn.* It is of red sandstone, with a quartzite cap. Three miles east of it is Canisp, rising from the shores of *Loch na Gainimh,* its summit an oval cone: W. H. Murray insists that 'the ascent is easy'.

To the north of Loch Inver is the Rhu Stoer peninsula, a desolate mass of rock, moss, heather and water accessible by the B869 road over the bridge from Lochinver. Along its coast, however, there is a surprising number of new houses, mostly

335

built for holiday homes, because of the many secluded little coves and sandy bays. The road, serving them and the older settlements, keeps to the coast because there is absolutely nothing to draw it inland. There are crofts along the shoreline because that is comparatively fertile, the climate is mild, and consequently the population is relatively high. Even on the headland beyond Clachtoll and Clashnessie there are crofting settlements. The northern point of the peninsula is distinguished by a pinnacle of rock called, like his namesake in Skye, the Old Man of Stoer. The Norse word *Staurr* means stake, but this one looks like an old, hunched figure. Ronald Faux, in *The West*, tells us, 'As the boat held a steady course into the bay, so the old man appeared slowly to be turning his head.' It is 200 feet high, and has, like everything else, been climbed. In 1966 Dr Tom Patey and Brian Robertson did so.

At Drumbeg on the northern side of the peninsula you can enjoy a wonderful view of Eddrachillis Bay, containing thirty-five islands, including the farthest, the bird-sanctuary Handa, and only just in view. In the clarity of the northern air, each island squats individually in the glittering water, inviting exploration; from the heights of Drumbeg you can see one or two small boats pottering about between the islands, each carrying two or more men, intent on their fishing. If they carried children, or naturalists, they would be enjoying the thrill of landing on uninhabited islands.

Drumbeg, since it is the biggest village in the peninsula, has a good hotel, which announces that it is 'an idyllic retreat for the fisherman', or anyone else, for that matter. The road on leaving the village drops suddenly 300 feet to sea-level at Loch Nedd, and here there are trees at last, alder and birch, but soon you are climbing back up to the stark moorland on the northern slopes of Quinag. This mountain has a series of seven peaks from about 2,500 feet to 2,600; its name is from *Cuinneag*, a churn or pail, which it does not resemble. In passing by the Churn, the road does a fair bit of churning itself, climbing and dropping without much warning, switching from right to left and back again like a rattlesnake, and behaving in fact like every other Highland minor road bar few. If you manage not to drive into a ditch you will reach the A894 road which had left Loch Assynt, and now makes for a bridge across a narrow strait called Kylesku.

At this point a long sea-loch from Eddrachillis Bay, Loch Cairnbawm or *a'Chairn Bhain*, forks into two, Loch Glendhu and Loch Glencoul. At the head of Loch Glencoul and rising in *Glas Bheinn*, 2,541 feet, is a stream which heaves itself over an open cliff at 825 feet. The Ordnance Survey gives the vertical drop as 658 feet. It is called *Eas a'Chual Aluinn* (pronouned Ess-kool-aulin), the Lovely Waterfall of Coul. There are no roads to it, and access is about as difficult as the approach to the Glomach Falls. There is a three-mile route to it, starting from the main road, and it is not easy.

Tiny settlements Newton and Unapool south of the bridge are not much smaller than Kylesku (*Caolas Cumhann*, the Narrow Strait) on the waterside, but it has a little pier from which boat-trips depart for loch cruises, since water is the best means of seeing the waterfall, and there is an inn. The Post Office rivals Lochbuie for size, it is a black weatherboard shed in someone's garden. The lochs are entirely surrounded by high, bare mountains, reminding one of Moussorgsky: they are bleak, inhospitable and rugged, and a night on one would certainly be a nightmare. When the weather is bad the people of Kylesku might be forgiven for thinking they were in Alaska.

The new bridge, high, wide, and handsome, replaces a ferry to Kylestrome on the northern side, and carries the good new road into the increasingly boulder-strewn, barren and bleak country of Reay Forest (pronounced Ray). It is an enormously wide area, the roughest and most intractable of all the northern Highlands, inhabited only along the coast and then sparsely. There are hundreds of lochs and little lochans. It is MacKay country: the Chief of Clan MacKay is Lord Reay, and it used to be the Chief's hunting ground until the Lord Reay in 1829 sold it to the Marquess of Stafford. It was he who built the road from Loch Assynt to Durness (but not the bridge), and it cost him £40,000.

There is scarcely any fertile land, even by the sea-coast, which is fretted by little bays and coves of Eddrachillis Bay (*Eadar da Chaolas*, Between two Straits). The biggest of the bays is Badcall, and at its head, just where the road starts off inland again to Scourie, is the Eddrachillis Hotel, much frequented by bird-watchers. The front windows have a superb view of the island-dotted bay, and a pair of good binoculars would obviate even leaving the room! So many species of sea-birds come and go that a list would swiftly run into dozens. Since the hotel itself is excellent, there is every reason to stay and none, apart from necessity, to leave.

Scourie is not far up the road, itself on a small bay, but situated in a wide plain fringed by low hills, where crofts can exist, growing potatoes, corn, and hay. Like Suilven, its name is a combination of Norse and Gaelic, from Norse *Skóga*, a copse, and Gaelic *Airge*, a shieling or summer pasture. It is not remarkably attractive, its houses functional rather than beautiful, and its hotel primarily caters for fishing devotees, but mentions bird-watching and hill-walking too. Despite its bleak appearance, Scourie's climate is yet mild enough for palm trees to grow; a hunting-lodge nearby was recently up for sale, with palms imported from New Zealand and planted in the 1820s, still flourishing.

Visiting bird-watchers have particular interest in Handa Island, out of Scourie Bay and across the Sound of Handa. It has been a bird sanctuary since being leased by the Royal Society for the Protection of Birds in 1962; 100,000 sea-birds inhabit the cliffs on its north-western shore, and 5,000 visitors arrive each year from other parts of Britain and abroad. It is only a mile and a half by a mile in area, but in the nineteenth century more than 100 families lived there, with their own queen and parliament. They were self-sufficient, like the St Kilda people, living on oats, potatoes, fish, and the sea-birds. The 1847 potato-famine finished them off, and the owner decided that sheep would be more profitable than people, so he cleared them all out: most of them emigrated to Canada and the U.S.A. Handa's 400-foot cliffs are of red Torridon sandstone, and off the north shore there is the Great Stack, a massive pillar of rock, 350 feet high, home to 12,000 birds like guillemots, kittiwakes and razorbills; its grassy summit is pocked with puffin-burrows. The gap between it and the island cliffs is about eighty feet, and Dr Tom Patey crossed it in 1967 with proper climbing gear. He was not the first, however: Donald MacDonald of Lewis crossed it in 1876, hand over fist along a rope!

From Scourie, habitations dwindle to nil, as the scenery becomes ever wilder, with water splashed about in a chaotic stony wilderness, lochans sited at every imaginable level. Laxford Bridge, on the map, is writ large as if it were important, yet there are no houses there, and it only achieves such fame because the road meets the A838 there, and stops being two-way. The bridge is where the Laxford river joins the sea at Loch Laxford, which has many bays and islands, and got its name from the Norse *Lax-fjord*, Salmon fiord. Salmon still frequent it. All the countryside from here is dominated by Foinaven, 2,980 feet, the last of the big ones. *Foinne Bheinn* means White Mountain: it has white quartzite screes. *Arcuil*, 2,580, to its south, is a hollow mountain, its summit ridge forming a three-quarter circle around a huge corrie containing a lochan. According to a seventeenth-century account, all the stags on *Arcuil* have forked tails. Perhaps Moussorgsky had it in mind. All around these mountains stretches the great gneiss moor, dotted with hundreds of lochans, 120 square miles of total desert. This is the country of the eagles and pine-martens, and the only humans ever seen are the hunting parties, after the red deer.

Through the verge of this strange moon-scape you come to

the head of Loch Inchard and Rhiconich, a tiny hamlet with an hotel commanding a splendid view down the loch, the northern shores of which are south-facing, are therefore more fertile and are crofted. A road from Rhiconich passes among the crofts to Kinlochbervie, another important fishing port, and nowadays offering various aquatic diversions to its visitors. There are sandy beaches along this coast on the fringe of the unspoilt wildness inland, and the road goes no farther than Oldshoremore, Oldshorebeg, Droman, and Balchrick, crofting townships blessed with caravan and camping sites, even in this remote corner. There are no roads at all from the last of these along the ten miles or so of coastline to Cape Wrath, so it is not surprising that such creatures as whales, seals, and mermaids frequent it.

Sandwood Bay (Norse *Sand-vatn*, Sand-water) is a good eight miles walk, there and back, from Balchrick, and one day Sandy Gunn was walking over the sands there with his dog, rounding up his sheep. Half a mile from the southern end of the bay, a reef of rock projects into the sea. The dog growled and stopped, his hair bristling, hanging back uneasily; Sandy went on to within about twenty yards of the rock and suddenly realised that there was a mermaid, sitting on the seaward end of the reef. She looked up and saw Sandy, and he, not wishing to be transmogrified into a lobster or worse, joined his dog in beating a rapid retreat. He was able to give a complete and detailed description of the mermaid when he returned home, and no doubt the story was worth many a dram to him in the years to come.

From Rhiconich the road goes straight through complete desert; to the left the last hills of north-west Scotland, to the right Foinaven's vast wilderness. There are no houses, no cover of any kind, and precious little vegetation, just a mass of stone interspersed with water. Into the middle of this bleak array comes Strath Dionard, and the road now follows its river down to the sea at the Kyle of Durness. There is a change of scenery here, since there is a change of rock; the Torridon sandstone of the hills gives way to Cambrian limestone, so there is grass, even if there are still precious few trees. The Kyle is long, an estuary winding out to sea between stony hills, and there is a ferry across it at Keoldale for foot passengers; it runs only from May to September, and it connects with a minibus service on the far side which will transport you along the little road, the only one of this last peninsula of north-west Scotland, to Cape Wrath (Norse *Hvarf*, a Turning-point), where there is a lighthouse, built in 1828. When we arrived at Keoldale it was April and the ferry was not running, so we went on to Durness.

Considering that it is a wind-swept, sand-blown and rather dreary place, Durness does pretty well for tourists. Its name is from the Norse *Dyra-ness*, Wolf Cape, and even the wolves have seen fit to evacuate it for some time now. It has three hotels, two guest-houses, some bed-and-breakfast houses and self-catering cottages, a camping and caravan site and a Youth Hostel. For amusement, there is Smoo Cave, a huge limestone cavern in the sea-cliffs which can be seen from walkways or by water, and along the way to Balnakiel Bay there is a hideous huddle of flat-roofed buildings, with W. D. written in every crack of them (it used to be a Radar station), which houses the Balnakiel Craft Village. The craftsmen and women make and market as many saleable objects as they possible can, from wool, wood, horn, metal, stone, and anything they can find on the beach. Balnakiel Bay is sheltered by a long northerly promontory called Fairaird Head, and it has a fine sandy beach curving round for a mile and a half, a perfect spot for sunbathing and swimming, if there is any sun and the water is above freezing. There is a nine-hole golf course nearby for those who prefer that more warming diversion, and a ruined chapel. Balnakiel means Township of the church, so there must have been a foundation long before the present ruin, which dates from 1619. There is a cracked recumbent stone in the churchyard inscribed with the name of Robert Donn, the Gaelic bard, known as 'the Burns of the North': he died in 1777.

As you stand on the sandy foreshore of Balnakiel Bay, the low dunes to your right stretching out to Fairaird Head, the high cliffs to the west leading to Cape Wrath, the wind fresh in your face and full of the familiar sea-smells of the whole coast, the ever-present gulls wheeling above, their vigilance undiminished, and you gaze out to the boundless, sparkling sea, you become conscious of the certainty that there is no more land ahead. There is the cold northern ocean, the great ice-packs of the polar seas, an infinity of frozen nothingness. The minibus trip to Cape Wrath apart, you are as far north as you can be in the West Highlands, just as you were as far west as you could be at Ardnamurchan Point, and as far south at the Mull of Kintyre.

The West Highlands, from Balnakiel Bay to Loch Lomond, and the inner islands, have yielded many secrets, but kept many more, and it takes years and more visits, or better still continuous residence in a part of them, to understand the nature of their moods. There is frustration and depression to be endured, when the dark ragged clouds hang low over the hills, and the rain sheets down with malign persistence for days at a time, weeks at a time; the Highlanders' Celtic temperament tends to swing between extremes of exultation and deep despair, and when the weather closes in they take to their *uisge-beatha* to lift them, and sometimes become suicidal. Yet there will be a sudden lifting of the sky, a hush of the wind, and the bright sun will lighten the mountain-tops, transform the whole scene with its magic, and the clarity of the air will show you faraway hills you thought you had never seen before. The hills and the lochs and rivers can become friends, whose character, temper and moods, like the Highlanders' themselves, you must work to know, understand, and love.

Appendix

Aids to Hill-climbers and Walkers
The uninhabited and trackless hills, moors and glens of the West Highlands are beautiful, fascinating, and extremely dangerous if you are not properly equipped and trained. The first essential skill is in map-reading and the use of compass-bearings. The second is knowing what to wear and what to carry; the third is knowing what to do if things begin to go wrong.

Wear or carry at all times:
Boots, socks, warm trousers, shirts, sweaters, underwear; waterproof jacket or cagoule and trousers; gloves, woollen headgear, gaiters.

Carry in your rucksack at all times:
Survival bag, extra warm clothes, extra socks, extra underwear; food or dextrose (or both), a small cooking stove, water, emergency rations, a knife with a tin-opener, first aid kit, fuel and matches, watch, torch with spare batteries, a small radio, map and compass.

When climbing or walking for the day only, one tent in a party is advisable, for use in an emergency. When out overnight or for several nights, one tent per two people is normal.

343

In Summer ADD:
Anorak, sleeping-bag, safety rope.
In winter ADD:
Ice axe, crampons, over-trousers, goggles, heavy gaiters, balaclava. *Always* when you set out for your walk or climb:
1. Tell your base or the people in your area WHERE YOU ARE GOING.
2. When you return, TELL THE SAME PEOPLE.

ALL WALKERS AND CLIMBERS must be aware that climbing in Scotland is particularly hazardous in winter above 2,000 feet, because of rapidly changing weather conditions which expose parties to the risk of getting lost in poor visibility, and subsequent danger from exposure in gale force winds and blizzard conditions.

SYMPTOMS OF EXPOSURE, and what to do:
How to prevent exposure:
1. A pack or load should never exceed one third of a person's weight. Generally avoid carrying a load of more than 40 lbs to 45 lbs.
2. Ensure that your clothing and equipment is of good quality, of the species listed above (i.e. boots, windproof and waterproof jacket and trousers), and wear woollen headgear. Heat loss from the head, in particular the face and forehead, must be avoided when not on the move. A balaclava prevents this.
3. Emergency rations, e.g. chocolate, glucose sweets (6 oz – 900 calories), first aid dressings, must be carried.
4. So must a survival bag (6 ft × 3 ft, 500 gauge polythene bag).
5. You *always* need your compass, map and torch: carry a whistle, and an inflatable splint.
6. Listen to and know the weather forecast, and the climatic conditions likely to be experienced.

7. Parties should be paired off to watch one another at all times, so that signs or symptoms of exposure or exhaustion can be recognised and reported quickly.

DO NOT go too quickly, as if rushing. DO NOT keep stopping for refreshment: too many stops will erode confidence in the leader, the party will begin to wonder is he is lost, and anyway they will indicate a lack of purpose and team discipline. DO NOT be over-clad: exercise creates heat, and more energy will be used as a result, and thus wasted. Strip down when on the move, BUT have your waterproofs handy: the body needs air. When the party does stop for lunch or refreshment, put on warm clothing for the duration of the stop, as the body will cool quickly. DO NOT drink too much water, a little goes a long way, so conserve it. If you are camping under canvas for the night, put on dry clothes from your rucksack *after* the tent is up but *before* supper. In the morning, stow away the dry clothes again in the rucksack and put back on the damp clothes. *Always* have the dry clothes in the rucksack. *Look after* your map: keep it in a large pocket of your anorak, or in the top pocket of your rucksack. Always keep it encased in plastic material. Hang your compass round your neck with plenty of cord, to facilitate use.

The above annotated observations are culled from two publications. The first is William McConnell's *Notes for Hill-walkers*, which contains, in addition to a much more detailed exegesis of the skills of hill-walking, a complete and clear explanation of how to read a map, take a compass-bearing and use it so as not to get lost. There are also several recommended walks in the area of Poolewe, Dundonnell, Kinlochewe, Achnasheallach, and Torridon, using OS map sheets 19 and 25 of the Landranger series.

The second publication is *Safety in Outdoor Education*, by the Department of Education and Science. It contains similar advice to McConnell's on equipment and procedure, and includes some addresses of organizations to contact if you want to arrange a hill-walking or climbing party.

Nature Conservancy
Council,
Scottish Headquarters,
12 Hope Terrace,
Edinburgh, EH9 2AR.

Countryside Commission for
Scotland
Battleby,
Redgorton,
Perth, PH1 3EW.

Loch Lomond Regional
Park,
Strathclyde Regional HQ,
Strathclyde House,
20 India Street,
Glasgow, G2 4PF.

Scottish Countryside
Rangers Association,
c/o Lochore Meadows
Country Park,
Crosshill,
Lochgelly, Fife. KY5 8BA

Bibliography

The Holy Bible

Ammianus Marcellinus: *Res Gestae* (trans. from the Latin by J. C. Rolfe), Loeb Classical Library, n.d.

Bell, Bozman and Fairfax-Blakeborough: *Hills & Mountains of Great Britain*, Batsford, n.d.

Blair, Anna: *Scottish Tales*, Richard Drew, 1988

Boswell, James: *Journal of a Tour to the Hebrides*, Dent/Everyman, 1958

Brooks, John: *Welcome to the Isles of Mull, Iona and Staffa*, Jarrold, 1984

Chadwick, Steve: *Short Walks around Gairloch*, Chadwick, 1987

Clayton, Peter: *Archaeological Sites in Britain*, Book Club Associates, 1976

Crichton-Smith, Iain: *Consider the Lilies*, Gollancz, 1986

Dept. of Education & Science: *Safety in Outdoor Education*

Downie, R. Angus: *All About Arran*, Blackie, 1933

Dunbar & Fisher: *Iona*, HMSO, 1983

Gardner, Arthur: *The Peaks, Lochs & Coast of the Western Highlands*, Macmillan, 1935

Gordon, Seton: *Highways & Byways in the West Highlands*, Macmillan, 1935

Gordon, Seton: *The Charm of Skye – The Winged Isle*, Cassell, 1929

McConnell, William: *Notes for Hill-walkers*, McConnell, 1990

MacDonald, Mairi: The West Highland Series: (all West Highland Publications): *The Appin Mystery*, 1981; *Crinan and Tayvallich*, 1986; *Exploring Moidart and Morar*, 1989; *Exploring Sunart and Ardnamurchan*, 1985; *Fort William and Nether Lochaber*, 1985; *Historic Kintyre*, 1984; *Lismore, Appin and Benderloch*, 1988; *Loch Awe and its Environs*, 1987; *Old Highland Folk Beliefs*, 1983; *Oban and its Environs*, 1985

MacGregor, Alasdair Alpin: *Strange Tales of the Highlands and Islands*, Lang Syne, 1977

Morton, H. V.: *In Search of Scotland*, Methuen, 1929

Morton, H. V.: *In Scotland Again*, Methuen, 1933

Munro, Neil: *John Splendid*, Blackwood, 1924

Munro, Neil: *Doom Castle*, Blackwood, 1924

Munro, Neil: *Para Handy Tales*, Pan, 1969 (1st pub. Blackwood, 1955)

Murray, W. H.: *The West Highlands of Scotland*, Collins, 1968

Pearson, Joan: *Kilmartin: The Stones of History*, Northern Books from Famedram, n.d.

Prebble, John: *Culloden*, Secker & Warburg, 1961

Prebble, John: *Glencoe*, Secker & Warburg, 1966; Penguin, 1968

Prebble, John: *The Lion in the North*, Penguin, 1973

Proctor, Carolyn: *Ceannas nan Gaidheal*, Clan Donald Lands Trust, 1985

Robson, J. E.: *Inverewe*, National Trust for Scotland, 1984

Scott, Sir Walter: *The Lord of the Isles*, (in *Scott's Poetical Works*), Warne, n.d.

Scott, Sir Walter: *Rob Roy*, Collins, 1817

Sharp & Matthay, Ed.: *Lyra Celtica*, Haskell House, (US), 1982

Stevenson, R. L.: *Kidnapped*, Nash & Grayson (reprinted 1951)

Sutcliff, Rosemary: *The Hound of Ulster*, Bodley Head, 1963

Thomas, Leslie: *Some Lovely Islands*, Arlington Books, 1968

INDEX

Index

Index

Index

Watson, Professor W. J, 39
Weir family, 50
West, The (Faux), 129
West Highland Way, 242, 254–5
West Loch Tarbert, 84, 94, 96, 115
Wester Ross, 304–17
Whiting Bay, 40–41

William III, King of England, 234, 250, 283

Young Pretender, 222–3, 227–8, 238, 257, 260, 264, 287, 299–300, 303
Younger Botanic Gardens, 15